The Dandy at Dusk

Born in Germany, Philip Mann has lived
in London since 1988 and has a degree in
the History of Art. He has written for
Frankfurter Allgemeine Zeitung and
Vogue and has lectured on matters sartorial
in Vienna, New York, Bern and London.

PHILIP MANN

The Dandy at Dusk

*Taste and Melancholy in
the Twentieth Century*

First published in the UK in 2017 by Head of Zeus, Ltd

Copyright © Philip Mann, 2017

The moral right of Philip Mann to be identified as the author of this work has been asserted in accordance with the Copyright, Designs and Patents Act of 1988.

9 7 5 3 1 2 4 6 8

A catalogue record for this book is available from the British Library.

ISBN (HB): 9781786695178
ISBN (E): 9781786695161

Designed and typeset by Lindsay Nash

Printed and bound in Great Britain by
CPI Group (UK) Ltd, Croydon CRO 4YY

Head of Zeus Ltd
5–8 Hardwick Street
London EC1R 4RG

WWW.HEADOFZEUS.COM

To my parents Anna Ritter and Hans-Joachim Mann and my late stepfather Henning Ritter without whose untiring encouragement this book would never have materialized.

CONTENTS

NICKY HASLAM

Preface

'The trouble with ghosts,' Margot Asquith once sagely remarked, 'is that their appearance is against them.' How different from a dandy, the very apparition of which is almost always – I realize there are some whose hackles rise at the sight – a delight to the eyes and senses. In his essay on dandyism, Max Beerbohm maintains that it is akin to the finer plastic arts, suggesting that 'so to clothe the body that its fineness be revealed or its meanness veiled' is as natural and valid an aesthetic aim as creating beautiful spaces, gardens, paintings or objects; that to make the best of one's build is no narcissistic sin, but an instinctive desire to hone it into something as near-perfect, say, as a Giambologna bronze.

The subject is of course a thorny one. The word dandy itself has given it a bad press. In some people's minds, dandies are simply preening popinjays obsessed with exaggeration and showiness, direct descendants of the mobs of Macaronis, and the Exquisites of the eighteenth century, such as my forebear, William Ponsonby, who, with his cousin Lord Harrington, 'went about drest in the last fashion, with diamonds, spotted muslin, silver turbans and feathers', or their friend George IV, whose 'fondness of dress even to a tawdry degree' was to be sobered up by Beau Brummell, naturally the *Übervater* in this book (and who, incidentally, was the first to advocate actually *washing* before donning that fustian palette). The flashiness of Count d'Orsay, for whom crowds gathered to watch him descend, 'insolent from his toilette', added to this general misconception, as did Oscar Wilde.

But Philip Mann handles such prickly problems with relish and historical insight, all the while endeavouring to give the dandy back to Brummell and tracing from him a decisive line into modernity and indeed modernism. Truly the incisive history of twentieth-century tailoring that this book *en passant* also recounts is not one of sartorial detail alone. As Mario Praz has shown in his classic *Illustrated History of Interior Design from Pompeii to Art Nouveau*, the history of design is one that justifiably prompts not only philosophical but also psychological musings. As such each object – be it a piece of furnishing or one of clothing – is a representation of the individual. Within his more confined period (the twentieth century) Philip Mann does for the sartorial arts what Praz has done for interior design; and more, finding as he does plenty of exquisite ironies within this history. One of the more obvious ones being the ever changing ideal of the perfect body the tailored self was to uphold. He writes that the narrow-shouldered, pear-shape, drawing attention to hips and stomach (and much else, since the Tudors' codpieces) considered desirable for centuries changed, in the late 1700s, and largely due to Brummell, to the upper part, with emphasis on chest and shoulders, thus paving the way for the silhouette of clothes, giving priority to bulk-free slimness and length of leg, via hose, pantaloons, britches, to the trousers of today – with a side-bar for the flapping Oxford

Bags on Harold Acton, Cecil Beaton, et al., worn as a cudgel to the bourgeoisie, and a cudgel taken up with a vengeance by Edward Prince of Wales who clearly, in those loud checks and strident tweeds, dressed to annoy his staid parents. In the 1960s one of course used to wear trews so tight, that someone so inclined might have told one's religion, for that very same purpose. Ironically I have now returned to the wide-legged trousers favoured by the Bright Young Things for my suits – no longer to upset my elders of course but as an expression of my admiration for those worn by Gary Cooper (notably the cinema plays a definitive role in this book as its last two dandies are great cinematic stylists).

It seems clear that the dyed-in-the-wool dandy – as opposed to the merely dandified, the 'nattily dressed' – is, *au fond*, an introvert. In all six examples under scrutiny here there is an underlying stratum of melancholy. That is their dusk. It is the dusk of modernism. While the Beau sombrely invented his present, and the Duke of Windsor his, with a lifelong flamboyance denied him in childhood, one reads the tears behind their mask of worldliness. That Adolf Loos, most avant-garde of modernist architects, loved and emulated the sartorial rigour of the Edwardian court comes as a surprise, and Bunny Roger, whom I knew well, and whose clothes represented his admiration for the perfection of former civilian and military cut and form, had, despite his apparent flippancy, a deep unease and distrust in the ethics of his time.

The personages in this book were interested not so much in fashion, but in the perfectly fashioned, which is the essence of Beerbohm's observation. To say they made this an art is not too strong. While there is still sartorial splendour around,

think of Hamish Bowles, or Lapo Elkann, or Will.i.am…
theirs is an external image. Too much glossy light is shed on
them. The true dandy inhabits the deeper, but not ghostly,
twilight of excellence.

Modernity out of Decadence

I. MODERNITY

One sensed that she did not dress only for the comfort
or decoration of her person; she was wrapped in her
wardrobe as though in the trappings – tender and
intellectual – of an entire culture.

MARCEL PROUST, *À LA RECHERCHE DU TEMPS PERDU,*
À L'OMBRE DES JEUNES FILLES EN FLEURS

In any truth you will find the natural and the artificial
linked arm in arm, and your joy at finding them so
united will compel you to embrace them both.

H. WALTON

The moment comes, in which it seems useless to us
to have to decide between metaphysics and dilettantism,
between the unfathomable and the anecdote.

E. M. CIORAN, *DE L'INCONVÉNIENT D'ÊTRE NÉ*

What is a dandy? In 1896, more than half a century after Beau Brummell's death, and after almost as many years of dandy discourse and dandy theory, the essayist, writer and (of course) dandy Max Beerbohm emphatically demanded a return to the roots, to the true source of dandyism. After giving a thorough dressing down to all the biographers who praised Brummell yet neglected his devotion to costume, so reducing 'to a mere phase that which was indeed the very core of his existence',[1] Beerbohm declared: 'To analyse the temperament of a great artist, and then to declare that his art was but a part – a little part – of his temperament, is a foolish proceeding.'[2] The ideal of the dandy is cut from cloth. His independence is expressed through the refusal of any visible distinction except elegance; his self-admiration in his self-adornment; his superiority to useful work in his tireless preoccupation with his costume. His independence, assurance, originality, self-control and refinement should all be visible in the cut of his clothes. To Beerbohm, the true greatness of the dandy lay in this reduction to the essential: the work of art itself.

When Thomas Carlyle had made essentially the same observation in 1831, in the chapter entitled 'The Dandiacal Body' in *Sartor Resartus*, it had been laced with a satirical disdain that was unmistakable: 'A dandy is a clothes-wearing Man, a Man whose trade, office, and existence consists in the wearing of Clothes.'[3] At this time, Carlyle was the leader in

England of the anti-dandiacal movement, a reaction to the Regency that had started with the death of George IV, formerly the Prince Regent, in 1830. The group, which attracted many Irish- and Scotsmen, gathered around *Fraser's Magazine*, and deplored the wit of the Regency, which they found an affectation, and its elegance, which they deemed superficial. There was a marked seriousness in the anti-dandiacals' sober commentary on the politics and literature of the day, which went along with an ideal of hard-drinking, robust masculinity. They also shared a preference for German philosophy: the principal character in *Sartor Resartus* is a cranky, provincial metaphysician by the name of Professor Teufelsdröckh.

That it was *serious* German philosophy is also relevant, in view of the reception of dandyism in present-day Germany. Still today, Germany is held to be the country of the anti-dandies. At the very moment of its birth, German identity defined itself in reaction to the cultural dominance of France. This entailed the principle of authenticity, or *Echtheit*, as opposed to the French sense of form, which was misunderstood as mere theatricality. So France, after England, became the second country in which dandyism manifested itself culturally. In Vienna an aesthetically conscious society similar to those of England and France developed in the nineteenth century, although it was hindered by the conservatism inherent in the rigid ceremonial of the Habsburg imperial court. In Germany today, the dandy is seen – if he is not confused with the aesthete, 'beautifully' dressed in silks and velvets – as a generally positive phenomenon that may be associated with almost any kind of artistic, literary or generally higher form of endeavour; but it must still be emphasized that what is interesting about the dandy is not his clothing, but also his attitude or, better still, his philosophy. Yet to the dandy, form and authenticity are not separate entities. The opposite is the case: to him they are virtually inseparable. As in the appreciation of any work of art, form and content are indissoluble. The dandy *is* his clothing, with all the multitude of references that this entails. Every tasteful socio-political nuance, every well-made subtlety of cultural history, even every uncomfortable existential thought that has worn him out, all these are present in his clothing. Indeed the nature of the dandy lies not only in his clothing, not just in his attitude, but also in the total fusion of the two: just as the dandy's suit is glamorous and his melancholy sombre, so his suit is sombre and his melancholy glamorous.

'What does such a man actually wear?' we may ask, perplexed. Perhaps something similar, as is so often assumed, to the 'aesthetic costume' that Oscar Wilde favoured at the time of his first successes – maybe a lavender-coloured velvet suit worn with patent shoes and silken handkerchief? Or should his clothes be of contemporary design but full of historical allusions and cultural politics, in the poetic vein William Burroughs described when he spoke of young dandies who had piss stains embroidered on their trousers in golden thread? In fact he wears neither of these: the dandy's costume is the most popular item of twentieth-century male attire, and at the same time the most abstract: a dark suit, classically cut from fine wool. On the surface, the dandy's costume is not very different from a business suit. The combination of trousers, waistcoat and coat forms the basis of his art; yet he is unlikely to be mistaken for a businessman.

The dandy masters convention, to which the businessman also adheres, to such a degree of perfection that he transcends it. The effect his form has is utterly calculated, and it is also this additional effort that fills it with content. The endless deliberations, even agony, which precede the choice of a particular cut, a particular material, or even the specific width of a turn-up are intrinsic to the fact that the dandy does not wear his clothing as fancy dress. Nor does his suit wear him: they are one. He might wear his suit like a uniform, but not a uniform for killing or making money. It is a uniform for living. Yet it has to be admitted that the hierarchies and distinguishing marks in this realm of sartorial art are based on nuances that might sometimes appear to blur the lines between the dandy and the well-dressed businessman.

In 1958, when it was still customary for most men to have their suits tailor-made, the costume historian Pearl Binder described a visit to that mecca of tailoring of the highest class, Savile Row: 'Here today contemporary English male dress is created, with all its complicated ritual processes, according to the gospel of George Brummell. The process begins when the customer calls by special appointment to discuss the suit he proposes to order. A middle-aged salesman, with the manners and the appearance of a courtier of the Court of St James's, helps the customer to choose the cloth of his suit. This is a most delicate process, involving the careful balancing of an infinity of considerations in the selection of one out of a multitude of varieties of only microscopically dissimilar patterns and materials, all extremely subdued in pattern and texture. It is, indeed, only by means of the refinements of subtlety that the English gentleman may today express himself sartorially, if at all.'[4] Judging from this, it could appear that there is hardly any difference between dandy and gentleman – indeed that both choose their suits by the same criteria. The reason for this, as Binder hints, is that the gentlemen's suit goes back to the first dandy: George Bryan Brummell, known as Beau, whom Max Beerbohm rightly called 'the father of modern costume'.

George Brummell was born 7 June 1778, the son of William Brummell, private secretary to the prime minister Lord North, and his wife Mary Richardson. His paternal grandfather was a servant. These humble origins he later obscured by making them even lowlier than they were anyway: 'Who ever heard of George B's father,' he would say, 'and who would ever have heard of George B himself, if he had been anything but what he is?'[5] Brummell's father, however, had acquired enough of a fortune to buy some land and send George to Eton, where the boy distinguished himself by taking fastidiousness to extremes in his choice of clothing, earning the nickname 'Buck' Brummell. During his time at Eton and especially later at Oxford, George was successful in acquiring friends among the 'first families of England'. He made the acquaintance of the 'First Gentleman of Europe', the Prince of Wales, later George IV, during his time at Oxford. Subsequently, it was the Prince who obtained an officer's commission for him in his personal regiment, the 10th Hussars. Despite his antipathy towards military service, Brummell managed to become very popular and win some aristocratic friends among the members of this supremely elegant regiment. Unfortunately, his division was soon transferred to Manchester, which Brummell considered beyond the call of duty; he promptly retired from the army with the rank of captain.

The beginnings of Brummell's existence in London coincided with his coming into the inheritance left him by his late father. Though modest in comparison with the fortunes of his aristocratic friends, this inheritance provided him with considerable means, and he now began his self-invention as a dandy, distancing himself from his family and completely ostracizing his brother and sister. In 1797 he moved into apartments that he furnished exquisitely yet not extravagantly. The next step in his evolution into a dandy came with the creation of a stage on which to show off his art: through the patronage of the Prince of Wales and the friends he had made in the army, he gained access with ease to the most exclusive gentlemen's clubs in London. Soon he became the most respected and – on account of his sharp tongue – the most feared member of Brooks's and White's; he was also the first non-aristocrat on the guest lists for the balls at Almack's. From the bay window at White's, this arbiter elegantiarum in the making delivered his often damning judgements on the clothing of passers-by. At Almack's balls, where he appeared late and stayed briefly in order to achieve maximum impact, his company was sought by the most beautiful women – yet it is not certain that he ever indulged in a single affair of the heart. All men sought to copy his style and the 'First Gentleman of Europe' followed his counsel more or less blindly. A baronet is supposed to have asked Brummell's tailor whether he would recommend the Prince's preferred cloth or the Beau's; 'I think Mr Brummell has a trifle the preference,'[6] the tailor dared to venture.

In the long run, the future king found the dandy's non-chalant superiority intolerable. Apart from Brummell's precisely aimed impertinence – 'Ring the bell, George,' he was once heard to command the Prince when a servant was needed – the admiration and friendship that the Prince had originally felt for this subject who was sixteen years his junior eventually turned into an unwillingness to bear his insufferable insubordination any longer, and in 1811 they fell out irrevocably. At first this falling out was of little concern to Brummell as he was still surrounded by influential friends – indeed he even proceeded to cut the Prince Regent dead in public. But in 1816 his prohibitively high debts, largely acquired at the gaming tables, forced him to leave London virtually overnight. The twenty years of his reign were followed by twenty-four increasingly bitter ones in exile. Initially he still managed to set himself up in Calais in somewhat inappropriate comfort – considering his debts – and kept himself entertained with visits from friends and curious travellers.

The final decline started when he got the first job – even if it was a sinecure – of his life. In order to help him to pay off his debts, the Duke of Wellington managed to have him appointed British Consul in Caen. But the required repayments were vastly disproportionate to his salary, and his situation deteriorated rapidly, culminating in the abandonment of the Consulate in Caen by the Crown. In 1835, at the instigation of his creditors, Brummell spent two months in debtors' prison. After his release, the remainder of his life was little more than a dance of death: he subsisted – despite his circumstances – on his favourite delicacy, the dainty and rather expensive *biscuit rose de Reims*; and his increasingly threadbare clothes were patched up for free by a sympathetic tailor. In 1840 the Beau had descended to a state of not only financial but also mental anguish that was intolerable (actually Brummell had suffered episodes of depression throughout his life. According to his biographer Ian Kelly these 'blue devils' in their chronic later form were probably symptoms of syphilis). Eventually Brummell was carried off to an asylum where he was soon to die, crying, 'Loose me, scoundrels! I owe nothing!'

The period of Brummell's influence coincided with the flowering of neo-classicism. This return to the chaste and simple formal language of antiquity, after the playful and rather arbitrary aesthetic of the rococo that had dominated architecture and the decorative arts, had its equivalent in costume. As Anne Hollander points out in her study of the development of modern costume, *Sex and Suits:* 'Aesthetic theory at the time is full of words like "virile" and "muscular" to describe the proper character of buildings created with the new simplicity of form based on ancient prototypes. An analogue in dress would thus naturally occur in male civil costume, and not in feminine fashion.'[7] This revolution in male attire extended to all aspects of clothing: cut, cloth and colour. Before Brummell, the ideal male proportions promulgated in art and fashion had been somewhat pear-shaped. Between 1650 and 1780, a gentleman's coat was cut to make the shoulders appear narrow and sloping; worn tight and open, it accentuated the stomach and emphasized the hips by falling open at that point on the body; it was also long, so making the legs appear rather short. The similarly almost knee-length waistcoat and breeches that sat below the waist emphasized these proportions. The rather feminine appearance of this ensemble (from a modern point of view, though this ideal seemed anything but feminine at the time) was further accentuated by a curly wig and high-heeled buckle shoes. The materials used for these garments, which had been adopted from the French court, were usually velvet and silk – fabrics which, while appearing opulent, were hard to manipulate during tailoring and did not move with the body. This gave them a dynamic of their own that can be seen in the arrangement of the folds in contemporary paintings. There was a marked preference for court colours such as old rose and pale blue, still associated with rococo interiors today.

The new interest in antiquity also led to a reappraisal of the physical ideal aspired to by the ancient Greeks, as might be admired in the figures of the Parthenon frieze and the Apollo Belvedere. Hollander notes: 'The system of clearly delineated limbs, heads and muscles, of harmonious stomachs and buttocks and breasts that was perfected in antique nude sculpture was adopted as the most authentic vision of the body, the real truth of natural anatomy, the Platonic form.'[8] It was not a question of advocating walking around naked or returning to the toga; rather it became the tailor's task to re-create this ideal in accordance with their skills and expertise and with the clothing already in existence. 'They offered the perfect Classical body, aptly translated into the modern garments that were the most traditionally "natural" in themselves, the ones that even further suggested the unfallen Adam in the Garden, the simple clothes of English country life.'[9]

Yet Brummell did not invent a completely new form of dress. Even in the realm of the aesthetic the dandy looks back: he is not an inventor. Instead, Brummell refined the look of the country gentleman in a way that was so elegant and simultaneously functional that soon it became not only acceptable to dress in this manner in London, but positively de rigueur. His day clothes consisted of a navy morning coat, a buff waistcoat made of chamois leather, trousers or breeches made of buckskin and soft Hessian boots. In the evening he wore a black suit with a white waistcoat and tight trousers, buttoned under the instep and worn with pumps. The wadding and roping that had traditionally been used on court dress to give the coat tails more weight, now travelled upwards to give the impression of a broad chest and shoulders. The coat tails were cut away to the back, to show off the short waistcoat and the pantaloons, which were cut to sit above the waist. The skin-tight pantaloons, which continued to the instep, fastening around the foot with a strap, further helped to give the impression of long legs.

Brummell's contemporary biographer William Jesse described the Beau as a man of Apollonian beauty, with a tall well-proportioned figure, beautiful hands and thin face. Other descriptions of his high forehead, his piercing eyes full of concentrated irony and his whole physique suggest a leaning towards the cerebral rather than the physical, however. According to his later biographer Barbey d'Aurevilly, Brummell was cerebral even down to the character of his beauty. Indeed, physical activity of any kind – which he found a nuisance at school and in the army – became anathema to him. In Brummell's case, the *corpus sanum* of classical antiquity was cut from cloth. And this cloth was wool. Easier to handle during tailoring and more forgiving to wear than velvet and silk, wool was not only the cloth of the toga of antiquity but was also the stuff of the costume of the English country gent: 'English tailors had long been superior to all others in the cut and fit of woollen garments; and wool was known to be the great staple fabric in England since the earliest period of its history.'[10]

The eschewing of superficial ornamentation and colour in Brummell's costume, described by the psychologist J.C. Flügel as 'the great masculine renunciation', reflects the cerebral quality of his work. In 1885, when Brummell's navy and beige had largely been usurped by black, Theodor Lipps analysed the meaning of the dark colours of men's clothing in his *Ueber die Symbolik der Kleidung* (to which Walter Benjamin referred in his *Arcades Project*): 'Grey is all theory; green, and not only green but also red, yellow and blue, is life's golden tree. So our preference for all shades of grey down to black clearly shows our way of socially and in other ways appreciating the theory of educating the intellect above everything.'[11] While the tenor of Flügel and Lipps is rather negative, it is precisely this need for abstraction that paved the way not only for the modern suit but also for modernity itself. Indeed, the principles of dress as laid down by Brummell read like axioms of modernist architecture and design. While the dark colour of Brummell's coat served to frame and emphasize the personality of the wearer, its subtle cut was an abstraction of the body underneath. The visible weave of its plain cloth expressed honesty; its proportions, precisely calculated after the antique ideal, rationality; and the shirt, of freshly laundered white linen with matching cravat, hygiene and cleanliness. Brummell's costume was a 'suit', not because all its components were made, as is the custom today, from one cloth – this would only happen a hundred years later – but because of its 'unified abstraction of form'.[12] When, in around 1815, trousers started to replace the tightly fitting pantaloons, the modern suit was born.

As has been suggested, the neo-classical style in clothing mostly affected men's attire. For a short while, admittedly, women wore dresses derived from Grecian models – flowing robes, with a high waist just under the bosom – but this remained a passing fashion rather than giving birth to a new kind of costume. But in men's fashion the classical mode persists to this day, despite countless attempts by clothes reformers and designers to supersede it. Since Brummell's day, dress has been divided into men's clothing and women's fashion. This was a division of labour that had already crystallized itself in France a hundred years before Brummell's day: in 1675, Louis XIV established the Parisian seamstresses' guild, and ever since then women's clothes have been made by dressmakers and men's by tailors. Even in an age when fashion designers are often male, the actual clothes are usually crafted by women, while tailors on the whole work in a male-dominated environment.

Hence the term 'fashion' is already anathema to the dandy. To him, his clothing follows a well-nigh mathematical system, which he seeks to master by finding a specific combination of numbers – his ideal measurements – among the endless variations within a given framework. The dandy subscribes to the core doctrine of all classical art: that it is precisely the limitation of form that generates the unfolding of the theme. Minute alterations to the shape of the basic components are made according to his individual cultural and social barometer and are never – even in the age of men's fashion – dictated by other people, such as designers or the general public. Women's clothing, being subject to fashion – as long as we are not discussing tailored suits – is an irrational mystery to him, into the shallows of which he dares not venture. Even if the 'normal' man is not prey to these preoccupations, the suit that he wears still goes back to Brummell's sensibility. After Brummell, developments in the form of the suit were 'subtle but fundamental alterations of cut, which meant overall changes of shape, with trim adjusted to match. These could count as basic innovations in the progress of a serious craft, rather like architecture.'[13] Even the terminology is similar: a suit is built like a cathedral. The dandy is the architect of his own person.

As the dandy defines himself through his clothing, dandyism also entails a general distance from the feminine. It seems that Brummell maintained mostly platonic relationships with women – he was a close friend of Georgiana, Duchess of Devonshire, and Frederica, Duchess of York, remained a strong support throughout his time of exile. It is not known whether this lack of *amours* was the result of a bad experience. What is clear, however, is that the possible consequences of love – a wife and children – would have meant an unbearable atavism for someone who had already divested himself of his birth family. Just as parents and siblings had hindered his self-realization, a wife and children would have hindered his self-cultivation. Even if we assume that he would have been capable of an *amourette* within the confines of the rules perfected by the previous century, he was clearly no Valmont. Of course the assumption that Brummell was homosexual, and even that the dandy as such is homosexual, is ever close at hand. Indeed the cultural historian Egon Fridell posited that the whole of classicism was homosexual in its approach: 'The homosexual eye predominantly sees contour, usage of space, outline, beauty of line, plasticity. The homosexual eye has no sense for dissolved form, blurring *valeurs,* purely painterly impressions. And so, looked at in the bright light of day, the whole *idée fixe* of "classicism" stems from the sexual perversion of a German provincial antiquary.'[14] He is of course referring to Winckelmann, who had the following to say concerning gender and the appreciation of art: 'I have noticed that those who are solely aware of the beauty of the female sex and are hardly or not at all touched by the beauty of our own gender, are not usually blessed with an easy, lively and general appreciation of beauty in art.'[15]

But his origins in masculine-dominated classicism do not necessarily draw the dandy to homosexuality. It is far more his leaning towards the cerebral – the rational paired with an over-developed sensibility directed exclusively towards one goal – that makes him wary of sensual abandon. Although woman is the opposite of the dandy, according to Baudelaire, he does not despise her. Because of his roots in classicism, he seeks to overcome the female principle by either ousting or incorporating it. An androgynous appearance and a vaguely effeminate manner serve to adorn him. Indeed, effeminacy is often a characteristic of the Englishman's portrayal of cultivated masculinity. Furthermore, the dandy's social life is necessarily dominated by men. To display his art he requires a public made up of tailoring cognoscenti. Generally these are male.

It is often claimed that the dandy is a snob. Some say that the word 'snob' is a contraction of *sine nobilitate*, and in its true meaning denotes somebody who seeks to emulate his superiors, usually the aristocracy. The term is often wrongly used to describe those who look down on their inferiors, even though these two vices often go together. Brummell sought to rid himself of his lowly origins, and from his Eton days onward cultivated aristocratic friendships. But this was a means to an end. He had to create a stage on which to display himself. And the only possible stage was the pinnacle of society, where the finest clothes were worn. Once he had reached the highest level, he could shape it and excel in it according to his own designs. So Brummell used aristocratic society in order to express his superiority to it through his distance from it. He demonstrated that superiority was no longer the exclusive privilege of those of high birth. Although his arrogant superiority was a confirmation of the aristocratic principle, and his way of life an exaltation of the aristocratic way of life, Brummell demonstrated his absolute independence through his subversive disregard for aristocratic hierarchies. The heroism of the hero created through dress consisted solely in his being utterly himself. While the attire of the *Ancien Régime* sought to express the glory and wealth of the wearer through luxurious materials and costly adornments, the position and deeds of the wearer were of no relevance to the refined yet simple cut of Brummell's coat.

Brummell did not have decorations on his uniform, his coach did not boast his coat of arms, nor did ancestral portraits adorn his walls. He sported no title except that of Mr Brummell, arbiter elegantiarum. In his contempt for the majority of his contemporaries he recognized no social differences, even if on the whole he seemed to apply the principle of *parcere subjectis et debellare superbos* (sparing the vanquished and subduing the proud). While he garnered the respect of the aristocracy through well-calculated impudence, the lower orders did not seem to him to offer any scope for attack. Owing to his over-developed sensibilities, he ironically saved his most barbed insults for the class whose clothing he had adapted for urban living. The country gentry were an insult to every fibre of Brummell's being, and he justified their exclusion from the most fashionable clubs with the contention that their 'boots smelled of horse dung and bad boot blacking'. Refinement and urbanity distinguished every aspect of Brummell's existence: his small but elegant London residence, his irreproachable dinners, his impeccably composed letters, his Boulle furniture and his Sèvres porcelain. But the most emphatic expression of his distinction was his personal appearance.

Hence the dandy is Janus-faced at his very birth; on the one hand he needs the aristocracy and its values, on the other he seeks to excel and overcome it. A few decades after Brummell's death, Baudelaire sought to find a socio-political causality for the dandy's ambiguous nature: 'Dandyism appears mostly in transitional periods, when democracy is not yet all-powerful and aristocracy has only just started to falter and has not entirely lost its dignity.'[16] Although his

values were anything but populist, the original dandy nevertheless pointed the way to democracy: Brummell's clothing
was suited to all classes and professions. He established the
golden mean of taste, appropriate for the last Georgian age,
which took pride in applying the principles of restraint, naturalness and simplicity to the modest fields of clothing and
interior decoration. It was again Max Beerbohm who pointed
out the universality of Brummell's achievement in being 'so
quiet, so reasonable, and, I say emphatically, so beautiful;
free from all folly or affectation, yet susceptible to exquisite
ordering; plastic, austere, economical... I doubt even if any
whatsoever gradual evolution will lead us astray from the
general precepts of Mr. Brummell's code. At every step in the
process of democracy those precepts will be strengthened.'
According to Beerbohm, the chaotic history of male costume,
which had always alternated between the too fine and the
too coarse, came to a close on 'that bright morning, when
Mr. Brummell at his mirror conceived the notion of trousers
and simple coats'.[17]

Because dandyism defined itself in opposition to the dominant French style of clothing and embraced the archetype of
English country clothing, its appearance outside England is
usually associated with notions of anglophilia. In France, the
phenomenon that became known as *anglomanie* had started
as early as 1740, with the adoption of British fashions by a
few aristocrats and rich merchants after visits to England.
Around 1760, *anglomanie* became a common concept in
France, which gained in strength with Brummell's growing
reputation. Yet in France a preference for either of the two
prevailing modes of dress could scarcely be separated from

political loyalties. *Anglomanie* was characterized not only by an enthusiasm for English clothing and manners, but also by a fascination with English ideas. As a counter-model to the absolutist system established through the long rule of Louis XIV, the British separation of parliament and monarchy was of great significance to, among others, Voltaire in his *Lettres anglaises* (1734). In this way, a gradual turning away from absolutist habits of dress preceded the Revolution in France. Two Englishmen who arrived in Paris in 1762 had suits made by a French tailor in the style of the *Ancien Régime* in order to equip them for their stay. One of them was to write later that the new outfits 'made complete Frenchmen of us. But for my part, Harry, I was so damned uneasy in a full-dressed coat with hellish long skirts, which I had never been used to, that I thought myself as much deprived of my liberty, as if I had been in the Bastille; and I frequently sighed for my little loose frock, which I look upon as the emblem of our happy constitution; for it lays a man under no uneasy restraint, but leaves it in his power to do as he please.'[18]

This seems an opportune point at which to weigh the dandy ideal against a much more obvious object of anglophilia, which dominated the bourgeois nineteenth century and retains a far-reaching appeal to this day: the notion of the gentleman. To the anglophile the attractiveness of the gentleman rests mainly in the assumption that the gentleman is generated by education and cultivation and is not necessarily a product of the accident of high birth. (In Britain the notion of the gentleman by birth still persists to a degree, but is increasingly becoming an anachronism.) It is, in short, an ideal that seemingly can be reached through personal endeavour. Hence Ian Buruma describes the anglophile notion of the gentleman as 'a bourgeois with aristocratic manners, a tolerant elitist who believes in fair play'.[19] In addition to dandyism, the definition of the gentleman is closely connected with aspects of moral judgement. But the ideal of the gentleman, which Evelyn Waugh called 'the most elusive in the world'[20] is not easy to pin down. In *The Gentleman in Trollope – Individuality and Moral Conduct*, Shirley Letwin observed: 'The gentleman's world does not require a choice between rebellion and submission, violence and reason, alienation and unity, certainty and apathy, it is a world full of nuances.'[21] While the dandy integrates form and content, the gentleman aspires to the integration of reason and emotion. The dandy is a work of art, hence moral questions are subsumed by aesthetic ones. To the question 'What is a gentleman?', that has obsessively exercised the minds of poets and philosophers, writers and theologians, liberals and conservatives, the dandy has a disarming answer. *He* is a gentleman: it is a visible fact, owing to an intangible something, a *je ne sais quoi*, that can be neither defined nor negated. The nuances of his world are an eighth of an inch on the heel of a shoe and the precise angle of a breast pocket. He does not need to integrate his emotions with his reason, as his nature is not animal but is already that of a gentleman. Of course the gentleman is also often defined through his appearance. Hazlitt, for example, assures us that a gentleman can be 'recognised infallibly at first glance'.[22] Others maintain that he 'always dresses as cleanly as he speaks, and is as meticulous about the things that surround him, as about his person and his clothing'.[23]

Indeed, as we have seen, the type of dress that to this day counts as 'gentlemanly' goes back to the principles established by Beau Brummell. This brings us back to the question of how the appearance of the dandy differs from that of the well-dressed gentleman. The effect produced by Brummell's dress was due to his behaviour and his manner. Many hours of concentration and preparation, of painstaking attention to detail, were necessary to create an impression of dignified simplicity. The ultimate result was one that was not entirely dissimilar to any other elegant gentleman; the distinction of the dandy was often only visible to the cognoscenti, and sometimes only to himself. What he desired was an abstraction of elegance, beyond all social signifiers. 'The dandy', as Roland Barthes says, 'is a man who has decided to radicalize the distinction in men's clothing by subjecting it to an absolute logic. On the one hand he increases the distinction: its essence to him is no longer a social one but a metaphysical one: by no means does the dandy confront the higher class with the lower, but only, and this he does completely, the individual with the common, in which the individual is not a generally perceived notion, but his own persona freed from any possibility of comparative recourse, so that in the end he, like Narcissus, subjects his clothing to his own and only his own judgement. On the other hand, he openly admits that the essence of distinction can, like that of the gods, reveal itself in a triviality.'[24] To the gentleman his dress is only one feature among many; to the dandy it is the existential problem per se. The 'visibility' of this attitude may be illustrated by an episode from the set of Visconti's film *The Damned*, described by the actor Helmut Griem. The table was laid for the grand dinner in the mansion of the von Essenbeck family, a thinly disguised portrayal of the Krupp family of steel magnates. Visconti approached the table, tried the wine, which had already been poured, and erupted into a fit of rage. 'Do you think for one moment that Krupp would drink your shitty Frascati?' he shouted at his hapless prop department. 'You have to put Mosel in there!' So they filled the glasses with Mosel, and *The Damned* became the film that it is.

The ideal of the gentleman is closely linked with that of the amateur. A gentleman and a scholar is a dilettante in the academic field. Not so long ago, the distinction between gentlemen and players, amateurs and professionals, was still of some importance on the sporting field. Unlike most countries, where the term 'professional' is praise of the highest order denoting not only high remuneration but also great skill, legend has it that the English gentleman is not only uncomfortable with being paid for something he enjoys doing, but also deems it vulgar to attract attention through undue success. Hence also the notion of fair play, of playing the game being more important than winning, and other similar principles. One of the oldest roots of the gentlemanly ideal is the Renaissance courtier, and a gentleman also has something of the Renaissance man. His knowledge is wide-ranging, he dabbles in many areas and avoids specialization, which could draw undue attention to him. Yet he is not necessarily a man of leisure, nor does he absolutely have to be of noble birth or in possession of a great fortune. As late as 1961 Simon Raven describes the gentleman as a demanding model of moral integrity, which is 'compatible with any form of social or practical endeavour'.[25]

Not so the dandy. As he is his own work of art, he does not strive for the state of doing, but rather for the state of being. In this spirit Oscar Wilde wrote of the dandy Thomas Griffiths Wainewright, who dabbled in the art of poisoning: 'This young dandy sought to be something rather than to do something. He knew life itself to be an art, and no less than art to have a style.'[26] Wilde himself would say that he had put only his talent into his works, whereas he had put all his genius into his life. Owing to his identity as a work of art, the dandy is of necessity idle. Brummell eschewed the earning of money as belonging to the lowly and vulgar sphere. His rejection of any profitable occupation was also a silent protest against useful and barbarized man. Brummell dabbled in the arts. He drew, wrote poems and even penned a history of the fashions of classical antiquity. But he was careful not to be so much of an original or a virtuoso in any of these fields as to risk being classified as an artist or a writer. What he probably also lacked was the 'naivety bordering on stupidity, which is necessary for somebody to label himself an artist'.[27] In this way, as Otto Mann puts it, the dandy's idleness is not 'a natural disposition towards under-achievement, but a phil- osophically determined lack of realization'.[28] This attitude makes financial independence a necessity for him – a neces- sity, however, that he is able to meet only very rarely: 'The complicated ability to develop dandyism in oneself has very rarely been paired with riches; on the one side is the born dandy without a fortune in the background, on the other side the rich fashion dandy without a real dandy concept.'[29]

As an artist, the dandy is a member of the leisured classes, but one who cannot afford his leisure. In theory poverty

does not compromise his dandyism, however: it even aids
the reductionism that is part and parcel of his striving for
perfection. Thus the Hungarian writer Sándor Márai notes
in his *School for the Poor*: 'Only very poor and highly tal-
ented men can fathom the heights of pleasure which the
poor dandy, and there are these as well, feels in the morning
when choosing between two ties, especially if he does not
own a third one. This pleasure of tying the only tie with the
greatest of care equals, if not exceeds, the one of discussing your wardrobe changes for the day with your English
butler according to mood or social obligations.'[30] Unfortunately, the dandy also has to operate by the principle of trial
and error, which necessitates a high consumption of ties.
Hence he is more often found in need of money than in a

state of blissful poverty. It was part of Brummell's genius to dominate the highest sphere of society on the strength of a 'modest' fortune of thirty thousand pounds. 'He was the most consequential of dandies by not acquiring money in other ways than at the gaming tables, and furthermore knew how to create principles which were appropriate to his means. He was victorious not through riches, through the opulence of his launch into society, but through exquisiteness and insurmountable taste.'[31] In the end, however, fate caught up with Brummell. Indeed, as Gilles Lipovetsky notes, 'the euphoria of fashion has its counterparts in dereliction, depression and existential anguish'.[32] But the dandy integrates the saturnine side of his nature into his being, without viewing it as a flaw in his existence. Melancholy, decline and an early grave are the flowers of evil that he sports in his buttonhole. Indeed the yearning for a tragic fate is the only motivation of the dandy, as he is free of worldly ambition. In death he realizes himself, as his life – like his suit – becomes a unified whole.

 Dear Philip,

FOR YEARS I WAS FORCING MR. WILKINSON TO CUT EXTRA
BROAD SHOULDERS FOR MY JACKETTS & SUITS
AND I WAS NOT COMPLETELY SATISFIED WITH
MY „BULKY LOOK"

SO, ONE DAY I HAD
TO FACE SARTORIAL
TRUTH: IT'S „NOT YOUR HAT,
MICHAEL, IT IS „
„YOUR HEAD"
said Wilkie very calmly,
„IT'S DEFINITIV: YOUR
HEAD IS TO BIG "
GOOD THING IS, THAT
YOUR SHOULDERS ARE
BROAD BUT LOOK QUITE
SLIM, SO, CONSIDERING
ALL YOUR DISPPROPORTIONS
THE RESULT IS A FAIRLY
ELEGANT SILHOUETTE
WHEN WE KEEP THE CUT OF
TROUSERS NARROW, SORT
OF LONG LEGS WILL BE
PRODUCING ANOTHER POSITIVE EFFECT "

M.W. 2019

Yours sincerely, ton ami

Michel Würthle

Berlin
November

II. DECADENCE

You always play around and joke. My friends, this pierces
my soul, for those who must joke are trapped in despair.

FRIEDRICH HÖLDERLIN, *DIE SCHERZHAFTEN*

We are crushed at every moment of our lives by the
conception and sensation of time. There are but two
means of escaping and forgetting this nightmare: pleasure
and work. Pleasure exhausts us. Work strengthens us.
We must choose. The more we have recourse to one
of these means, the more the other repels us.

CHARLES BAUDELAIRE, *JOURNAUX INTIMES, HYGIÈNE*

That explained why my worries concerning my death
ceased at the very moment when I had unconsciously
recognized the taste of the little madeleine, because
at that moment the being that I had been stood outside
time and for that reason could face the vagaries of the
future without apprehension.

MARCEL PROUST, *LE TEMPS RETROUVÉ*

How is a dandy made? While the decision to be a dandy is a conscious one, in the true dandy there seems to be an element that is innate. Being a little bit of a dandy is as impossible as being a little bit pregnant. It seems the dandy is born as such. Yet his vocation is confirmed by strokes of fate. The Damascene moment for Barbey d'Aurevilly came when he was a young man, with his meeting with – or rather mere sighting of – Brummell in Caen. Although Ernst Jünger talks of dandyism as merely a stage before greater goals, naming Caesar and Frederick the Great as examples of eminent personalities who in their youth spent months and years 'frittering away their time'[33] (Disraeli would be another obvious example), it would seem that actually they lacked the natural inclination to live their dandyism to the full. They turned, as Beerbohm put it, to 'some less arduous calling'.[34]

While Jünger describes more convincing dandies, such as Prince Pückler-Muskau, the fictitious Pelham and of course Brummell, as stuck in the prelude of dandyism, he denies them the fulfilment that flamboyant failure must have meant to them. It seems legitimate, however, to say that dandyism is a compulsion that is never far from the pathological. In *L'age d'homme*, Michel Leiris recounts an occasion when his girl-friend raised the issue of his wardrobe: "'I love you enough (meaning she loved me in the full sense of the word but only a little bit), but to be perfectly frank I don't love the way you dress." I am mortified; I think of the hat I'm wearing (while so many young people go bareheaded), of the bowler hat I used to wear, of my waisted topcoat, my gloves, my whole stiff manner, I think of everything this entails, my formality, etc... I know I can't change and if I tried I would only lose. I explain to my girlfriend why it is necessary to use one's clothes in order to erect a wall around oneself.'[35] And so the dandy appears frequently to be very much aware of his problematic nature, yet he differs from the merely neurotic by (instead of seeking a cure) manifesting himself for what he is.

What the outside world perceives as the dandy's physical vanity has often been developed through his perception of his own inadequacy, which he seeks to disguise: 'I prefer to dress with a maximum amount of elegance; because of the physical faults I have mentioned, I generally think of myself as inelegant; I have a horror of suddenly catching my reflection in a mirror, as if I am caught unawares I seem to myself of a humiliating ugliness each time.'[36] Indeed, a good tailor knows how to compensate for all kinds of physical shortcomings: a nineteenth-century cutting guide mentions, for example, the 'pigeon-breasted figure' and the 'fore-and-aft humps'.[37] 'We improve on the perfect fit,' a cutter for Huntsman remarks. 'A perfectly fitting suit can't satisfy us if there are physical faults to correct or hide.' While this refers to obvious and very real defects, the dandy has a hypersensitive and extremely critical perception of his own physique. His total self-control serves among other things to keep his often hysterical perfectionism within bounds. Yet when the desired state of perfection is apparently attained, alarming thoughts of a different nature soon crowd to the fore. The essayist

Dolf Sternberger describes the satisfaction he felt when, after many false starts and failures, he finally succeeded in tying a Windsor knot: 'I felt progress had been made in my life, since I had mastered this humble art, these simple hand movements. Or rather not progress, that's not the right word. It is more than progress, it is the final and perfect knot. All previous ones were at best preliminary stages or projects in development, probably even mistakes. Yet finally I am privy to the secret, the right instruction, and I am glad of it.' But this joy is inevitably marred by the one thought that associates itself with perfection. It interjects 'like a fine, sharp cut and destroys all contentment within an instant: I am going to die'.[38] At the very moment when life proper is about to begin – with each new item of clothing the dandy expects a new, better life that renders all previous experience incomplete – it is also almost at an end.

The dandy knows to hide the pathological side of his character through masks, which are second nature to him. Poise and mannerliness serve him as a shield against the world. It was Brummell's mien of imperturbability – the *nil admirari* of the stoic – that he passed down to his successors. While a certain degree of emotional control has always marked and eased communication in the 'best' society, since Brummell a cold and imperturbable calm has been the main characteristic of those who move successfully in society. To Baudelaire, the very opaqueness of the dandy's mask marks his aesthetic standing: 'The character of beauty that distinguishes the dandy consists mainly in his cool mien and manner, which express the unshakeable resolve not to allow himself to be moved.'[39] The philosopher Otto Mann, in his

description of the state of disorientated despair that made
Barbey d'Aurevilly reach for the dandy mask, identifies this
stance as the lid on Pandora's box: 'He found himself without
religion, without *Heimat*, without political beliefs, without the support of a creative force as such; furthermore
without the possibility of anaesthesia, without a soothing
relationship to nature and quickly sated and wearied by
women.'[40] Indeed, convinced of nothing except his own existence, the dandy finds himself at a disadvantage in questions
of faith, even compared with the atheist and the nihilist.
His nihilism is timid, as he needs society – the workings of
which he despises – in order to express himself. His atheism
is comparable to that of Luis Buñuel: 'Thank God I'm an
atheist.'[41] Thus the external veneer of imperturbability lends
him an inner calm. Once he has gone through this process,
it is enough for him to express his creative force through his
person. His imperturbability is an instrument of classicist
regulation; within the classicist framework he can give full
expression to his individuality.

In addition, particularly in the twentieth century, the
dandy also makes use of another mask. 'Camp' has been written about at length elsewhere; what seems interesting here
is to shed some light on the relationship between camp and
the dandy sensibility. At first glance, camp – the theatrical
gesture that declares the trivial tragedy or epiphany – is the
polar opposite of stoic imperturbability. Yet what seems to be
the opposite of camp, the laconic remark that minimizes the
event, is part of the same sensibility. Camp uses stylization,
the over- or understatement that just stops short of a lie, to
express a truth. What lies behind camp is also a feeling of

powerlessness, the dramatic sensation of not belonging. The old-school dandy substitutes the will to power with the will to absolute stylization, which transcends all worldly hierarchies of power. With a limp-wristed wave, camp renders the abdication from power ironic. Camp is simultaneously inside and outside the dominant culture. In its subtler forms, camp wanders on the knife-edge between superficiality and depth, not always to the disadvantage of the latter. Camp seeks to blur the line between life and art. And it is precisely here that the difference between camp and old-school dandyism lies. Susan Sontag describes camp as 'a certain mode of aestheticism. It is one way of seeing the world as an aesthetic phenomenon. That way, the way of camp, is not in terms of beauty, but in terms of the degree of artifice or stylization.'[42] The dandy is art, that is manifested artificiality. As such he is part of the camp sensibility, part of its idealized self-image. The dandy does not knowingly oscillate between the above poles, instead he integrates them. He has no need to good-humouredly embrace this good old ambiguous world. It is part of him.

Mentally, it is the dandy's deep fear of the banality he perceives around him that enables the absolute will to be original to develop within him. He feels ill at ease in the time in which he lives. When Baudelaire describes the transitional period between aristocracy and democracy as fertile ground for dandyism, this should also be taken metaphorically. The dandy lives in a superannuated society, the forms of which – to the extent that they still exist – have been separated from their content. Where Brummell was both keeper of the aristocratic flame and harbinger of democracy, the dandies of progressive democracies are increasingly nostalgic. The contemporary dandy longs to return to modernism, to a time that was obsessed with the integrity of form and that made such frequent reference to classicism, with its male representative in the dandy. Thus what is still today referred to as the 'classic suit' was developed in the 1920s and 1930s in a dialectic relationship with modernism: 'In the 20th century, as old fashion plates show, the abstract shapes and plain textures of modern suits were linked to the visual vocabulary of modern abstract art; but even more tellingly and more consistently, they shared in the formal authority of modern practical design.'[43]

At the same time, the standardization and mass production espoused by the Bauhaus and Le Corbusier, combined with the industrial design of classic modernism – America had a flourishing ready-to-wear industry as early as the late nineteenth century – had a detrimental effect on dandyism. Ready-to-wear is indeed the dandy's nemesis. The industrialization of his art form robs him a priori of any claim to uniqueness. Even greater anathema to him is the faux individualism offered by fashion. As Roland Barthes remarked, 'to buy the newest Italian shoes or the latest English tweed is an entirely banal gesture'.[44] With the arrival of men's fashion in the 1960s, the dandy's path was strewn with obstacles that he could contrive to circumvent – like an Impressionist in the era of Pop Art – only by remaining stuck. If the 1950s was the last decade in which tailor-made clothing was the norm, 'uniform in its essence, yet adaptable in its details',[45] then the 1960s and 1970s were a period of transition that gave rise to the paradoxical illusion of a democratic dandyism. With the arrival of the designer in the 1980s, the topicality of dandyism as part of the zeitgeist disappeared completely. No matter how 'exclusive' designer fashion may be, it is from the outset an impossible compromise, a fraud based on individualism for sale, 'a medium between the absolute individual and the total mass'.[46]

The twenty-first-century dandy yearns for the time before the dissolution of these parameters, which from about 1973 seemed irretrievably lost. If he also longs to go back to the 1960s and 1970s, it is because dandyism seems to have been particularly prevalent during that period of transition. The 'dandy after modernism' likes to wear out his father's old bespoke suits, because even when worn-out and threadbare the one-offs of the past are infinitely more precious than contemporary ready-to-wear. He seeks to regain times past, with a Proustian attention to detail: dressed in a neo-Edwardian 1950s suit remade with the help of his tailor, with a Georgette Heyer novel in the inside pocket, he is ever eager to conjure up not only the image but also the truth it contains. To truly regain lost time, he must unearth not only the dates, names and places of times past, but also his own subconscious memories of them. The childhood photograph, the prawn cocktail, his father's old tie and an episode of *Columbo* first viewed thirty years ago are the madeleines of those born after 1950. For earlier post-Brummellian dandies, a slightly melancholic nostalgia already formed part of the way they defined themselves: d'Aurevilly remained faithful into old age to the redingote that had been fashionable in his childhood; Max Beerbohm was an Edwardian until his death in the 1950s; and Bunny Roger even reinvented the Edwardian style in the late 1940s.

As the twentieth century reached its mid-point, there was already a longing for its beginnings – for the pre-media, pre-industrialized glamour of the Belle Époque and the Edwardians: the Hôtel de Paris, Felix Krull's Monte Carlo, *Last Year in Marienbad*. The yearning for the 1950s, '60s and '70s that began as early as the mid-1970s reinforced this nostalgia. Sándor Márai, as old as the century in which he lived, had already started to miss the rationality of early modernity in 1934: 'In these times I have to live and work as well as possible. It is very difficult. With great consternation, I sometimes notice that sixty-year-olds are closer to me in soul and tastes than twenty-five-year-olds. All of us who were born in the last, victorious moment of the class, feel this way. It is almost as if those writing today merely want to give testimony for times to be – testimony that the century in which we were born once proclaimed the triumph of the mind. And I will testify to this until the last moment, as long as I am allowed to put letters onto the page: that there was a time and a few generations, which proclaimed the victory of rationality over animal instincts and believed in the resilience of the mind, that is capable of taming the desire for death.'[47]

Given the dandy's nature as work of art, the passing of time poses particular problems for him. His life is only partially the natural progress from naivety to maturity. Having realized himself early, he faces eternity. He is conscious of the fact that he cannot do justice to traditional modes of maturity, and they cannot do justice to him. Nor does he fit within conventional patterns of masculinity. Thus the fully formed dandy has to develop strategies for coping with the passage of time; strategies that allow him to remain unchanged. The most radical solution to this problem is suicide. In his study of Baudelaire, Walter Benjamin identified suicide as the *'passion particulière de la vie moderne'*: 'Modernity must stand under the sign of suicide, an act which seals a heroic will that makes no concessions to a mentality inimical toward this will. Such a suicide is not renunciation but heroic passion. It is the conquest of modernity in the realm of emotions.'[48] Suicide not only solves the problem of time, it also confirms the art-like or artificial nature of dandyism.

Jacques Rigaut, Surrealist poet and friend of André Breton, was to offer one of the most influential dandy suicides of the twentieth century. At the age of twenty, Rigaut resolved – unprompted by feelings of duress or unbearable despair – that one day he would commit suicide. From that point on he patiently awaited the right time, which he found in his thirtieth year. The dandy's goal of triumphing without ever having taken part can scarcely find a better example than in Rigaut: 'I will be a great dead man. Try if you can to stop a man who travels with his suicide in his buttonhole.'[49] The writer Pierre Drieu la Rochelle, to whom suicide was also an *idée fixe* that he would eventually realize, immortalized his friend Rigaut in his great suicide novel *Le feu follet*. His protagonist, Alain Leroy, is a dandy whose identity has led him into a *cul-de-sac* early in life. He removes his mask when he laments the first principle of the dandy, distance – to not touch and to be untouchable: 'I cannot touch, I cannot hold, and basically it comes from the heart.'[50]

In Louis Malle's eponymous film of the book, Alain, played by Maurice Ronet, has the date of his planned suicide written on the mirror in his room – quite literally a memento mori.

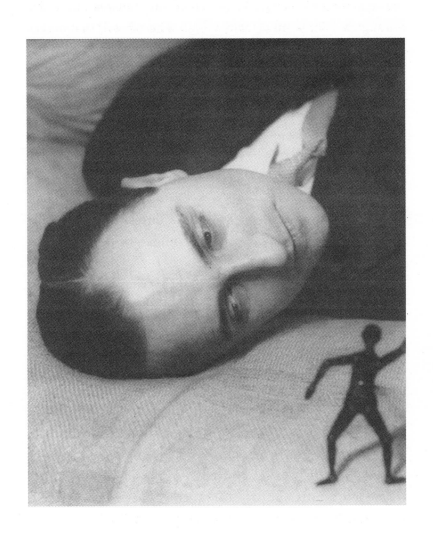

This resolve is also illustrated by his farewell note to the world, which combines triumph and despair: 'I kill myself because you did not love me and I did not love you.' This dialectic between 'I cannot' and 'I don't want to' – or as Herman Melville's Bartleby rather more succinctly puts it, 'I prefer not to' – is also characteristic of the dandy's love life, or rather his lack of one. The dandy is not a misogynist; he merely defies the dependency and vulnerability that love implies for him. Again, Drieu was an *homme couvert de femmes* more than an *homme à femmes*, of whom André Malraux observed: 'Misogynist? Not the elementary and cretinous misogyny that regards woman as less intelligent, less sensitive than man, no... But the misogyny of the man who understands the indispensability, the necessity of woman, and rebels against this fate.'[51]

A less final way than suicide of defying time is illness. In illness, the dandy can legitimately retreat from doing to a state of being. As Sándor Márai noted in 1947, 'Modern scholars of the soul tend towards the assumption that humans only become ill when they want to flee the responsibilities of life. Is there a more beautiful journey than a bout of appendicitis, when the poor man can have a holiday from life, does not have to engage in the daily struggle for existence anymore and is gently rocked towards the miraculous shores of death?'[52] In his attempts to seek rest and recovery through suffering, the dandy frequently cultivates more than an interesting limp. Otto Mann even finds the dandy's true nature in his pathology: 'In the convulsive desire for a fulfilling content to life, all possibilities are exhausted. Barbey d'Aurevilly sought redemption in suffering in the decadent manner.'[53] Yet Mann denies the dandy the desired release: 'As such, a wretch never suffered a clearly delineated materiality, never found the sweet consolation of being the willing victim of circumstances beyond his control, his suffering remained the sad delight of tearing himself apart, which in the end leaves nothing behind but a dissected, repugnant cadaver. The impotence and lack of dignity of this suffering, the shameless analysis, the reopening of self-inflicted wounds, the oscillation between emotionless torpor and violent agitation – in the end, all were felt by the late aesthetic type [Mann's art-historical and psychological categorization of the dandy] himself.'[54] To the modern eye, what Mann describes here is not so much reprehensible indulgence as the infinitely painful state of depression. The dandy's philosophically determined idleness, his complete self-absorption and his coolly analytical nature rather predispose him towards pathological melancholy. Precisely because of his excessively rational nature, he is susceptible to escaping into the irrationality of mental illness, which in the case of depression is not a helter-skelter of emotions but their terrifying absence.

Before presenting hundreds of different kinds of melancholia and their origins in his comprehensive *Anatomy of Melancholy*, Robert Burton concedes in his introduction that Plutarch knew that idleness was the sole origin of all melancholy. This concurs with Benjamin/Baudelaire's tragic view that the dandy is a Hercules bereft of labours and a tragic hero of modernity: 'Modernity proves to be his undoing. It has not provided for the hero; it has no use for his type. Modernity anchors him forever in the safe harbour; it abandons him to an eternity of idleness. In this, his last incarnation,

the hero appears as dandy.'[55] If melancholy to Baudelaire seemed virtually the natural state of modern man in general and the dandy in particular, which he has to bear stoically and through no fault of his own, it can hardly be denied that the desire for a tragic fate is also the dandy's motor. To him, in the ancient manner, life is comedy or tragedy. Thus Oscar Wilde writes in *De Profundis*: 'I thought life would be a brilliant comedy. I found it to be a revolting and repellent tragedy.'[56] Comparing himself in his customarily modest fashion to Jesus, he sees his fate perfected only through suffering, as it is through suffering that the spiritual side of his soul is fulfilled: 'Pleasure for the beautiful body, but pain for the beautiful soul.'[57] What is really unbearable is the banal drama of real life. To Brummell, mental illness was merely the last stop before the unconsciously desired end.

A third and more agreeable possibility for defying the unbearable passage of time is geographical flight, as embodied in travel. Leaving the familiar behind is more important here than arriving in the unknown, since upon arrival it is only a matter of time before its passage becomes unbearable again. So it is the departure, and – as Edward Gibbon knew already – the journey itself that approach closest to a form of relief: 'I am always so much delighted and improved with this union of ease and motion that, were not the expense enormous, I would travel every year some hundred miles.'[58] The state of movement that a train journey entails, for example, allows the dandy to 'move with the times' rather than watch time dwindle away. Sometimes there is not even the necessity for actual departure in order to gain the refreshing sensation of leaving the familiar. Des Esseintes, the protagonist of

Joris-Karl Huysmans' *À Rebours* (1884), decides in the latter half of the book to take a trip to London in order to recover from a spell of fatigue. After extensive packing, and the careful choosing of a grey-on-grey check Savile Row suit to reflect the rainy mood that pervades his being, he is delivered to Paris by his servant in time to catch the evening train to London. Having studied his Baedeker, which sets him off on an intense series of daydreams ranging from Millais' choice of colours to the characters in Dickens, he enjoys a rich English meal in a restaurant frequented largely by English travellers, before deciding to go home again: 'In fact I've experienced and seen what I wanted to experience and see. Ever since leaving home I have been steeped in English life. I would be insane to risk losing, by an ill-advised journey, these unforgettable impressions.'[59]

Sándor Márai recounted how in times of particular poverty – for which reason the dandy has frequently to deny himself the pleasures of travel – he would go to the railway station, enquire about the departure time of the Rome Express and buy a platform ticket, sandwiches and magazines. He would then place his foot on the running board of the smoking carriage and his gloved hand on the brass door handle, before hopping off again at the very moment of departure and going home refreshed. Indeed, the names of the various *trains de luxe* that still existed in the first half of the twentieth century seem designed for this kind of spiritual refreshment through daydreaming: Orient Express, Le Train Bleu, Das Rheingold. But as with so many other aspects of modernity that made the dandy's life bearable, the quality of civilized travel becomes diluted some time towards the end of the 1970s. An easyJet flight doesn't inspire any kind of fantasy. The wish to travel, the desire for flight and obscurity, is yet another utopia that nourishes the natural death wish of the dandy. *Partir, c'est toujours mourir un peu*; therein lies its attraction.

Yet the microcosm of a short trip also satisfies another of the dandy's desires, which precedes that for death: perfection. For the manageable period of a journey, the perfect wardrobe can be planned. There is no room for experimentation – everything that was wrong has already been eradicated in 'normal' life – and the amount of luggage is restricted by the paramount need not to compromise the flight aspect of travelling by weighing the traveller down with physical burdens. It is possible to plan every day to allow the frittering away of time in agreeable ways, without these rituals becoming wearisome through constant repetition. This ascetic, minimalist aspect of dandyism finds particularly powerful expression in the twentieth century. In *Enemies of Promise* (1937), Cyril Connolly identifies this contemporary type of dandy: 'At the moment dandyism in its most extreme form, perfectionism, is on the increase, for perfectionists, like the hermits of the Thebaid, take refuge from the world in private salvation. I have known many perfectionists, all of whom are remarkable for the intense stripping process which they carry out. Their lives are balloons from which more and more ballast has to be cast; they never have more than one suitcase, wear no pyjamas or underclothes, travel constantly and are the mystics of our time, *pressés de trouver le lieu et la formule*.'[60] It is true that at this period an unusual number of dandies went into exile. But although exile as an attempt at permanent flight seems to attain a utopian state, time exposes it as false. Both Brummell and Wilde died wretchedly in exile.

What remains are the most immediate ways of escaping time, labelled 'pleasures' by Baudelaire: alcohol, fornication and *'les paradis artificiels'*, excessive enjoyment of which equates most closely to the common definition of decadence. They lie at the heart of *fin-de-siècle* dandyism, the 'naughty nineties' of the nineteenth century. The archetype of the decadent dandy is again Huysmans' fictional Des Esseintes in *À Rebours*, the book which the cultural critic Mario Praz described as 'the pivot around which the psychology of the whole decadent movement centres'.[61] We meet Des Esseintes at a point in his life when he is already greatly weakened by the excesses of active decadence and has retreated into a self-created hermitage in the *banlieue*. Here he fights his *ennui* with virtual excesses, such as the creation of symphonies of taste for the palate from exotic liqueurs and the study of ecclesiastical literature. The last of an aristocratic line that over the years has become increasingly anaemic, Des Esseintes is neurasthenically sensitive to everything and everybody. Like Wilde with Dorian Gray (whose bible, the 'yellow book', is arguably *À Rebours*), Huysmans conveys only a vague impression of exactly what pleasures have so sated Des Esseintes that his 'cold, steel-blue eyes' look on the world with universal disdain. Sexually, however, he descends from encounters with singers and actresses, via 'evil' mistresses experienced in every art and ever less refined whores, to 'unnatural' love affairs and 'perverted pleasures'. The seemingly inevitable results of this polymorphous perversity are 'lethargy and impotence'. The *fin-de-siècle* dandy replaces Brummell's asexuality with the celebration of sexual marginality and pathology. Where effeminacy was an adornment to the Regency dandy, in decadence it becomes a weakness.

What emerges as the definition of decadence is the progressive replacement of the harmony of form and content by sensual stimulation. Otto Mann sees parallels to this emphasis on sensuality in the modern art of the late nineteenth century: 'A new irrational melody, its strength revealed by Schumann, its weakness by Mendelssohn, a new perception of the soul, far removed from Bach's dryness and depth, far removed from the sweet yet measured clarity of Mozart, a diminishing of rationality, a surplus of sensuality...' 'Baudelaire,' Mann continues, 'whose instincts were always so accurate, occasionally found in the fervent, despotic music of Wagner, painted on a backdrop of darkness, the swooning traces of opium... Equally, one is struck by the transition from the superior deep harmony of Rembrandt's colours to the brilliant inflammation of a Delacroix, from the sculptures of Michelangelo to those of Rodin, from the sonnets of Shakespeare to those of Baudelaire.'[62] The inherent problem of this survival by sensual stimulation lies in the law of ever diminishing returns, of dulling of the senses. To retain its power, the stimulus has to become ever finer or coarser. To the dandy, who is already defined by being excessively sensitive, the ceiling in terms of refinement is soon reached – he needs stronger, coarser incitements. Thus the relative failure of *fin-de-siècle* dandyism seems to derive not so much from its decadence as from its vulgarity.

The most prominent example of late nineteenth-century dandyism in England is found – it is generally thought – in the person of Oscar Wilde. Wilde was born into a middle-class Irish background with a strong streak of bohemianism on his mother's side, and his London debut bore a passing resemblance to Brummell's in its brisk conquest of the aristocracy. Hindered by a fatal, if romantic, snobbery, however, he was never to surpass his idols or rise above the status of bourgeois intellectual. In the long run, he merely dominated the bohemian milieu into which he was born, described by Yeats as 'the fine life which we look at with affectionate eyes out of our garret windows'.[63] This apart, his early understanding of dandyism could not have been further removed from Brummell's. He championed an 'aesthetic costume', consisting of a lace-trimmed velvet jacket and velvet knee breeches worn with silk stockings and buckle shoes. During his American lecture tour he presented himself as a clothes reformer, declaring contemporary dress too gloomy and advocating colour and decoration, as were the custom in the eighteenth century – precisely the type of dress, in other words, from which Brummell had sought to disassociate himself. Only in later years, when Wilde had established himself as an artist, was he to return to the type of dress that conformed to the axioms laid down by Brummell.

In Wilde's defence, it could be said that he regarded himself chiefly as an artist, to whom dandyism was just a phase. But true dandyism is not satisfied with a phase. Even as an artist-dandy, Wilde trailed a long way behind Baudelaire, for example, to whom the label might also apply. Baudelaire was always an artistic dandy, rather than a dandified artist. He did not get lost in the artisanal and remained an outsider – in bohemian circles as well as in fashionable society. If Wilde's

aphorism describing dandyism as 'the assertion of the absolute modernity of beauty'[64] sounds promising initially, the
problem lies precisely in his emphasis on beauty. Brummell's
modernity consisted in the economy, severity and function-
ality of his clothing. If it was commensurate with an ideal of
beauty, it was a beauty that evolved from the adherence to
these principles, and that was not an end in itself. The beauty
of Brummell's clothing was the final product, not the starting point.

John Ruskin and Walter Pater, whose lectures Wilde had
attended during his time at Oxford, had left their traces in
his thinking. Ruskin's Christian/moral understanding of art,
long suppressed by Wilde, resurfaced in his 'serious' work
De Profundis (the distinction between being serious and
posing is undandyistic in itself: the dandy takes his appearance seriously), when Wilde had been sobered by the prison
experience. Pater's influence appeared in his former *l'art pour
l'art* hedonism; and both were reflected in his blind ador-
ation of beauty. Proust was to remark on Ruskin's idolatry
'of pursuing the external beauty of symbols rather than the
truth they conceal'.[65] Ruskin and Pater led Wilde to antiquity
and the Renaissance but not to classicism. On the contrary,
he expressly opposed classicism, which he saw as a canon of
dead rules, opposed to his own Christian romanticism. Hence
his love of the Renaissance was restricted to the early Christian Renaissance that produced Giotto, Dante and the artists
of Chartres, while he scorned the classical Renaissance of
Raphael, Petrarch and Palladio. Wilde's understanding of
individualism as an amorphously unfolding inwardness is
the polar opposite of the dandy's art, for which the rule and

the occasional transgression of the rule create a framework for the expression of individualism. Ironically, Wilde returned to dandyism at precisely the point at which he believed he had left it behind. In believing suffering to be the secret of life, which nourishes the soul and transcends the banality of pleasure, he brought the dandy's unconscious to the surface. The decline to which both Brummell and Wilde fell victim, and that decadence celebrated, is as inherent to the dandy as it is to the antiquity that guides him. Yet he does not consciously seek it. The true dandy is more Stoic than Epicurean.

Even though the dandy's life is, in most respects, alienated from conventional definitions of happiness, it is neither entirely meaningless nor without salvation. The success of a dandy's life is marked by the transition from lacerating self-analysis to shedding light on his own opaqueness. Suffering and pleasure are reflected in order to enter the work of art that is his life. As Cyril Connolly wrote in *The Unquiet Grave*, 'Present pleasure kills time, it is like sleep, a harmless anaesthetic: harmless when once we have recognized that our life is so painful as to need what otherwise must distil only guilt and remorse. If, however, we understand that the love of pleasure can be increased or decreased according to need, then as the pleasure fades into the past it will leave behind only a sense of nostalgia, and this nostalgia can be converted into art, and, once so converted, all sense of guilt attaching to the pleasure is washed away.'[66] This condensed summary of Proust's *Time Regained* also points at the essence of dandyism. It is the reflection of even the most quotidian aesthetic gesture that elevates it. The dandy is the poet of applied aesthetics – he fills the superficial things of life with content beyond the banalities of discourses on lifestyle. When Cioran said 'To fuck up one's life means getting access to its poetry – without the help of talent,'[67] he meant that a ruined life also has its poetry. Baudelaire demanded a poetic prose, and in the twentieth century, especially, the poetic is mostly found in the prosaic. As Jean Gassou noted in 1932: 'There is more poetry in the jazz opera of Kurt Weill or the miraculous novels of Georges Simenon than in most books which pretend to contain poetry because they are printed in irregular lines.'[68] The essence of dandyism is the elevation of the prosaic life into the poetic.

No one could accept himself as he is if some miraculous circumstance offered him a full knowledge of what he was and what he is. Man recognizes *Himself* only... in *Another!*

PAUL VALÉRY, *MONSIEUR TESTE*

ADOLF LOOS

The Architecture of the Suit

Art is for people who have no culture.

J. MEIER-GRAEFE

When a lean man with ligaments of steel, dressed in a red tailcoat made from soft cloth and snow white breeches without a single crease from the knee downwards, his arms held closely yet lightly against his body, stands in the stirrups of a hunter at the gallop; or when a young lady during a light conversation – you gentlemen of course do not know what a light conversation is, and if I were now to ask you would cite the name of some Danish author in whose work you presume to have found one – when a young lady in a gown which once put on belongs to her like her hair (the young ladies of your acquaintance are firstly not ladies and secondly do not wear gowns but rather fancy dress) – when during a light conversation a young lady rises to pour tea for the person facing her, from white porcelain which a servant has silently placed before her – you see, gentlemen, these are some of the things that culture means to me.

RICHARD VON SCHAUKAL, *LEBEN UND MEINUNGEN DES HERRN ANDREAS VON BALTHESSER*, 1907

Painted on the back of a large nineteenth-century building in Taborstrasse in Vienna's second district until late 2009 was an enormous picture of the head of a bowler-hatted gent. Beneath it was the word 'Windsor', advertising the firm of gentlemen's outfitters housed in the premises. To this day there is a *Café Engländer* in Postgasse, and rather characteristically it bears little similarity to English hostelries of any kind, whether today or a hundred years ago. However it would have appealed to the man who was largely responsible for Austrian anglophilia in the twentieth century. Adolf Loos is known to posterity chiefly as one of the harbingers of modernist architecture. Yet to view Loos merely as an architect would be to overlook his copious work as an essayist, presenting a cultural philosophy that reveals him as a highly radical and advanced reformer of everyday life, who was to have a major – if largely indirect – influence on twentieth-century thinking in this field. For Loos, the exemplary culture that had replaced that of ancient Greece was the Anglo-Saxon one. This idealized view curiously encompassed some areas in which England has since been regarded as rather backward, namely food and plumbing. But central to Loos's thinking about culture and modernity was tailoring, a realm in which England leads the field to this day. While Loos's writing was to be given far more attention in Austria after his death than during his lifetime – a comprehensive edition of his essays was published only in the 1980s – it was through his own clothes and lifestyle that he showed himself a living exemplar of his perception of England – its interiors, its food and above all its suits – as the measure of all things 'modern'. All through his life, the procurement of correct clothing of the highest quality was an existential priority to Loos, and was closely connected to his thoughts on architecture. To Loos the dandy, 'the clothes-wearing man' of Carlyle's *Sartor Resartus*, was not a marginal phenomenon but was more or less the foundation of his cultural and ethical ideas. The arbiter elegantiarum that Brummell had been and that Loos later became to Viennese society was a pillar and patron of culture.

In her memoirs published in 1968, Loos's second wife Elsie Altmann wrote of her late husband: 'Loos looked like a typical Englishman, had good English manners, it was easy to love him. He was always very well dressed. He loved English cloth, and he loved it well cut. He never bought a suit off the peg, he always had the best tailors. Yet as beautiful as his suits were, his trousers always lacked a crease. He wouldn't allow a crease at the front of the trouser leg, his trousers had to be ironed along the side seams. That's how King Edward of England wore his trousers, when Loos and the King were young men. He thought the crease at the front of the leg had no right to exist.'[1] Indeed, there seem to be no photographs of Loos in a lounge suit with a central crease to his trousers. Yet although in most photographs Edward VII himself sports side-creased trews, curiously he is also credited with the invention of the front crease, as he is with almost all male fashions of his day: having got wet while at an inconvenient distance from his tailor, he is said to have had his trousers

pressed quickly by a nearby tailor, who presented them to him with a front crease. By the time Loos adopted the side crease, around 1910 (earlier photographs show him frock-coated and front-creased), it was – rather typically – already something of an anachronism. The only man in public life who now still sported the side crease was not the late King Edward but his son George V, who notoriously adhered to Edwardian dress in every detail. When, a decade later, pleats became commonplace, allowing the front crease to fall perfectly from the waist, Loos's insistence on sticking to his old habits can only be regarded as peculiar. Yet what may seem like a quirk actually provides a fairly comprehensive key to Loos's character and particular brand of dandyism: an anglophilia paired with an element of snobbery that was more romantically inclined than he would have cared to admit, a dogmatic functionalism and a militant sticking to his guns that defied all evidence and expediency.

Adolf Loos was born on 10 December 1870 in Brünn, in what is now the Czech Republic. His father was a stonemason and sculptor who had his own business. He was by all accounts a genial man to whom the young Adolf was extremely close, in stark contrast to the relationship with his harsh and disciplinarian mother. Sadly Adolf senior died when Loos was just eight, leaving him at the mercy of a mother who was fundamentally unsympathetic to the boy's temperament. Yet Loos's mother's attempts at moulding young Adolf only succeeded in making him less compliant and increasingly idiosyncratic. After leaving school, Loos attended the Staats-Gewerbeschule (State-Trade-School) in Reichenberg and Brünn (in the building department) but had to leave when he was called up for military service. Subsequently he resumed his studies at the 'Technische Hochschule Dresden'. Even at this early stage in his life, Loos asserted his individuality by refusing to join a 'Studentenverbindung' or student guild – viewed as *de rigueur* among his contemporaries – and acquiring the fencing scars that went with it. He left Dresden without gaining a diploma. Equally, he failed to follow his mother's ambition for him to take over the family business. Instead he decided to visit the 1893 World's Fair in Chicago, using it as an excuse to escape his mother's clutches. To cut himself loose from all family ties, he also agreed to give up his inheritance. He ended up staying in the United States for three years, mostly in New York, first in the YMCA, then sharing with some bricklayers and then on the sofa of a tailor in the Bowery, interspersed with occasional days out at relatives of his father's in Philadelphia and Long Island. He survived by taking a variety of jobs, including bricklayer, architectural draughtsman and dishwasher. His often precarious financial circumstances helped him to develop a talent for thriftiness that would not only come in useful periodically throughout his life, but would also form a cornerstone of his ethical beliefs. This stay in America, his equivalent of the Grand Tour, would prove to be the most significant event in the shaping of his aesthetic and cultural ideas. Here this young man who had been born into the Austro-Hungarian Empire, which by its very nature was heterogeneous both socially and geographically, realized that an inclusive culture common to all was possible. It was also in New York that Loos experienced what might be described as his aesthetic epiphany. Hitherto, he had not been disinclined towards the decorative in everyday objects and in dress, but now, in a department store window, the young man's gaze fell on an utterly simple yet exquisitely crafted suitcase. Suddenly the scales fell from his eyes, affording him an unblinkered view of the modern style: 'The practical is beautiful!' The all-embracing nature of this Damascene conversion was probably later exaggerated by Loos. It was from this moment on, however, that he began to realize that following what he termed the style aberrations of the nineteenth century – though he greatly approved of the Regency and Schinkel's neo-classicism – the style of the dawning twentieth century had to break away from the idea of consecutive periods defined by changing tastes in ornamentation. The style of the coming age was to be found not in the applied arts, nor even in art itself, but rather in objects of daily use. 'Loos found the new forms he was to develop in his architecture, in inconspicuous objects like suitcases and simple furniture, in which plain surfaces and good materials were combined to pleasing effect.'[2]

Never claiming to be an inventor (revolution), but always with an eye to tradition (evolution), Loos soon identified the origins of his new credo. They were to be found not in the new world but in the realms of antiquity: 'The Greeks worked only for practicality, never giving any thought to beauty.'[3] Yet it was the Anglo-Saxon world (oddly, Loos seemed to think that England had remained chastely classical from Georgian times to his own day, thereby ignoring the horrors of the Gothick and Victorian styles among others) that in his view had inherited the mantle of the ancients: 'Is there a people today who work like the Greeks? Yes, the English people, the engineers.'[4] Of course, Loos was not the first to rediscover classical antiquity as an aesthetic form in keeping with the contemporary. As Anne Hollander has shown, the neo-classical artists and designers of the late eighteenth century used antique forms to formulate modern ideas. While classical elements had been in use in Europe for centuries, it was after 1760 that the visual awareness of the vocabulary of antique forms – Pompeii and Herculaneum had just been excavated – was greater than ever before. What was new was the usage of antique sources not merely for their decorative vocabulary but as an inspiration for basic forms. Now the classical orders and architectural principles of antiquity became mandatory once again, later leading the architectural historian Nikolaus Pevsner to describe neo-classicism as the 'first chapter' of modernism. In England, Sir John Soane – like Karl Friedrich Schinkel in Prussia – was one of the first architects to emulate the simple proportions of antique buildings, rather than their decorative features. Loos was an ardent admirer of Schinkel, declaring himself the official champion of Schinkel's memory towards the end of his own life.[5]

The pivotal role played by Beau Brummell in applying classical theories and proportions to the realm of dress has already been discussed in the introduction to this book. But this backward glance to antiquity was not the only common feature shared by the father of modern costume and the pioneer of modernism. In the modern suit, with its emphasis on the utter simplicity that Brummell had brought to it at its inception, Loos found the prototype for his philosophy of design and architecture. And clothing itself – an existential problem to Loos – remained one of his basic themes. What struck him particularly in America was the way in which people of all classes had access to modern clothing. While the Austrian peasant would come to Vienna in his loden coat and hobnail boots, Loos was surprised to find American farmers attending a funeral in faultless morning suits and frock coats. This was the result not only of the seemingly classless society he found there, but also of the phenomenon of off-the-peg clothing, which had originated in North America. In the US, ready-made suits were becoming popular as early as the 1820s, when such a thing had hardly been heard of in Europe. 'Observers in the New World, however, remarked that American gentlemen, who had always quickly adopted elegant English fashion, were already becoming very hard to distinguish from American farmers, shop-keepers and artisans who were appearing in the park or at church in well-cut, well-fitting ready-made town clothes.'[6] Loos, by now an ardent admirer of all things American (according to his second wife Elsie Altmann he would continue to favour the 'foreign' over the homegrown Austrian to the end of his life), saw in this a fundamental American attitude that was superior to that of the Middle European: 'An American philosopher says somewhere: "A young man is rich, if he has a brain in his head and a good suit in his closet." This philosopher knows his way around. He knows his people. What good is a good mind, if you cannot set it off to advantage with good clothing? Thus the English and the Americans demand of every man that he be well dressed.'[7] Ironically, Loos himself only ever wore bespoke clothing, always adhering to the hand-crafted over the industrially manufactured – an attitude that was also the fundamental feature of his Janus-like position within modernism.

Loos did not acquire the clothes that were to arm him for the fight awaiting him in Vienna in America, however, but rather on a lengthy stopover in London on his way back. There he had a comprehensive new wardrobe made by the finest tailors he could afford, thereby sealing the process of gradual identification with Anglo-Saxon culture that he had been experiencing in the preceding years. When Loos passed through London in 1896, Queen Victoria was still on the throne and the start of the golden age of male elegance presided over by her son was five years away. Yet in the eyes of the world, Edward was already the king of fashion. Whatever the future Emperor of India wore last year at Marienbad set the trend for the wardrobe the whole male world aspired to wear the next. Wherever the Prince of Wales went on his travels, tailors would gather to make copious notes and take surreptitious photographs. And he returned the compliment in part by adopting items of clothing that he had come across and bringing them back to England. The Homburg hat, for example, was a great success, later becoming the emblem of the diplomatic service, while the Tyrolean hat, for obvious reasons, was not. Edward was 'one of those pivotal figures so crucial to the history of men's fashion in the way they orient, regulate, and accelerate change when the world shifts from one era into another. They adopt and lend their prestige to sartorial changes, endowing them with the legitimacy needed to enter a stylish man's wardrobe.'[8] He is particularly significant for initiating the introduction of 'sportswear' into the world of fashion. This of course did not mean sweat pants and matching top, but rather shooting tweeds or tennis 'togs': off-white flannels and single-breasted blazer, which were gradually adopted for more general summer wear. The *fin de siècle* was infatuated with all the new sports then appearing, and cutting a dash was often more important than displaying sporting prowess. 'A man's wardrobe is now almost as varied as that of a woman,' observed the author of *Manners for Men* in 1897: 'He has special clothing for walking, riding, coaching, visiting, boating, hunting, shooting, playing golf, bicycling, tennis and cricket, for dinner, smoking and idling, for football, for the races and sailing, not to mention uniforms and attire at court and also the new motoring fashions.'[9] Edward – or Bertie as he was known – would also have had difficulty in becoming too accomplished a sportsman, as his taste for good living fairly soon made him run to fat. Yet his very portliness was another reason for him to promote an *élégance pratique*, ingeniously making a stylish feature of comfort. The most famous example is supposed to have come about when – after indulging in one of his usual rich meals – he undid the bottom button of his waistcoat, so initiating a custom that remains de rigueur to this day. This official sanction also eased the renaissance of the waistcoat, this time as an integral part of what would become the male uniform of modernity: the three-piece lounge suit. Loos was naturally convinced not only that the English shape was the correct one, but also that the British royal family was the ultimate authority in matters of taste: 'Everything we wear on our bodies directly relates to the King of England, since the English king is the visible symbol of the character of the English people.'[10] Just how far he was prepared to go in pursuit of his sartorial convictions is illustrated by an anecdote he told some years after his return to Austria, in an essay entitled 'Gentlemen's Hats': 'The correct hat is sold only in London. When my London hats were wearing out, I went in search of the correct shape [English in the original] here. What I found was that the English hats sold here were not the same as those sold in London. I asked a hatmaker to procure for me, from England, a hat of the precise form worn by members of the royal family. I made a guarantee from the London hatter regarding this a condition of my order. Cost immaterial. I had embarked on a wild goose chase. After months of excuses, after a sizeable sum spent on telegrams, the English firm brought negotiations to a definite close.'[11]

When Loos arrived back in Vienna in 1896, the *fin-de-siècle* dream was already about to measure itself against reality. During the second half of the nineteenth century, Vienna had been dominated by the liberal bourgeoisie; as the historian Carl E. Schorske points out, Vienna's cultural heyday was the product of an ideal combination of factors: 'Political, academic and aesthetic cultural factors were not only closely connected in principle and practice, but the whole of social life and the cultural life of the elite were also supported by the synthesis they created.'[12] Indeed, the 'high culture' of the liberal bourgeoisie engendered a domination of the arts in the Austrian empire, and in Vienna in particular, that was unparalleled anywhere in Europe. The Austrian middle class valued aesthetic culture as a visible sign of personal development and social status. In this process, the aristocracy served as a model for the bourgeoisie. This assimilation of the aristocracy and the bourgeoisie manifested itself in the most visible legacy of the 'liberal ascendancy':[13] the architecture of the Ringstrasse, the grand boulevard encircling the centre of Vienna. Schorske describes how, 'On account of its stylistic homogeneity and its extent, the Ringstrasse became a standing reference that enabled Austrians to recall the characteristics of an era, like the Victorian age for the English, the Gründerzeit for the Germans or the Second Empire for the French.'[14] Yet the 'tenement palaces' on the Ringstrasse emulated not only the baroque and classical mansions of the city centre, but also the town houses of London. Both classicism and anglophilia were far from alien to the Viennese bourgeoisie.

The aesthetic culture of the Austrian aristocracy had itself developed from the highly ritualized Catholicism of the Counter Reformation. Through the influence of court and church, the theatrical elements of religious worship also permeated the secular world. The significance accorded to aesthetic rituals occasionally assumed grotesque proportions. As Sándor Márai recalled in his autobiography, *Bekenntnisse eines Bürgers*, in his youth the Hungarian provinces saw a vogue for suicide among rank-and-file soldiers that only ended when the attendance of an imperial and royal military band was restricted to the funerals of officers. The idea of the Austrian nobleman was in many respects closer to dandyism than, for example, that of the Prussian Junker, which was characterized above all by total discipline and adherence to strict regulations (in a telling passage in Karl Kraus's *Die letzten Tage der Menschheit*, an Austrian general addresses his officers: 'Say what you like about the Germans... they have organization... We also have a few things over them, for example that certain indefinable something, charm, a *je ne sais quoi*'). Yet the charm of an Austrian officer and nobleman (usually the two went together) was a theatrical affair that had been scripted many years earlier, and that could therefore often be quite as predictable as the Prussian *Offizierscomment*. While the dandy's wit grows out of his more or less empirically determined role as an outsider, the charm of the Austrian aristocracy derived from the security of belonging to a privileged class.

As Joseph Roth described with peerlessly elegant melancholy in his novels, towards the end of the nineteenth century and the beginning of the twentieth, as the aristocracy faded and democracy loomed, the Austrian upper classes went through a period of decadence comparable to that of dandyism at the same time. The growing realization of their own obsolescence leads Roth's ambiguous heroes down the only path open to them: the aestheticization of their impotence. Yet Roth's Barons von Trotta and Taittinger lack the deep-seated ambivalence of the dandy, who works towards democracy even as he clings to a notion of aristocracy. Roth himself, however, experienced a good deal of the ambivalence that is an integral part of dandyism, as a lifelong socialist monarchist who affected the style of a military man. An anecdote sheds some light on his dandyism, which was one of grace and defiance in despair: his affluent friend the writer Stefan Zweig – who was also exiled by Nazism – ordered a pair of trousers for Roth, since he only had one pair, and they were unfit for the sort of restaurants Zweig liked. Roth insisted that they should be cut in Austrian cavalry style, making them immensely expensive. The next day, sitting in a bar in Ostend with his cronies, Roth ordered a vividly coloured liqueur which he proceeded to pour all over his jacket. He

was 'punishing Stefan Zweig', he explained, and was going to embarrass him by turning up for dinner in a stained and smelly jacket: 'Millionaires are like that! They take us to the tailor and buy us a new pair of trousers, but they forget to buy us a jacket to go with them.'[15] The Austrian aristocrat had a role to play in the grand theatre of empire, which entailed grace, charm and a touch of civilized decadence. The Marschallin in Hofmannsthal's *Rosenkavalier* sums up the thespian ethos of her aristocratic class rather aptly, as Schorske notes: *'Und in dem "wie", da liegt der ganze Unterschied'* (and in the 'how' lies all the difference). As they feel their luck has run its course, Roth's charming barons are more or less happy to settle into a permanently provisional arrangement of bittersweet nostalgia.

The decadence of the *fin de siècle* was not restricted to the aristocracy. No period in history is more closely associated with the terms 'modernity' and 'decadence', and no place more so than Vienna. While the Ringstrasse reminds Austrians of the period that preceded it, Vienna in 1900 is redolent of the tortuous labouratory that brought modernism to the world. Towards the end of the nineteenth century, aesthetic culture had started to detach itself from its synthesis with politics and science. The bourgeois dream of a cultural continuity of structures of expression and feeling had begun to reach its limits. These structures were in danger of being undermined by a culture of sentiment, which entirely lacked the moral dimension the middle class needed to maintain its identity. This atmosphere of social upheaval heightened the nerves of the bourgeoisie to a state of hitherto unparalleled sensitivity, which is well documented in Freud's writings and provided the pathology on which psychoanalysis was built. In artistic terms this meant a turn towards the aestheticism that could now also be seen in England and France. Yet unlike in London or Paris, the evolution of modernity out of decadence in Vienna took place within a comparatively confined geographical and chronological space. As Schorske observes again, 'In France, the post-liberal question of modernity in culture arose in the wake of the revolution of 1848 as a kind of avant-garde self-criticism of the bourgeoisie, and slowly spread with many advances and retreats, from the era of the Second Empire to the eve of World War I. In Austria, however, the modern movements appeared in most fields in the 1890s and were fully matured two decades later. Thus the growth of a new higher culture seemed to take place in Austria as in a hothouse, with political crisis providing the heat. Backward Austria, in sudden travail, became, as one of its poets [Friederich Hebbel] said, "the little world in which the big one holds its tryouts".'[16] The curious mixture of cosmopolitanism and provincialism, of traditionalism and hunger for innovation that was to be found in the capital of the heterogenous Austro-Hungarian Empire provided a rich sphere of influence for the dandy. As well as the London clubs and Paris boulevards, the coffee houses and salons of Vienna were a stage from which he could address the whole intellectual elite of Austria.

It was to this hothouse that Loos – newly attired both inside and out – returned from America and London in 1896. Now ideologically developed, Loos found himself caught between two fronts: on the one hand, traditional bourgeois Austrian culture, which he thought backward, describing its architectural manifestation the Ringstrasse as 'Potemkin-esque' for its richly decorated façades; and on the other, the manifestations of the new aestheticism emerging mostly from the Secession and the Wiener Werkstätte. The 'applied arts' – a genre that a priori should not exist, in Loos's view – especially emerging from the Werkstätte, were later tellingly fictionalized in Roth's *The Emperor's Tomb*. When Baron Trotta returns from the Great War, his mother asks him, with some foreboding, to guess what has become of his wife, with whom he has lost contact during his time as a prisoner of war in Russia: 'I suspected the worst, or rather what in the eyes of my mother might appear as the worst: "A dancer?" I asked. My mother shook her head earnestly. Then she said sadly, almost mournfully: "No – an arts and craft person."' To the elderly aristocrat the inherent deception she perceives in the applied arts – a belief she shares with Loos – is a cardinal sin: 'If you start making things that look valuable from worthless materials!'[17]

Completely unknown and fairly inexperienced in the archi-tectural field that he had envisaged as his profession, Loos set about creating a fertile climate for his ideas. He began with a series of articles in the *Neue Freie Presse*, concerned chiefly with questions of dress and the design of everyday objects. These brief essays were to serve as his credentials for the rank of arbiter elegantiarum, a rank already proclaimed by his appearance. His express aim was to shock the Viennese into a new awareness. He shared with the writer and essayist Karl Kraus, who had become his friend, the slightly super-cilious tone of a particularly Viennese form of irony, which ridicules the enemy by endorsing his views with obviously over-emphatic hyperbole. Kraus and Loos, whom Schorske calls 'the last two Puritans',[18] were ploughing the same lonely furrow. Both wanted to banish cloying ornamentation: Loos in architecture and design; Kraus in language (not using 'decorative' phrases was of course one of the three hallmarks of impeccable breeding that made Proust's Saint Loup such a perfect gentleman). In addition to styling himself a prophet, or even a messiah ('My children, fear not…'), Loos also had frequent recourse to one of the most basic tools of dandy rhetoric: the lie that tells the truth, the paradox. He later described the success of this tactic: 'That sounded paradoxical. But there were brave souls who diligently filed this and many other of my paradoxical ideas and had them reprinted. This happened so frequently that in the end people thought they were true.' When it came to the burning issue of dress, Loos did not tarry with generalizations for long, but soon moved on to personal attacks: 'When I returned to Vienna after a three-year absence in 1896 and saw my colleagues, I could scarcely believe my eyes. All these architects were dressed like artists. Not like other people, but – as the Americans would say – like buffoons. They had trained their own tailor, who created this costume from cloth… I – as was clear from my dress – was not an artist. I had engaged the services of Goldman & Salatsch [a Viennese tailor who worked in the English style and who had significantly dropped the second 'n' of 'Goldmann' in order to appear more Anglo-Saxon] and tried to convince my colleagues to stop fooling around and do the same. I was derided.'[19] Yet there was one person who heeded Loos's example, albeit with consequences that allowed Loos in turn to pour ridicule on his 'acolyte'. From around 1898, Loos had started to design the interiors of apartments and shops. His interiors were conceived as 'gentlemen's homes' to please clients who were very much like himself, bourgeois men with aristocratic ideas, and featured Persian carpets, brass fittings, open fires, mirrors often used to make rooms appear bigger, parquet floors, Chippendale-style chairs and tables, wooden panelling and plenty of marble. Loos gave a tour of his first interior to Josef Hoffmann, founder of the Wiener Werkstätte, and afterwards declared: 'He went straight to my tailor from this flat and flung his clothes where his clients would fling his designs a few years later... following this excursion, all his designs are influenced by me. But how! A Chesterfield is an upholstered cube, a teapot a silver one. Embarrassing!'[20]

Just as Loos condemned the applied arts in design and architecture, so he pointed the finger at the 'applied arts dress', with its flamboyant array of broad checks, velvet collars and eccentrically knotted neckties, that was the mark of the 'artist' around the turn of the century (Wilde had notably tried to promote his 'aesthetic costume' before reverting to more sober, Brummell-inspired attire). Loos had already attacked this contrived bohemianism in dress in an essay from 1898 entitled simply 'Die Herrenmode' (Men's Fashion), identifying it as a characteristically German habit: 'The English and Americans expect every man to be well dressed. But the Germans go a step further, they also want to dress beautifully. If the English wear wide trousers, the Germans immediately find proof – by referring to old Vischer, perhaps, or the golden mean – that these are unaesthetic and that only narrow trousers can be considered beautiful. Blustering, railing and ranting, they allow their trousers to become wider, year after year. Fashion is a tyrant, they protest. But what is this? Has somebody had second thoughts? The English are wearing narrow trousers again, and by precisely the same process the Germans find evidence for the beauty of the wide trouser. Who can make sense of this? But the English make fun of the German craving for beauty. The Medici Venus, the Pantheon, a Botticelli painting, a song by Burns – these are beautiful! But a pair of trousers!? Or a coat with three buttons or four!? Or a waistcoat cut with a high or low V!? I always feel uneasy when I hear people discussing the beauty of such things. I get nervous when someone asks facetiously of an item of clothing, "Is that supposed to be beautiful?" Germans in polite society do as the English do. They are happy to be well dressed. They relinquish beauty. The great poet, the great painter, the great architect are dressed like them. But the poetaster, the Sunday painter and the minor architect turn their bodies into altars on which they make sacrifices to beauty, in the form of velvet collars, aesthetic trouser fabrics and Secessionist neckties.'[21]

He identifies an archetype of the petit-bourgeois German/ Austrian thirsting for beauty in the form of the *Gigerl* (Austrian for popinjay, or dedicated follower of fashion). Though often confused with the dandy, the dedicated follower of fashion is his polar opposite. The Gigerl thirsts for originality, wanting to stand out from the crowd. The dandy, following Brummell's dictum, 'If John Bull turns around to look at you, you are not well dressed; but either too stiff, too tight, or too fashionable', seeks a distinction so subtle that it is recognized only by the cognoscenti, and sometimes only by himself. Baudelaire expanded on this: 'Dandyism does not consist, as many thoughtless people assume, in an inordinate delight in dress and material elegance. To the consummate dandy, such things are merely a symbolic expression of the aristocratic superiority of his mind. Hence – in his eyes, enamoured as he is with distinction – perfection in dress lies in utter simplicity, which is indeed the best way to distinguish oneself. What then can this passion be, which has crystallized into a doctrine and has generated such devoted acolytes, this unwritten code that has created so haughty a brotherhood? It is above all the burning desire to create a true originality just outside the limits of social conventions.'[22] Indeed, the dandy is concerned less with an arbitrary notion of beauty than with correctness as defined by the rules set in place by Brummell. Perfection lies in absolute familiarity with the rules and their application, an application which can also include the occasional transgression, or solecism. Loos elabourates on this point: 'To be correctly dressed! It seems to me that with these words I have lifted the secret with which our fashions in clothing have so far been surrounded. We have tried to define fashion with words such as beautiful, chic, elegant, dashing and smart. But that is not the point. The point is to be dressed in such a manner as not to attract attention.'[23] There is of course an irony here: in Vienna, Loos's appearance was far from the anonymous one he himself prescribed. His clothing was correct to an excessive degree. Loos's admirer and contemporary Richard von Schaukal expressed this ambiguity through his fictional character Andreas von Balthesser: 'The dandy stylizes his conscious correctness and treats his consciousness ironically.'[24] And it is indeed in this way that the dandy transcends

convention and attains distinction – by pushing the convention to its furthest limits, and so transcending it. There can be no doubt that Loos also enjoyed this role of dandy as outsider or 'the Englishman', the gentleman who towers above his ill-dressed compatriots.

The knowledge and application of the rules is an arcane matter, not easily acquired. It requires a noble and infinitely cultured soul. And not just any culture, but what Loos refers to provocatively as occidental culture, in order to distinguish it from the oriental or rather Balkan culture that – in the heterogenous and hierarchical Austrian empire – coexisted side by side with Western influences. To Loos, the cultural epicentre of the world was of course London. Loos began his essay on men's fashion with an attack on the backward culture of the old regime of his native land ('The nature of Austria is not centre but periphery,' Count Chojnicki declares in Roth's *The Emperor's Tomb*): 'Is there anybody who does not want to be well dressed? Our century has abolished hierarchies in clothing. Everybody now has the right to dress like a king. We may use the percentage of people who take advantage of this libertarian achievement as an indicator of the cultural level of a nation. In England and America it is the whole population; in the Balkans only the upper crust. And in Austria? I dare not answer that question.'[25] Two broader issues underlie Loos's argument: modernity and class. Modernity is Loos's primary concern. Yet this is not modernity as manifested in the latest development in any field, or indeed the latest fashion. Instead, Loos's notion of modernity combines the established with the contemporary: to make use of the achievements of one's time while upholding the traditions of culture without regard for superficial trends. According to Loos, the forms of correct clothing, which have developed in a quasi-evolutionary manner, need no changes, or hardly any. With him this aesthetic position was linked inextricably with his enthusiasm for the traditional crafts, which he preferred to industrial production. So on the one hand the term 'classical modernism', of which Loos is now widely seen as the pioneer, could not be more appropriate. On the other hand, however, his persona and beliefs were – in true dandy fashion – a way of marrying seeming opposites, and grew out of the circumstances of his own life. The love of craft and the belief in its inherent nobility that had been instilled in him by his adored father never left him, even in the 1920s, when figures such as Le Corbusier and his followers, whom Loos to some degree viewed as his heirs and even imitators, regarded industrial production as the true basis of modernity.

Again, Loos's notion of modernity, and indeed of modern man, is inextricably linked with the concept of the gentleman, and indeed of the dandy. He sums up the application of the principles of correctness and anonymity thus: 'An item of clothing is modern, if when wearing it at an event in the best society at the epicentre of one's culture, one attracts as little attention as possible.'[26] The principle of anonymity also serves to protect the wearer. In 1894, Loos's near contemporary Oscar Wilde remarked: 'In so vulgar an age as this we all need masks.' The famous mask of the gentleman, of which his clothing forms only one aspect, is also a mask behind which he is protected against the increasingly threatening and seemingly uncontrollable forces of modern life.

Behind this standardized mask, modern man is free to live his individuality. Curiously, Loos also applied the principle of the mask to the houses he designed for private clients, to the extent that the windows in his otherwise featureless façades sometimes look like holes cut out for eyes and mouths. To the dandy, the creation of his subtly individualized and consummately perfect mask is of course an end in itself and his *raison d'être*. His salvation, as well as his tragedy, lies in the fact that the work of art, the persona he has perfected, becomes, in the words of Ernst Jünger, 'the gilded, unchangeable mask over the horrors of the void'.[27]

It is also Loos's evolutionary concept of how something comes to be modern that roots him deep in tradition. The frantic chasing of the modern by the dedicated follower of fashion is of course a deeply un-modern act. Just as the 'effortless elegance' of great dressers lies in its apparent artlessness, so the quest for the modern can only result in its loss. Modernity is an unconscious effect, not something declared by artists or designers. This elevation of the unconscious practice of craft over the calculated effect of 'design' runs like a thread through all of Loos's early articles. In parallel with Loos, the German architect Hermann Muthesius, whose three-volume *Das englische Haus* (The English House) referenced an earlier volume by Robert Dohme formulated his understanding of the modern in an essay on the English country house in 1903: 'This is the unconsciously modern. To want to be modern as a matter of principle is not objective and hence very un-modern. One is modern by being as objective as possible and thinking of nothing but what is immediately required. To seek modernity in superficial detail is the erroneous way of the 19th century, a way of looking at artistic matters from the wrong point of view.'[28]

As far as class was concerned, what Loos bemoaned in Austria was the lack of occidental culture at all levels of society. Yet his concern was not one of standard egalitarianism. Loos wanted everybody to be an aristocrat. By this he of course meant the idealized notion, rather than the real thing. In this desire he was 'more Nietzschean than royalist'.[29] It was a desire for a consistency between the ideal of citizenship and the aristocratic claim for superiority that was not only inherently paradoxical but had also not been approached since the Greek *polis* of antiquity. And it was also, of course, the aristocracy of Brummell, whose nobility was 'entirely personal, unsupported by armorial bearings, ancestral halls, vast lands, or even a fixed address, and he was also known to be able to live on nothing a year'.[30] The initial claim for aristocracy hence shifts towards a desire for individuality and distinction, the latter necessarily lacking in the born aristocrat, who sees it as his birthright. Baudelaire continues: 'All [dandies] are prone to the characteristics of dissent and revolt; all represent what is best in human pride, the desire that is so rare in contemporary society to fight triviality and to destroy it. This desire is expressed in the dandy as a haughty, patrician attitude, cool and challenging.'[31] Loos's notion of aristocracy is inherently one of revolt: not only was the ideal implicitly far superior to the reality lived by the contemporary Austrian aristocracy, but he also wanted to impart it to every citizen. He embraced the inherent paradox that in a society where everybody has achieved the ultimate distinction, distinction ceases to exist. While the art of the dandy makes no allowance for compromise, contradiction is another matter.

Quite at home with the dandy's position of ambivalence, Loos then goes on to qualify his egalitarianism with a snobbish confirmation of the status quo. The only people in Austria whom Loos perceives as part of occidental culture are the nobility: 'Polite society, which finds such concerns too petty, will only embrace changes in fashion that are too subtle to be noticed by the middle class. Its members are no longer protected by sumptuary laws (as in the Middle Ages), and they would find it disagreeable to have their fashions copied the day after they have worn them. In order to be released from the eternal pursuit of the latest clothes and cuts, they operate by the most discreet of means. For years a new cut will be protected, an open secret among the great tailors, until it is leaked by some fashion journal. Then it will be another few years before everybody knows about it. The great tailors of the world, those who are capable of dressing a man according to the noblest principles, number only a handful. The fact that we have a few of them in Vienna is due only to the fortuitous circumstance that our nobility are frequent guests in the Queen's [of England] drawing room and have many clothes made in England. This in turn introduced good taste to Vienna, so raising Viennese tailoring to heights that are admired abroad. It is fair to say that Viennese high society is the best-dressed on the Continent, and that other tailors have been raised to greater heights by these firms.'[32]

In his follow-up essay, 'Die Damenmode' (Women's Fashion), Loos gives us a clearer glimpse of the underlying psychological fears that were part of his aversion to ornament. The battle fought by Kraus and Loos was not only against the old Austria and the new aestheticism, but also against sensuality. The embodiment of all the irrationality and threatening sensuality they perceived – and in which it may be assumed they were not particularly out of step with the attitudes of the time – was woman. In counteracting this perceived threat, they tended to be patronizing rather than openly hostile. In his essay 'Sittlichkeit und Kriminalität' (Morality and Criminality) Kraus had already touched on the subject, and had sided with women as victims of society. In his notorious study 'Geschlecht und Charakter' (Sex and Character), Otto Weininger had meanwhile advocated the female principle should be superseded entirely. From today's point of view, Loos's personal relationships with women – he was married three times – can only be described as flawed. All of his wives were considerably younger than himself, and he adopted a pseudo-paternal attitude towards them. While he found it useful to employ them as captive pupils for his theories of 'noble living', he failed on the whole to provide for them – in fact they often had to support him. Though she always spoke admiringly of Loos, his second wife, the dancer Elsie Altmann, recalled a telling episode in her memoirs, when towards the end of their relationship Loos tried to convince her in all seriousness to have her legs broken and lengthened, so as to conform to a more modern ideal of beauty and increase her success as a dancer. Though in some ways a great lover of women – he was also a great admirer and friend of Josephine Baker, though unlike Le Corbusier he did not succeed in seducing her – Loos came up time and time again against the obvious obstacle: the dandy's life is not suitable for sharing. Curiously, the only woman he had a slightly more equal relationship with was his English companion Bessie Bruce, who though deeply in love with Loos was too much her own woman to be moulded by him.

In 'Die Damenmode', Loos ultimately supports the notion of female equality, but only after first relegating woman to a lower rung on the evolutionary ladder: 'Woman's fashion! You dreadful chapter of cultural history! You tell humanity of its secret lust. As we browse your pages, our soul shudders at the prospect of your terrible aberrations and unbelievable vices.'[33] He views women's fashion as an ancient ruse by which women seek to ensnare men. While he believes that the 'noble' in woman seeks to be equal to man, he adds that at present time this is only possible if she wins his love. As men grew bored eventually with the costume of Eve, woman invented fashion to tease man with sphinx-like mysteries that he must endeavour to unravel. In parallel to his views on men's clothing, Loos also sees women's fashion as expressing something of the existential nature of its wearer. Yet he does not differentiate between different types, as he does with man: every woman is 'forced to appeal to man's sensuality through her clothing – unconsciously compelled to appeal to that perverted sensuality of his – for which only the culture of the times can be held responsible.'[34] Clothing is thus given to man as a permanent creative device, to be utilized among other things to express his social position, which enables him to dominate woman. To woman, on the other hand, it is a means to an end – marriage – at which point her existence becomes entirely subsumed by her husband's social position, and the subtleties of her own persona become irrelevant.

Man aspires to nobility, woman aspires only to man. Changes in women's fashion are thus driven by changes in the sexual ideal. In the light of this, Loos identifies the fashion leaders in both sexes: 'The leader in men's fashion is the man who occupies the highest social position, while the leader in women's fashion is the woman who has developed the highest sensibility in the arousal of sensuality: the cocotte.'[35] This theory would appear to be borne out by Proust, who created in Odette the most sophisticated of cocottes, whose fashion sensibility is so highly developed that she appears to be 'wrapped in an entire culture'.[36] Apart from a few salient points about the fundamental differences between tailored clothing and women's fashion, running through the pages of 'Die Damenmode' is also Loos's only half-unconscious fear of what Kraus had termed the 'vaginal age'. Man hides not only his sensuality but all aspects of his private life behind his mask: 'Masculinity in essence is the ability to keep a secret, and all secrets are ultimately of a sexual nature.'[37] The dandy seeks to neutralize the unsettling sensuality of the cocotte – expressed through silks and velvets, ribbons and flowers – which threatens his rationality. He wants to banish it. By putting her into a tailor-made (woman's) suit he turns her into a version of himself, something he can understand, a comrade.

This is not the place for a detailed discussion of Loos's architectural work, which has been done admirably elsewhere. It is important, though, to consider a few characteristics of his built work and interiors in relation to his dandyism. Remarkably, it is Loos's private houses and commercial interiors – controlled environments serving a specific purpose or the needs of one person or family – that constitute his masterpieces. Despite his messianic and in some ways socialist approach towards the public good, and towards ideas of redemption of the common man through aristocratic aesthetics, his designs for larger-scale public buildings remain less convincing. The reason for this largely unacknowledged (by him) preference is to be found in his article 'Prinzip der Bekleidung' (Principle of Clothing), which is an adaptation of the older architect Gottfried Semper's *Bekleidungstheorie* (Theory of Clothing): 'In the beginning there was clothing. Man sought shelter from the inclemencies of the weather, and shelter and warmth during his sleeping hours. He sought to cover himself. The most ancient architectural feature is the blanket.'[38] Loos assigns to the architect the primary task of providing a spatial shell for the human being within. The building structure, plan and façade are secondary considerations in his view. Loos sought to progress from the innermost layer to the outermost, from clothing to interiors to architecture, starting with the construction of a three-dimensional shell, covering the individual according to his needs, like a bespoke suit. Hence he took issue with the historicists and secessionists of 1900, as well as with the modernists of the 1920s, with their fondness for standardization and two-dimensional thinking. Loos buildings are based not on a ground plan but on a three-dimensional room plan. All the rooms have different ceiling heights according to their use – as may be observed specifically in his villas – and no space is wasted for the sake of uniformity. As a result, the exteriors frequently appear as a complex agglomeration of interlocking boxes.

Economy to the point of thrift is of course one of the dandy's prime virtues, very much in contrast with his lavish image. In itself, it is an inevitable concomitant of the eternal search for perfection. Furthermore, it is a necessary virtue in a life that oscillates continuously between the poorhouse and the Ritz. Loos was a veritable emperor of thrift: no one was more 'pressé de trouver le lieu et la formule' than him. His painstaking use of space has its equivalent in the economical architecture of travel: a sleeper train compartment or a ship's cabin, their interiors fitted so precisely to make full use of minimal space. But this urge is not purely economical. Psychologically, it is driven by a kind of claustrophilia, as well as by a fetishistic attachment to the 'perfect fit': the bedroom is a cosy cabin, the house a direct extension of the inhabitants' needs and individuality. The dandy desires to live in his wardrobe, both literally and metaphorically. The architect Herbert Schleicher describes attending some lectures Loos gave at the Technologische Gewerbesmuseum (Museum of Technology and Trade), in which he spoke on the organization of flats and specifically the storage of clothing: 'The first strong impression I got was of the description of desks and wardrobes equipped with so-called "English drawers" [Englischer Zug], which was an entirely new term to me.'[39] The dandy's perfect microcosm will be full of sliding doors, brass hinges and devices that snap into place: things that are balanced and indeed fitted. Parallels with the tailored suit are never far away, a fact that was not lost on Loos's contemporaries. Ludwig Hevesi, then spokesman for the Secession, compared the geometrical elegance of Loos's architecture to his suits, remarking of his interior designs for Goldman &

Salatsch: 'Well, Loos! That's just like him. It really is just like him. He dresses like that too. And his tailor's shop and flat on the Graben are furnished like that too. Folding, snappy, so formally and mechanically correct.'[40] It was hardly surprising that the style best suited to the furnishing of tailors' and of gentlemen's outfitters' premises should be that of the dandy.

When his London suits started to wear out, Loos started to cultivate Viennese tailors with a view to rebuilding his wardrobe. He settled his substantial tailors' bills, which he was often unable to pay, through his architectural work. His earliest interior was for the tailor Eberstein, which Loos furnished in the American style with dark stained wood, even importing brass fittings and door knobs from America. He also introduced as a customer his protégé Oskar Kokoschka, who not only waxed lyrical about the tailor's art and august standing but also followed the method of payment favoured by his mentor: 'Neither he nor I ever had any money, but he knew the best tailors in Vienna, for example the court tailor Herr Eberstein, who dressed the old emperor Franz Joseph. He was a distinguished old gentleman and *the* tailor in Vienna. He dressed me in bespoke suits as though for one of his noble customers. In return I painted his portrait, depicting this conservative figure in a way that no court photographer could have managed. As he took my measurements I learned anatomy for the first time, from him, the court tailor, as this is also of great importance in the making of a suit, so that the body can move freely in its clothing. This is true elegance.' Gentlemen's outfitters remained one of Loos's specialities. Their interiors evoked the atmosphere

of the clubs of St James's (the most august of which were furnished according to Brummell's prescriptions) with wood panelling, brass fittings and buttoned leather chairs and sofas. In an atmosphere that was masculine without being too stuffy, Loos managed to reflect the luxurious simplicity of the wares offered for sale. His design of 1910–13 for the shop of the renowned Viennese tailor Knize – for whom Loos also designed their Berlin and Paris branches – alas remains the only surviving example of his mastery of this genre that was so close to his heart.

There was also another home from home for the dandy. Later in life, Loos was to become a familiar figure in the musical theatres and cabarets of Europe and his second wife Elsie Altmann described how the couple were regulars at the

Variétés Apollo and the Ronacher in Vienna. But it was much
earlier, in 1908, when he was still under the influence of his
American trip, that Loos created his dandyistic masterpiece,
unifying as it does in one tiny room the apparent opposites of lavish opulence and utter simplicity: the American
Bar, which survives and thrives to this day in the Kärntner
Durchgang in Vienna's first district. In his memoirs, entitled
My Last Breath, Luis Buñuel devoted a memorable chapter
to 'earthly pleasures' in which he described his ideal bar, a
space of exiguous proportions inhabited only by men who
drink and think in silence, a 'school of loneliness'. The Loos
Bar, as it is now known, a dimly lit space of just 27.4 square
metres, is a claustrophiliac's dream come true, a womb-like
space of mahogany and marble, bathed in a diffuse light by
the backlit onyx of the entrance area. Mirrors ring the room
above eye level, reflecting the heavy marble ceiling, its oblong
cassette pattern tapering inward to infinity, along with the
drinkers' thoughts. The geometric, labyrinthine impression
of an all-encompassing microcosm is further enhanced by the
black-and-white chequerboard of the floor. Yet while these
optical illusions suggest the possibility of flight – the Lilli-
putian stairway to the downstairs lavatory gives the perfect
illusion of being on a cruise liner or a luxury train – all the
materials are of reassuring and luxurious solidity, and all
the lines leading to perdition are straight, never threatening
a loss of control along the way.

Loos's attitude towards the Great War is best illustrated
by a dandyistic gesture of almost comical proportions:
as soon as he was called up he went to Knize, by now his
favourite tailor and good friend, and ordered a uniform he

had designed himself. Following his preferences, the design was not only the colour of American uniforms but was also as close to them in cut as could be imagined. He wore this uniform in the field, blithely unperturbed by any fear of disciplinary consequences, and – even more bizarrely – never threatened with any. His other contribution to the war effort consisted of a published appeal to his fellow soldiers not to wear elastic-sided boots, as they caused sweaty feet which could lead to frostbite in winter. He addressed the relevance of matters of dress in wartime in 1919, when the Viennese newspaper *Das Neue 8-Uhr Blatt* commissioned him to answer readers' queries on sartorial matters. He had already started a sartorial agony column in his own *Das Andere* before the war. In 1921, Loos was appointed chief architect in the *Siedlungsamt* (housing department). Only one of his housing projects was built, but it seems that what disappointed Loos even more was the lack of appreciation of his small cottages by the workers for whom they were intended. Loos's ideas of a self-sufficient, small-scale aristocracy inevitably clashed with more 'common' ideas of self-advancement. Irritated and slightly bitter, Loos gave up his post in 1924 and sought to make a new start in Paris, the capital of (Baudelaireian) modernity and his favourite city. What doubtless had given him hope was his invitation to and membership of the Salon d'automne the previous year.

In Paris, the self-styled cosmopolitan could put his standing as an 'international gentleman' to the test. The writer Julius Klinger had earlier remarked, on watching Loos crossing the Ringstrasse, 'Your deportment is very Viennese, Adolf Loos; but this local note in your habits and your movements

is sure to go unnoticed in Paris, London, New York or anywhere else in the world. The French, English and Americans are highly unlikely to take you as a foreigner.'[41] Ironically, it was not long before Loos, the arbiter of modernity, was to enlighten the Parisians in such matters. In 1926, he gave a lecture with the title 'Walking, Standing, Sitting and Lying Down' at the Sorbonne, as part of a series of lectures entitled *Der Mensch mit den Modernen Nerven* (Man with Modern Nerves). In this, Loos imitated the attitude of the humble subordinate, for example, by perching on the edge of his seat, so highlighting the assumption that people are at their most respectful when they are sitting as uncomfortably as possible. He contrasted this with the casual manners of the Americans, who for instance did not see the need to doff their hat when entering a shop. This assumed nonchalance of course also references Brummell's famed imperturbability. Loos's reforming zeal also extended to food. He had already upset the Viennese by advocating replacing their rich cuisine with a diet of raw tomatoes, roast beef and cabbage (Loos himself for years subsisted exclusively on ham and cream to cure a stomach ailment). Brummell had also pronounced on food. Principally a beefeater himself he deemed vegetables on the whole inelegant, though he did concede, 'I once ate a pea.'

As far as modern sartorial nerves were concerned, by the 1920s the metropolitan cityscape was dominated by the three-piece lounge suit, which had almost entirely replaced morning suits and frock coats except on formal occasions. Whether its comparatively loose cut encouraged lounging, or whether increasingly relaxed attitudes demanded a more casual approach to dress is of course a chicken-and-egg question. Loos had already addressed the eternal existential choice between loose and tight fit and low and high buttoning in his role as a sartorial agony aunt. Answering a question about the belted overcoat, Loos found modern nerves not yet entirely in tune with the possibilities of the lounge suit: 'Sometimes people feel more comfortable when they are casually dressed, sometimes when they are smartly dressed. We are living in an age when people want to dress smartly, more buttoned-up. Even our "lounge-suit", which by virtue of its visible waistcoat is designed to be worn open, was already worn increasingly buttoned before the war. Obviously the nerves demand it. The more modern man's nerves are, the more buttoned-up his coat will be.' As an example he cited his friend Peter Altenberg, who fifteen years earlier, and somewhat ahead of his time, had had belts fitted to all his coats, so that he could pull them in more snugly at the waist. Altenberg was also a warning of the closeness of perfectionism to pathology. So modern were his nerves that he not only had a belt fitted to his dinner jacket (behind Loos's back), but also spent most of his life in psychiatric institutions.

Sadly, architectural work in Paris was not as forthcoming as Loos had hoped it would be. The only built reminder of his time in France is his house for the Dadaist Tristan Tzara, while a house for Josephine Baker and the Grand-Hotel Babylon remained at the planning stage. But those three names are enough to conjure up an idea of the time he was having in the City of Light. Despite being constantly broke, he assured Elsie (whom he had married in 1919), that 'the main thing was to be able to live in Paris'.[42] It seems that

Loos was making the most of his enforced idleness, the positive virtue of which he had already pointed out in his essay
'Lob der Gegenwart' (In Praise of the Present). Once again he
praised the woollen clothes of the Englishman, and – with
a degree of poetic licence – his country and its acceptance
of the unemployable: 'It is the clothing of the people who
include the strongest characters, where the strong character
without money, the tramp, is not locked away in the work-
house, and where he is shown goodwill and interest. Where
work is nothing to be ashamed of but even less something
to be proud of, where everybody can work or not, where
everybody lives life according to his free will. The tramp is
the heroic expression of a strong individuality. It is hardly
heroic to have money and not work. But he who goes through
life without either money or work is a hero.'[43] To Elsie, who
found the couple's hand-to-mouth existence increasingly
trying, he added rather ruefully: 'Only the true aristocrat can
live without working. Other people do not have the nerves
for idleness.'[44] A poignant reminder that the dandy and the
tramp are merely two sides of the same coin.

The less aristocratically inclined Elsie had moved back to
Vienna, where she found it easier to make a living from her
dancing, and only came to Paris on visits, when she inevitably had to pay Loos's hotel bills. She also failed to share his
enthusiasm for the nightspots of St Germain, the company
of idle youths (Loos was now fifty-five) or his new-found
love of whisky (or, though not mentioned by Elsie, brothels).
Eventually, she could no longer bear the combination of emotional distance – Loos's behaviour had become irrational and
even callous in her eyes – and the financial demands of her

husband's babylonian lifestyle. Elsie divorced Loos in 1926. It took Loos another year to return to Vienna himself, not exactly with his tail between his legs, but a little defeated by his lack of built projects and considerably weakened by a taste for decadence discovered comparatively late in life. Despite some built work, mainly in Czechoslovakia – the Villa Muller in Prague, his late masterpiece, was finished in 1930 – this last Viennese period was overshadowed by a growing feeling that he had not received the recognition he deserved. Ever the mythomaniac Loos was not beyond stylizing his 'failure' into a legend of unrecognized genius: his writings from 1900 to 1930 were published under the title *Trotzdem* (Despite). Despite, indeed, a grand celebration of his life and work on the occasion of his sixtieth birthday in Prague, he remained a largely unheard and unheeded prophet in Vienna. The last five years of his life were also darkened by increasing physical and mental ill health. Having long suffered from bad hearing, he was now more or less completely deaf, which compounded his feelings of isolation and depression. In 1928, he had received a suspended prison sentence for child abuse. In 1932, his last marriage to Claire Beck, thirty-five years his junior, ended in divorce after just three years. By this point Loos was already a patient in the sanatorium of Kalksburg, where he died on 23 August 1933 in a state of partial dementia.

In retrospect, the year of Adolf Loos's death cannot fail to seem significant. After a lifetime of preaching cosmopolitanism and modernity, and of condemning the atavistic aspects of Austro/German culture, he died in the year that Adolf Hitler came to power. So began a period that was the devastating and disastrous culmination of Germany's revolt against

modernity, of which the formation of the German nation had itself been the beginning. If Nazism was the antithesis of everything Loos believed in, parallels can be found between his thinking and that of a more recent Austrian with dandy-ist leanings. Like Loos and many dandies before and after him, Thomas Bernhard believed that only hyperbole and repetition can create clarity. Like Loos, Bernhard sought constantly to attack and undermine the Austrian culture of which he himself became a representative. Like Loos and Baudelaire before him, Bernhard was a self-declared enemy of the establishment, who was equally ill at ease with the aes-thetic follies of bohemianism. Like Loos, Bernhard employed the services of Knize. But there the similarities end. To most people, Loos's legacy lies in the misquotation of his most famous essay 'Ornament and Crime' as 'Ornament is Grime': a misrepresentation that not only renders this man who was steeped in ambiguity unambiguous, but also overlooks the most important section of the essay, in which Loos preaches aristocratic tolerance. Ornamentation was indeed a crime, but it was one that Loos was willing to commit each time he ordered a pair of shoes, as he was reluctant to deprive his bootmaker of the pleasure he derived from applying the brogueing pattern. From the dandy's point of view, the essence of Adolf Loos's legacy is an assertion that is as mod-ernist as it is unfashionable: 'There can be no development of perfected forms.'[45]

THE DUKE OF WINDSOR

Rule and Transgression

On est bien changé, voilà tout.

BEAU BRUMMELL

To Dolf Sternberger the mastery of the Windsor knot seemed a major stepping stone; in at least one aspect of his life he had 'arrived'. Curiously, the Duke of Windsor himself never tied the knot he is supposed to have invented. To achieve the sumptuous plumpness of his knots, he had his shirtmaker and haberdasher Hawes & Curtis put extra inter-lining in his ties. The knot remained a simple four-in-hand. The duke, formerly Edward VIII, King of Great Britain and the British Dominions and Emperor of India, would certainly have been in agreement with Sternberger, however, over the importance he invested in what to most people would seem a trivial choice. To the Duke of Windsor, clothing was not merely one aspect of life, it was the existential problem per se. In his sartorial autobiography *A Family Album*, published in 1960 and intended as a light addition to his official autobi-ography *A King's Story*, he analysed the various aspects of trouser-widths and lapel-lengths with a lively energy that he never quite managed to devote to the state of the Empire. *Sinn und Wirken der Kleider* (the meaning and effect of clothes) the title Thomas Carlyle gives to the imaginary work of Professor Teufelsdröckh in *Sartor Resartus*, were to him a real and pressing concern. The way he dressed was not only the creative expression of his dandyism but also a means of subverting the role that had been assigned to him.

In his book he described his own style of clothing in some detail, and also set it in the context of the sartorial preferences of previous monarchs. The irreconcilability of an excessive interest in clothing with the role of a responsible monarch is highlighted in a letter from his great-grandmother Queen Victoria to her son, later Edward VII, in 1851: 'Dress is a trifling matter which might not be raised to too much importance in our own eyes. But it gives also the one outward sign from which people in general can and often do judge upon the inward state of mind and feeling of a person; for this they all see while the other they cannot see. On that account it is of some importance particularly in persons of high rank. I must now say that we do not wish to control your own tastes and fancies which, on the contrary, we wish you to indulge and develop, but we do expect that you never wear anything extravagant or slang, not because we don't like it but because it would prove a want of self-respect and be an offence against decency, leading, as it has often done before in others, to an indifference to what is morally wrong.'[1] To the dandy, each new item of clothing brings with it the promise of a new life. To Edward Windsor, the way he dressed initially expressed the kind of life he wished for, yet was prevented from having by the position he was born into. He had arrived when he was born. As soon as he became aware of this fact, he longed to depart.

His was a buttoned-up childhood in every sense of the term. Born Edward Albert Christian George Andrew Patrick David on 23 June 1894, he was the eldest great-grandson of the reigning monarch, Queen Victoria, and first child of the Duke and Duchess of York, Prince George and the former Princess Victoria Mary of Teck. When the Victorian age ended with the death of Victoria in 1901, Edward was too young to have any real sense of the momentousness of the occasion. When his parents set off soon after on an extended tour of the Empire, Edward and his siblings were left in the care of his grandparents, the new King Edward VII and his wife Queen Alexandra. Much later in life the duke was to declare: 'I had a wretched childhood! Of course there were short periods of happiness, but I remember it chiefly for the miserableness I had to keep to myself.'[2] The time he spent with his grandparents seems to have been just such a period of happiness, which left an indelible impression on the child and went some way to explaining his character as an adult. When he recalled Edward VII in later life, the duke's memories seem to have crystallized into a figure of gilded geniality, the personification of ease: 'the portrait of my grandfather seems bathed in perpetual sunlight. He was in his sixties, in the twilight of his life, when his personality began to mean something to me. Few men could match his vitality, his sheer *joie de vivre*. The Parisian term *un bon boulevardier* might have been invented for him. And while I can remember him of course as the regal figure of solemn ceremonies, I like best to recall him presiding over a well-laden table or making gallant gestures towards beautiful women.'[3] The writer Osbert Sitwell, who was on familiar terms with many members of the royal family, would later recall how he was told by Edward's maternal uncle, Lord Athlone, 'that for many years he had seen trouble coming to his nephew, the Duke of Windsor, who, even as a boy, had shown himself fascinated by the gallant career of his grandfather, King Edward VII, and would frequently question his uncle about it. Lord Athlone would try to discourage him, and the talk would invariably end with the young Prince asking, "But Uncle Algy, wasn't my grandfather very popular with everyone?" to which Lord Athlone would always reply, "It was alright in his time, but nobody would stand it today!"'[4]

Edward was not the first member of his family for whom clothing acquired an almost existential significance. His uncle the Duke of Clarence, nicknamed 'collars and cuffs' on account of his high starched collars, was rumoured (however improbably) to have died from influenza contracted from an infected double-breasted jacket. His grandfather had of course launched a great many fashions during his long tenure as Prince of Wales. Though a stickler for correct apparel and the minutiae of etiquette, he was almost as indulgent to his grandchildren as he was to himself. Edward basked in this obvious affection, which was in marked contrast to what he perceived as his father's authoritarian coldness. In his memoirs, the duke portrayed his father as a rather strict and uninspiring man who disapproved of his heir from an early age. As the duke's biographer Philip Ziegler puts it: 'The Duke of York loved and wanted the best for his children but he was a bad-tempered and often frightening man; he was never cruel, but he was a harsh disciplinarian who believed that a bit of bullying never did a child any harm...

a summons to the library almost always heralded a rebuke, and a rebuke induced terror in the recipient.'[5]

Of course Edward – both because of his status as heir to the throne and because of his early propensity towards 'easy living' – came in for a good deal of this kind of discipline. These measures were doomed to fall on fallow ground, however, as the young prince appears to have been a sensitive child who would have benefited more from lighthearted encouragement and praise. When Edward was just eleven years old, Lord Esher, a close aide to the royal family, found him to be an unusually courteous and considerate child for his age, but also remarked: 'The look of Weltschmerz in his eyes I can not trace to any ancestor of the House of Hanover.'[6] A year earlier, his parents had had Edward's royal skull examined by an eminent phrenologist. Whatever the accuracy of the procedure, his findings now seem rather prescient: 'He would show his talents to greater advantage were he possessed of powers of concentration and greater self-confidence.' The learned man attested that his subject had a good eye for painting and a liking for music, though mainly of the lighter kind, 'for example songs and dancing tunes'. He also doubted that he would have much time for organized religion, although he would respect the views of others.[7]

The Duke of York, although unlike his father in being entirely lacking of flamboyance, still placed the utmost importance on clothes as an outward sign of convention and tradition. Apart from a liking for rather loud tartans in some of his country suits (worn for shooting teas) – one of which was to be the only item the Duke of Windsor kept from his late father's wardrobe – he was a man very much in tune

with his grandmother's precepts for dressing appropriately. It was a difference in approach that was described by the Duke of Windsor in *A Family Album*: 'Now that I come to think of it, clothes were always a favourite topic of his conversation. With my father, it was not so much a discussion as to who he considered to be well or badly dressed; it was more usually a diatribe against anyone who dressed differently from himself. Those who did he called cads. Unfortunately "the cads" were the majority of my generation by the time I grew up, and I was of course one of them.'[8] It was this concern for correctness in dress, among other things, that made him appear somewhat staid to the next generation. When George V died in 1936, John Betjeman wrote a poem entitled simply 'Death of King George V', which satirized this obsession, as well as his similarly pedantic fondness for hunting and stamp collecting.

What distinguished George V from his contemporaries was his lifelong adherence to Edwardian custom. The Duke of Windsor later gave a description of his father's wardrobe: 'My father's gloves were invariably blackpointed, as his own father's had been. I never saw him in a soft collar, though he did adopt the modern turned-down collar, in place of the wing collar. His shirts were seldom striped and never coloured. His socks were always of wool, usually hand-knitted, never of silk. He continued to prefer the sideways crease in his trousers. He hardly ever wore shoes, adhering faithfully to the buttoned, cloth-topped or even elastic-sided boots of earlier days. He preferred a hard hat to a soft one – remarking that it was easier to lift. My father set few, if any fashions. Certainly his habit of wearing his tie passed through a ring, instead of tied in a knot, was not imitated by many of his subjects. An essential accessory to the well-dressed man in the 19th century was the walking stick. My father would not have dreamt of going out without carrying one of these elegant weapons, surmounted by gold or tortoiseshell knobs or handles, of which he had a large collection.'[9]

Clothes were more a liturgy to George V than a means of individual expression, a liturgy that was intended to uphold the dignity of the upper classes and the monarchy. Consequently the clothes he made his sons wear reflected the fact that they were always on parade – a fact that he would never let them forget. Kilts and sailor suits were the only dress he considered appropriate for children, and he applied the same standards of perfection to the way they were worn as a general inspecting his troops. On one occasion, when he discovered Edward with his hands stuffed in his pockets, he immediately ordered the young prince's nurse to sew up the pockets of all his sailor suits.

It was at his father's wish that in 1907, aged barely thirteen, Edward was sent to Naval College at Osborne and then Dartmouth, rather than to an ordinary boarding school. The then Prince of Wales had been a naval officer himself, and the Royal Navy was seen as a good training ground for future monarchs: 'Its officers were recruited largely from the gentry or aristocracy, it offered less opportunities for debauchery or any kind of escapade than its land-based counterpart, it inculcated those virtues which it was felt were above all needed in a future king: sobriety, self-reliance, punctuality, a respect for authority and instinct to conform.'[10] At naval college, every item of his clothing was of course precisely specified, with severe restrictions including the banning of trouser pockets, to which he was by now reluctantly accustomed. Although the Prince of Wales wanted his son to be treated like any other navy cadet, he still made sure his hair was not cut by the college barber but rather by his own London barber in Piccadilly.

Edward felt ill at ease in uniform, a discomfort that extended to all kinds of ceremonial wear, of which he was obliged to wear rather more once he had become Prince of Wales after his grandfather's death in 1910. In this he differed markedly from earlier generations, including most notably his cousin the Kaiser, who was never seen out of uniform and devised special ones even for leisure activities such as hunting. In fact Edward harboured an almost pathological dislike of dressing up, which might seem paradoxical in a young man who was soon to become the world's icon of masculine dress. Yet it was of course completely consistent with his dandyism that he should have felt comfortable only in clothes that expressed his individuality, rather than the institution he represented. Later on, he was to give an inkling of some of this in what might well be called his credo: 'All my life I had been fretting against those constrictions of dress which reflected my family's world of rigid social convention. It was my impulse, whenever I found myself alone, to remove my coat, rip off my tie, loosen my collar and roll up my sleeves – a gesture aspiring not merely to comfort but in a more symbolic sense to freedom.'[11] It was when Edward went up to Oxford that he finally attained some of this social and sartorial freedom. This freedom was still very much contained within the boundaries set by Brummell, however, as noted by the *Tailor and Cutter* (formerly the official magazine of the trade) on his arrival at Oxford: 'There has been nothing daring or original in his sartorial equipment, but rather the unobtrusive shades and outlines that always distinguish the well-dressed Gentleman.'[12] A photo of him boarding a train shows him in a checked suit, with the trousers just a fraction wider and the coat a little less skirted than his father would have approved of.

He went up to Oxford in 1912, so preceding by a decade the between-the-wars generation of largely Oxbridge-educated young men whom Martin Green, in *Children of the Sun*, described as a generation of dandies. It was after the First World War, in which Edward served as an officer in the Grenadier Guards instead of continuing into his third year at Oxford, that the dandy as a cultural type came to the fore. After 1918 there was an air of rebellion in England, a rebellion that took the form of conflict between the generations, as exemplified at the very top of society by the problematic relationship between the Prince of Wales and his father. Within the upper and upper-middle classes, the trauma of the Great War gave birth to a new ideal of masculinity that was to dominate English culture for almost forty years. That so many brilliant young men, including the poet Rupert Brooke to mention only one, had been sacrificed to the ideals of the older generation, the generals, the statesmen and indeed the king himself, led to a disillusionment not only with the virtues of soldiering and war, but also with the cultural values of a whole generation of fathers. Suddenly, young men born into what would later be called the Establishment did not want to grow up to be fathers, husbands and masters.

This conflict between the generations proved fertile ground for the development of dandyism in the widest sense, as expressed in a preoccupation with style and with the perfection of self through rituals of taste; and a freedom from all human commitments – passion, morality, ambition, politics, work – that are in conflict with aesthetic considerations. The generation that followed those who had fought was inclined to take a sober view of the ideal of maturity, one that had been prevalent in Victorian and Edwardian times, the heyday of the Empire. The dandy idealizes the young man, is consciously immature and selfish, because maturity and dedication to values outside the self are the core values of the orthodoxy he seeks to undermine. The dandies of the 1920s were of course well aware of their predecessors in those historical periods when dandyism had been a cultural force before, the Regency and the *fin de siècle*. The Duke of Windsor made frequent reference to Brummell in *A Family Album*, sometimes to the detriment of his own family in the areas of sartorial influence and wit. While Brummell's reputation remained largely unchallenged, the dandies of the 1920s sought to distance themselves from the more recent 'naughty nineties' and their morbid aestheticism. The new 'dandies' sought to embrace the twentieth century, as embodied in America and modernism, jazz and cocktails, Picasso and T. S. Eliot. 'Old England' perceived these cultural phenomena not only as alien but even as hostile. Through their adoption of them, the 'dandies' forged a new English identity, a new kind of Englishness.

It was only now that Edward had properly to face up to his role as Prince of Wales. His ascendancy to the title in 1910 had been rapidly followed by naval college, Oxford and the Great War. Furthermore, in 1910 he had been very young, as indeed he still was, in actual age and even more so – as he was well aware – in mental age. In 1921 he told his mistress, Freda Dudley Ward, that he had been reading Max Beerbohm's essay on King George IV, Brummell's erstwhile friend and foe: 'I've found a sentence in it that I think must be amazingly suitable and applicable to me and somewhat an apology for my doings and behaviour... "He was indeed still a child, for royalty not being ever brought into contact with the realities of life remain young far longer than other people." No one realizes how desperately true that is in my case [more] than I do.'[15] Most of all, though, he looked very young indeed. By no means a tall man, he was also a modest eater, never taking lunch in later life, which meant that he retained a boyish figure to his death (in his sixties he tried on the robes of a Knight of the Garter that he had worn at fifteen and was overjoyed to find they still fitted). More than this even, his impish face and golden blond hair made him the consummate fairy-tale prince. The role of Prince of Wales is purely ceremonial in a representational monarchy: it is simply a matter of waiting to be king. Edward filled this wait with extended tours of the Empire and extensive amusements in London. Appearing in various costumes on various continents – pith helmet in India, kimono in Japan and sitting on a bull in a ten-gallon hat that made him look like a twelve-year-old playing at cowboys in Canada – he resembled nobody so much as Tintin, the intrepid cartoon character, ageless and asexual, but with that quality of immediate recognizability that is ultimately the secret of glamour.

In London, he was not only at the pinnacle of the ruling

class but was also the perfect figurehead for the 1920s generation. Being twenty-six in 1920, he was just old enough to be taken seriously as a role model, but still young enough to be accepted by them as 'one of us': 'Whether he was seen sympathizing with the out-of-work miners in South Wales or dancing the Charleston in Mayfair, he was the symbol of the "new England", of the forces that would change the old England.'[14] Edward enjoyed nightclubs, drinking and Americana (he saw the *Blackbirds of 1928* Broadway revue twenty times). As he himself pointed out in *A Family Album*, the 1920s were the "Golden Age" of the restaurant and the night-club, often with floor show, and I would escape to the Embassy Club, that Buckingham Palace of night-clubs, the Kit-Kat, Quaglino's or the Café de Paris, with its "Champagne and Chandeliers"... Afterwards I would sometimes continue the party at York House. I remember an evening when Fred and Adèle Astaire, at that time drawing large audiences in London, danced for us there to the gramophone.'[15] As far as his love life was concerned, he preferred affairs with married women, the most significant of whom, before the arrival on the scene of Wallis Simpson, was Mrs Freda Dudley Ward. A style icon in her own right, she took a quasi-maternal interest in his life, taking in hand the interior decoration of his residences (first at St James's Palace and later Fort Belvedere), and also advising him a great deal on matters concerning his role. One of the prince's equerries later called her 'one of the best friends he ever had in his life'.[16] It was in 1927, at the height of Edward's popularity, that Herbert Faqeon wrote the famous song 'I've danced with a man, who's danced with a girl, who's danced with the Prince of Wales.'

The generation of 'dandies' encompassed famous figures such as Cecil Beaton and Evelyn Waugh, infamous characters such as Brian Howard, aesthetes such as Howard Acton and traitors such as Guy Burgess. Whether they were homosexual or not, what united many of these figures at the time was the idealization of the young man. This influence of course also spread to the boyishness of women's clothing, demeanour and even bodies in the 1920s: in the words of Cecil Beaton *à propos* Mrs Dudley Ward, women were now 'concave instead of convex'.[17] The intellectual foundation for this new mood of dandyism had come from France at the beginning of the century, in the form of Proust's *À la recherche du temps perdu*: 'It turns the experience of young men, young men who refuse the adult commitments of politics, government, power, and marriage, who occupy themselves with questions of social and sexual and aesthetic taste, into the material of great art. The English dandies of the 20s, typically during their years at Oxford, were profoundly influenced by Proust – more than by any other writer. Proust had been reproached by his literary rivals – by André Gide, for instance – for betraying literature in his pursuit of social success of the most snobbish and dandified kind, and this novel was, among other things, a self-justification.'[18] Although both Swann and Charlus display characteristics of dandyism, the *recherche* is not a dandy novel in the way that Disraeli's novels and Bulwer-Lytton's *Pelham* had been. Far more importantly its pages contain the very substance of dandyism.

At this point we should introduce a caveat: the duke was no reader. As Osbert Sitwell recalled, at an official dinner he tried to impress Lady Desborough, whom he knew to have literary

interests, by informing her: 'Lady Desborough, I know you're a bookish sort of person. At the moment I'm reading such an interesting novel. I think it would appeal to you: it's called *Dracula!*' According to his prime minister Stanley Baldwin, as king he wasn't even much of a thinker, taking his ideas from the daily press instead of working them out for himself: 'He never reads – except, of course, the papers. No serious reading: none at all.'[19] William Gore-Langton, the Coldstream Guards officer who oversaw the Duke of Windsor's embarkation for France, just hours after the abdication, put it even more succinctly: 'He wasn't overly burdened with brains.'[20] From this evidence it is unlikely that the duke would have read Proust, if he was aware of him at all. Similarly, judging from the artworks in his possession, we cannot assume that he was a great admirer of Picasso. Nor is it likely that he was a great admirer of the poetry of T. S. Eliot, whose dandyism, in its strict adherence to Brummellian principles, was so 'exquisitely modulated to a level of seriousness'[21] that in terms of gravitas it would have left most of his generation far behind anyway ('Remarkable man, Mr Eliot,' his tailor remarked. 'Nothing ever quite in excess').[22] Indeed, as far as modernism was concerned, the duke was the first to admit that he was not strictly speaking 'with it': 'At a dinner party where he had been talking with some pride of his old-fashioned and "outspokenly suburban" rock garden, Emerald Cunard turned to him and told him he was the most modernistic man in England. The King blinks his fair eye-lashes and says with the utmost simplicity: "No, Emerald, I am not a modernist, since I am not a highbrow. All I try to do is to move with the times."'[23]

In his emblematic youthfulness and his craving for pleasure, the Prince of Wales was more the figurehead of the inter-war generation than a member of it. This does not by any means make him unworthy as a subject of study; quite the opposite, indeed, as Osbert Sitwell (who does not seem to have been too fond of the duke) makes clear in a paraphrase of Proust himself: 'He [Proust] proposed, in short, the theory that what always most interests the ordinary reader in any book of reminiscences are details concerning the lives of princes, because for him royal personages form a separate caste and creation, set apart from all others than themselves by birth, heredity and upbringing: and so the plain man likes to be reminded that though princes may be descended from the deities and in themselves be godlike as the Roman emperors or the mikados of Japan (an opinion of their derivation and standing in which those potentates were formerly happy to concur) they are also men – some wise, some silly, some gay, some dour.'[24]

There was one area in which the duke was closer to the visual vocabulary of modern abstract art than other members of his generation, and that was in his suits. While many of the 'dandies' of the period devoted their creativity to a process of dissection of their own role, so reinventing the suit almost as a by-product, for Edward clothing was the sole creative expression of his dandyism, and of its inherent rebellion. As he was to acknowledge in the 1920s and 1930s, the fact that he was so 'with it' in terms of fashion and lifestyle was one of the accusations levelled at him around the time of the abdication by the protectors of the old order.[25] In the name of comfort and freedom, Edward adopted or launched almost all of the

sartorial changes of the 1920s, endowing them with the legitimacy they needed in order to enter stylish men's wardrobes.
What made him so suited to this role – apart of course from
his position as royal Prince Charming – was that despite
being a very small man he was very well proportioned, which
meant that most types of clothing tended to look good on him.
A large proportion of the 'dandies' went to Eton and Oxford,
and it was in these 'factories for gentlemen' especially that
their dandyism manifested itself in the most literal sense.
What was taking place was more a rebellion than a revolution as – for the time being – the changes taking place were
limited to the ruling class, and did not affect the class system
as a whole. This peculiarly British phenomenon has been
described by the French fashion historian Farid Chenoune as
the combination of 'the power of social segregation with openness to stylistic change, orthodoxy with outrageousness'.[26]

'Oxford bags' were one of the fashions that developed
among undergraduates in the 1920s. These very wide trousers with extremely deep pleats, falling fan-like from the
waist, expressed not only a desire for greater comfort but
also a rejection of the military associations of the close-cut,
straight-legged Edwardian style. Extreme cases might reach a
bottom-width of twenty-four inches, recalling the wide skirts
worn by women at the time. Confronted with these culottes,
the *Tailor and Cutter*, the voice of sartorial orthodoxy, sighed:
'The Almighty deliver us from suchlike excesses.' The prince's
trousers also grew wider, if only by an inch or so at first.
From greater excesses he was restrained on two sides: his
trusty equerry Major Dudley 'Fruity' Metcalfe, whom Edward
fancied as the Brummell to his George IV; and his stern

Dutch-born tailor, Mr Scholte, who 'had the strictest ideas as to how a gentleman should and should not be dressed, he disapproved strongly of any form of exaggeration in the style of a coat... As befitted an artist and craftsman, Scholte had rigid standards concerning the perfect balance of proportions between shoulders and waist in the cut of a coat to clothe the masculine torso.'[27] To anchor the flapping bottoms of the wider trouser leg, turn-ups became indispensable. Turn-ups had already existed in Edwardian times, originating from the habit among gentlemen of literally turning up their trousers to protect the fine cloth in rainy or muddy conditions. At this period they were rarely fixed, and consequently shortened

the appearance of the trouser leg. When Edward dared on one occasion to enter one of the royal drawing rooms with turn-ups on his trousers, his father asked curtly: 'Did it rain in here?' The sartorial battle in the palace raged on. Even at the age of thirty, Edward was still reprimanded by his father, in front of a number of guests, for appearing for tea still dressed in his shooting clothes.[28] To George V his son was quite simply 'the worst-dressed man in London'.[29]

While trousers grew wider, coats got shorter and were cut without a skirt, the flaring at the waist that had been a leftover from the morning coat. In tandem with this, the buttoning was reduced from three or four to two, to give an appearance that was literally less 'buttoned-up'. Later on, Edward began to favour the double-breasted jacket, which brought with it the added convenience of not requiring a waistcoat. Here he was also keen to reduce the number of 'working' buttons from six to four, sometimes even fastening the coat only on the lowest button (in a fit of insolence worthy of Brummell, Brian Howard observed: 'In clothes the double-breasted coat is being made vulgar by the Prince of Wales').[30] In the 1930s, the double-breasted suit made of chalk-stripe or Glen plaid (sometimes known as 'Prince of Wales check' on the continent) material became acceptable as town wear, and a sound alternative to the single-breasted coat with peaked lapels and double-breasted waistcoat, which was considered quite simply wrong by anybody with a due respect for the histories of both coat styles (a solecism of a different kind, of which Edward would never have been guilty). Yet time and again Edward managed to cause excitement in the fashion world by flouting the rules of 'correct clothing'

and the conventional taste endorsed by the staider represen-
tatives of the established order. He had materials intended
for single-breasted suits made up as double-breasted (a habit
taken up by his great-nephew Prince Charles), and wore
suede shoes with town clothes, a fashion that had also originated in Oxford. When Edward, Prince of Wales, set his
suede-shod foot on American soil in 1924, it was explained
to him by embarrassed bystanders that in the United States
only homosexuals wore suede shoes – a revelation that he
greeted with the nonchalant indifference it deserved.

Yet the cult that grew up around the Prince of Wales
would not have had such an enormous impact if he had not
formed a fashion and social alliance with the United States of
America, which had emerged from the Great War as the most
powerful nation on earth. He fell in love with America first,
on his world tour, and with Wallis Simpson second; in the
1950s he went so far as to declare to the actress Lili Palmer:
'My tragedy is that I couldn't stand England from the start.
But the first time I set foot on American soil – I was still a
very young man – there I knew at a stroke that this was the
place for me.'[31] The American press kept a watchful eye on the
prince at all times. Following his return to Europe, whenever
he wore a new outfit a selection of photographs, with samples
of fabrics, collars, ties, socks and so forth, was rushed to
America, where overnight a new fashion might be born. One
of the prince's biggest admirers was Fred Astaire, who did
not mind revealing the source of his inspiration: 'HRH was
unquestionably the best-dressed young man in the world and
I was missing none of it.'[32] And America's sartorial love affair
with Edward was reciprocal. His style of dress, then and in

later life, amounted to a hybrid that has been described as the Anglo-American gentleman. The other famous example of this successful transatlantic style was of course Cary Grant. The duke's suits were in fact literally transatlantic. Like American men, he preferred to wear his trousers on the waist and held up with a belt, a habit that presumably went back to the time when men still wore guns. Scholte made trousers in the English manner, sitting high above the waist and held up by braces. The duke therefore had his coats made by Scholte and his 'pants', as he soon tended to call them, in New York – a habit the duchess referred to as 'pants across the sea'. Perceiving the substitution of belts for braces as disastrous, the *Tailor and Cutter* presciently commented: 'Slackness in dress will in the long run make for slackness in behaviour, and it is not so wild as it sounds to say that society will fall to pieces and man will revert to a state of savagery.'[33]

In evening wear, Edward was similarly a harbinger of comfort or savagery, depending on which way one is inclined to look at it. He made the dinner jacket, a garment his father and grandfather had worn only for informal dinners within the immediate family, acceptable for general evening wear. Up to the end of the 1920s, any evening occasion in society required a tail coat and starched shirt. In a speech to the Jewellers' and Silversmiths' Association, Edward reflected on the starched or boiled shirt: 'This horrible garment we have to wear now, which has given us such untold misery... Have any of you ever stopped to think why we are all dressed up in these stiff, armour-plated shirts tonight?'[34] He concluded that it was the studs, which refused to stay put in soft shirts, that were to blame. Consequently he soon popularized the soft shirt with turn-down collar. Having started to wear a single-breasted dinner jacket with a white waistcoat, he then went on to sport the double-breasted version in midnight blue (blacker than black in artificial light), first seen on Jack Buchanan, the debonair Scots-born film star of early musical comedies. Already as Prince of Wales, Edward had developed a liking for Mediterranean holidays – much to the chagrin of his father, who thought it more appropriate for a member of the royal family to spend his holidays in Britain. Suntanned complexions – hitherto looked down on by the leisured class because of their associations with manual labour – became popular in the 1920s, in tandem with an increasing idealization of physical athleticism. Edward liked to 'toast his skin to a rich brown tan',[35] and adopted the clothing of the indigenous populations of his holiday destinations, such as Breton shirts and summer trousers of heavy linen. The baring of royal flesh made the physicality of the royal personage all too apparent. The shock of this revelation is hard to imagine nowadays. Presciently, George V commented, 'You might as well be photographed naked; no doubt it would please the public.'[36] On a cruise of the Adriatic with Wallis in 1935, Edward often went ashore wearing only shorts, a singlet and espadrilles. He was rarely recognized, precisely because so much of him was on view.

Though not a particularly accomplished sportsman, Edward nonetheless indulged in many sports. Golf, which in the 1920s became particularly popular in America, was one of his favourite pastimes. And – appropriately enough – it was in the field of sportswear that his guiding principles of comfort and freedom came into their own. Edward's plus-fours were considered extremely wide at the time, even though – according to him – they were only an inch or so wider than conventional ones. It was also in sportswear that Edward felt free to indulge his penchant for bright colours and bold patterns. He caused widespread shock in France in 1930, when he emerged from his plane at Le Touquet dressed for a round of golf, sporting a pink shirt with a military tie, a checked plus-four suit with bright red-and-white checked stockings, and black-and-tan correspondent shoes. Noticing the disastrous impression he was making, he said in rather dismayed tones: 'I thought that in France one could dress as one liked.'[37] Edward loved tweed suits in bold checks, and in the country tended to wear Highland evening dress, consisting of buckled shoes, kilt and short velvet jacket. In the 1940s, the Rothesay hunting suit he had inherited from his father launched a fashion for tartan in America that was to spread to every part of the male wardrobe, from dinner jackets to swimming trunks. Especially in his later years, the duke liked to mix loud, dissonant colours and seemingly incompatible patterns. As he noted in *A Family Album*, this tendency to sin against conventional notions of 'good taste' had its precursors among the more eccentric members of the British aristocracy. He quoted the example of Lord Lonsdale, the 'Yellow Earl', so called because everything around him – his cars, his carriages, his servants' liveries – was canary yellow.[38] And Edward VII had already incurred the disapproval of the *Tailor and Cutter* when he was spotted in Marienbad wearing, 'A green cap, brown overcoat, pink tie, grey shoes and white gloves. We sincerely hope His Majesty has not brought this outfit home.'[39]

In letters of instruction 'for the guidance of gentlemen appointed to attend on the Prince of Wales', Prince Albert had enlarged on the precepts impressed on their son by Queen Victoria: 'The appearance, deportment and dress of a gentleman consists perhaps more in the absence of certain offences against good taste, and in careful avoidance of vulgarities and exaggerations of any kind, however generally they may be the fashion of the day, than in the adherence to any rules which can be exactly laid down... In dress, with scrupulous attention to neatness and good taste, he will never give in to the unfortunately loose and slang style which predominates at the present day. He will borrow nothing from the fashions of the groom or the gamekeeper, and whilst avoiding the frivolity and foolish vanity of dandyism, will take care that his clothes are of the best quality, well-made, and suitable to his rank and position...'[40] While spicing up one's style with a few forbidden fruits was perfectly acceptable for an independent member of the aristocracy ('A little bit of bad taste is like a nice splash of paprika,'[41] as Diana Vreeland was to opine more than half a century later), it simply would not do for a personage born to represent an entire country. As many commentators have noted, the royal family has always been very middle class.

In addition to being a fundamental characteristic of a certain type of British chic, raised to yet more exalted heights in New England – as seen in the pink-and-green dolphin-embroidered trousers in the *Official Preppy Handbook* – 'bad taste' is also associated with the camp sensibility for which Edward created a larger space in the stylish male wardrobes. Camp is an important key to the dandyism of Edward's

generation. As Cecil Beaton pointed out, many mannerisms that might nowadays be perceived as 'classic camp', not to mention turns of phrase that have passed into normal speech, such as the over-use of 'terribly' or 'frightfully', have their origins in the 1920s.[42] The camp sensibility, which belittles true gravitas and dramatizes the detail, might to some seem wilfully perverse, but is in fact a valid survival strategy. The appreciation of kitsch is part of the ironic counselling that camp can provide. The camp person is unable to identify with traditional modes of maturity, partly out of feelings of inadequacy and partly out of healthy arrogance, and seeks refuge in various modes of marginality – for example that of the film star who is leisured, apolitical, charismatic and attractive, and spends his life indulging in conspicuous consumption. The Duke of Windsor was of course far from camp in any of his mannerisms, and would have been horrified had anybody suggested anything of the sort (even though he did once dance with Noël Coward at a late-night party). What Edward expressed through the way he dressed was his fundamental discomfort with the role assigned to him. Already in his boyhood he had frequently envied 'ordinary boys', even putting on a slight cockney accent in emulation of his beloved nanny Charlotte 'Lalla' Bill. As Osbert Sitwell noted, he later replaced it with the American accent he adopted from his wife.[43] Sitwell also observed that during his brief reign as king he lacked the natural confidence in his own kingship that his younger brother George, though naturally shy, quite clearly possessed when he succeeded him.[44] Sitwell viewed Edward's abdication in 1936 as the natural 'climax of this royal philistine rake's progress'.[45]

Despite his undoubted talents as a media star, the Prince
of Wales was already subject to frequent bouts of depression.
His doubts about his own suitability for his role, induced by
a temperament that his biographer Philip Ziegler described
as one of 'restlessness, recklessness and febrile rejection of
any kind of discipline', came to a head when he ascended the
throne. Now there were no more escape routes open to him:
he had to face the solemnity of his duties and responsibilities.
Viewed in this light, his abdication in favour of a marriage
with Wallis Simpson, 'the woman that I love', sometimes portrayed as one of the great romances of the twentieth century,
appears rather more complex. This does not mean that the
sincerity of his motives is necessarily in doubt. But from an
outsider's point of view, the events leading to 11 December
1936 acquire a certain logic in the light of his character. It
was the character of a dandy, who for a long time had avoided
even the commitment of marriage: 'Whether he was aware of
it or not, the argument goes, he was resolved never to marry;
by falling in love with a married woman he was providing
himself with an alibi against having to marry anyone else.
He was temperamentally unable to accept such a commitment, or perhaps he sought to leave open a route by which he
might one day escape the throne.'[46] One might even suggest
that the choice of a twice-divorced American woman as the
object of his affections was comparable to the combination
of checks and stripes in his clothing. To Baudelaire, the connection between love and dandyism was at best an accidental
one: 'If I speak of love à propos of dandyism, this is only
because love is the natural occupation of the idle. But for the
dandy, love is not a goal he sets himself.'[47] Abdication and

marriage to Mrs Simpson were necessary steps in Edward's self-realization as a dandy. If he had disappointed the expectations he was born to, he had ultimately remained faithful to himself.

Edward's fully fledged existence as a dandy began at the moment when the heyday of other dandies ended: in exile. Apart from an interlude as Governor of the Bahamas during the Second World War, exile largely meant permanent homes in France, permanent globetrotting, permanent idleness and a life spent 'at the wrong end of the table'. George V had earlier remarked, 'My son hasn't a single friend who is a gentleman;'[48] now the Duke of Windsor was forever banished to the world of Café Society. Like other dandies before him, Edward found himself finished long before the end, forever preserved in his gilded heyday as Prince of Wales: 'At fifty, the Duke remains the royal Peter Pan... his wizened jockey's face, his fair hair and his debonair appearance contribute towards this persistent youthfulness and make one understand the note of novelettish sentimentality in his abdication.'[49] What might seem like a Wildean dream come true equally had its nightmarish qualities. Nancy Mitford thought the Windsors looked 'ravaged with misery',[50] while Cecil Beaton observed that the duke's face 'now begins to show the emptiness of life... He looks like a mad terrier, haunted one moment, then with a flick of the hand he is laughing fecklessly.'[51] There could hardly be a more succinct diagnosis of the 'Hölderlin dilemma'.

If travel offers a valid form of escape for the impoverished dandy, how much more true is this for the rich one. In the 1950s and 1960s, the allure of travel was at its height, and

the jet set was still in its not yet entirely charmless infancy.
Few things can better create the illusion of a fulfilled life
than constant travel, and the Windsors spent the post-war
decades flitting between North America (in the winter),
Biarritz and more exotic locations, always with quantities of
trunks and servants in tow. The at first enchanting rituals
of time-wasting inevitably palled, although the duke made
sure that the gilded, unchangeable mask over the terrors of
the void stayed in place. Harold Nicolson observed: 'He pre-
tends to be very busy and happy, but I feel this is false and
that he is unoccupied and miserable.'[52] The mask did crack
occasionally, though, as when he told a journalist: 'You know
what my day was today? I got up late and then I went with
the Duchess and watched her buy a hat.'[53] Presumably to
allow for late rising, meals at their homes were put forward
by an hour from the conventional times. Cocktail hour – the
highlight of the duke's day – came at seven, and it was clear
to visitors that the drinking hour sometimes seemed to him
a long time in coming.

Yet it was also in his homes, the Paris mansion in the
Bois de Boulogne and the country house, Le Moulin de la
Tuilerie, that the duke could fully live out his dandyism. The
style was the substance (albeit a slight one) for both the duke
and the duchess, and in France they could live to perfection
the 'minor arts' of dressing, interior design and entertaining.
His kingdom had been reduced to a much smaller realm:
one that he felt confident he could manage and that was
devoid of any true responsibilities except for himself. Every
aspect of his life was thought out to perfection. The historian
James Pope-Hennessy stayed at Le Moulin in the 1950s, and

described the guest room in which he slept: 'The room in the stables… was very pretty and convenient, and once more planned or prepared by a perfectionist: there was nothing on earth you might conceivably want that wasn't there – every kind of writing paper, nail-file, brush, fruit ice-water: the bathroom loaded with scent bottles like a counter at a bazaar – a delicious sense of self-indulgence.'[54] The duke had a valet to look after his wardrobe, which was a far more demanding job than might at first appear: 'His Royal Highness was so fussy about his suits. They had to be hung in the closet in order and then rotated. And I would iron his shirts just the moment before he put them on, or otherwise the Duchess would come in saying, "Sidney there's a crease."'[55] Similarly, it was also in his houses that the Duke of Windsor expressed the limitations of his dandyism. Having achieved the independence that he owed to his nature so painfully, he still found it impossible psychologically to break free from the royal reins. At their Bois de Boulogne house, the footmen wore royal livery and visitors entered under the duke's personal garter banner. Even the carpet had the three feathers of the Prince of Wales woven into it. The interior of Le Moulin, meanwhile, was a monument to the duke's past, and for decades the sparse communications he had with his family were devoted largely to his demands for the title of Her Royal Highness for the duchess. Curiously – or perhaps logically for a figure who had escaped the constraints of the 'serious' establishment – the duke's dandyism remained less abstract and less serious than that of any other figure in this book. Anaesthetized by a surfeit of money and its concomitant luxuries, he perhaps also lacked the sensitivity to pain that could have heightened the experience of his dandy-ism. The Duke of Windsor was too unreflecting a person to embrace the tragedy of his fate, an embrace that could have unified him – a fact that according to Cecil Beaton showed in his very features, which were 'too impertinent to be tragic'.[56]

In the aftermath of the Great War, the old-style dandy became an anachronism. Bourgeois ideals were adopted by kings, and Brummell's ideal of subtlety and discretion in clothing become that of George V. The new dandy no longer held a silken handkerchief to his sensitive nostrils; instead he flirted with the driving force of the twentieth century, vulgarity. Having been an arbiter and pioneer of excessive and transgressive taste in clothing in his youth, he remained forever faithful to the new styles he had helped to forge. When a guest at Le Moulin de la Tuilerie appeared dressed for the weekend in trousers without turn-ups, the duke greeted him with mock indignation, prompting the American guest to have outsize turn-ups sewn on to his 'pants' overnight. Having – with his father's encouragement – been a heavy smoker since his early teenage years, Edward, Duke of Windsor also remained ever faithful to the vice that, on 28 May 1972, was to kill him.

d.

BUNNY ROGER

A Certain Kind of
Englishman

This cellar and this wilderness I took as my special
province, thus early falling victim to the common English
confusion of the antiquated with the sublime, which has
remained with me.

EVELYN WAUGH, *A LITTLE LEARNING*

Good old England, you're my cup of tea, but I don't want
no drab equality.

JOHN OSBORNE, *THE ENTERTAINER*

There may be a handful of Londoners who remember
the apparition that graced the Underground train on
the westbound Piccadilly line one autumn day in the late
1980s. The septuagenarian gentleman was resplendent in an
immaculate neo-Edwardian suit with breathtakingly tight
trousers, a long coat adorned with a mauve carnation, and a
diminutive bowler hat perched on the luxuriant silver hair
that framed his discreetly made-up face. Declining to risk
sullying his pale yellow chamois gloves by clinging to any

part of the train – no matter how unsteady the journey – he leaned on the handle of his furled umbrella with perfect poise and deportment. Like Beau Brummell, Bunny Roger, possibly the last great dandy to concentrate almost solely on self-cultivation, understood that *le style c'est l'homme même*. This self is revealed through clothes, manners and interior decoration, and Bunny Roger was not shy of self-revelation. He hugely enjoyed the attention his attire invariably drew, countering Brummell's dictum, 'If John Bull turns around to look at you, you are not well dressed', with, 'I should be very upset if he didn't!' Born in 1911, Bunny Roger was part of the generation of Bright Young Things who had dominated the between-the-wars era. A contemporary at Oxford of the poet John Betjeman and the cartoonist Osbert Lancaster, among others, he nevertheless remained on the fringes of that generation in the 1920s and 1930s, being of a less literary turn of mind. In his brief account of Osbert Lancaster's life, *Cartoons and Coronets*, James Knox lists some of the personalities which dominated Oxford's social scene at this time: 'His friends included the civilized plutocrat Harry d'Avigdor Goldsmid, raconteur Denis Kincaid, literary tyros Alan Pryce-Jones and Graham Shepard, a Dada-ist in the person of Tom Driberg, the romantic swain James Lees-Milne, poets John Betjeman and Louis MacNeice, jazz musician Graham Eyres-Monsell, and maverick intellectual Christopher Hobhouse. Their chatter, antics and jokes were assiduously reported, usually by themselves, in the gossip column of *Cherwell*. Readers learnt that the dandy Bunny Roger, who favoured a green suit and yellow hair, had complained of a recent social event: "It's not easy being the life and soul of this sort of party."'[1] Indeed Bunny Roger was only fully to forge his style and receive the attention he desired and deserved after the Second World War.

By this time the members of the dandy generation had reached or were approaching their forties, and had usurped the Bloomsbury set as the mandarins of British culture. Some were now famous writers like Evelyn Waugh, some had inherited the executive desks in the literary world like Cyril Connolly, while others were ensconced in the Foreign Office, a branch of the Civil Service that was curiously welcoming to eccentric and pleasure-seeking individuals. Few escaped the banality which seems to beset the middle-aged rebel: Brian Howard ended his life of flamboyant failure by his own hand in 1958, and Guy Burgess and Donald Maclean more famously and symptomatically escaped to Russia in 1951, having subverted the system from within for some time. In a variety of ways, the scandal that followed their defection involved every member of their incestuous class and generation. Brian Howard, who holidayed with Bunny Roger in Toulon in the 1930s, had first met Burgess at parties earlier in the same decade, and spent time with him again after himself being sacked from MI5, the Secret Service, for drunken indiscretion in 1942 (bizarrely being mistaken for Burgess in flight in 1951, immediately after the news of the latter's disappearance had broken). Although they were not strictly speaking dandies, the case of the Cambridge spies sheds some light on the characteristic dandy temperament. It appeared that – in the case of Guy Burgess, at least – a taste for 'luxury and display, suites at Claridge's, fast cars and daily hungover breakfasts at the Ritz'[2] could coexist with a stringently dialectical mind.

Connolly summed him up as 'Marxist in his mental processes and anti-Marxist individualist in his personality'.[3] In striving for modernity while retaining a taste for decadence, Burgess was of course far from alone among upper-class types of his generation, as evinced by Count Luchino Visconti di Modrone's very public support of the Communist Party, and the many young men of wealth and privilege who fell fighting on the Republican side in the Spanish Civil War. In Burgess, the two personas simply happened to be equally strong. In fact the strict logic of Marxism would hold a strong appeal for the dandy's rationalism, while his puritan streak might be inclined to seek a painful solution precisely because of its painfulness.

Spying would therefore appear as one of the few occupations to match the dandy's inverted value system, as in the world of espionage minute and seemingly trivial details also take on an existential significance. The act of treason itself appears more as a consequence of the dandy's psychological make-up than as something actively sought by him. The inability to take institutions and politics seriously was combined with the pressing fear of being subsumed by their banality, and the absolute precedence of aesthetic and personal loyalties over those that to the dandy must seem arbitrary, including patriotism and public morality (not surprisingly, Burgess did not adapt well to life in the Soviet Union). The essence of this attitude was famously summed up by E. M. Forster in 1938: 'If I had to choose between betraying my country and betraying my friend, I hope I should have the guts to betray my country.'[4] And weighty approval came thirty years later when Graham Greene asked with regard to Philby: 'Who has not committed treason to something or someone more important than a country?'[5] Although Greene wrote this on the cusp of another era, it expresses what the middle-aged Bright Young Things felt in 1951, that 'subtlety was on the side of the traitors'.[6] What shocked sections of the British public who were less discriminating when it came to nuances of taste and the political classes of the rest of the world was not so much the defection itself, but the way it was played down by the Establishment. In fact the very term 'Establishment' was first used in its derogatory sense in relation to the protection of Burgess and Maclean by their peers.[7] This public unease led slowly but surely to the unmasking of a whole class, to an increasingly earnest style within the literary and artistic intelligentsia, and to a general feeling that the running of the country was a task too serious to be entrusted to a gentlemanly elite. The dandy's inherent ambivalence, embracing both modernity and decadence, was to split into different factions in the post-war era, eventually leading to the democratization and dissolution of the ideal.

Yet dandyism was ready for one last Baudelairean flowering, resembling – in the words of Baudelaire himself – the setting sun, splendid yet devoid of warmth and filled with melancholy. This melancholia was certainly evident in Cyril Connolly's characteristic summing up of the post-war mood: 'Here, the Ego is at half-pressure; most of us are not men or women but members of a vast, seedy, overworked, over-legislated neuter class, with our drab clothes, our ration books and murder stories, our envious, strict, old world apathies and resentment – a careworn people. And the symbol of this mood is London, now the largest, saddest and dirtiest of the great cities, with its miles of unpainted half-inhabited houses, its chop-less chophouses, its beerless pubs, its once vivid quarters losing all personality, its squares bereft of elegance, its dandies in exile, its antiquities in America, its shops full of junk, bunk, and tomorrow, its crowds mooning around the stained green wicker of the terias in their shabby raincoats, under a sky permanently dull and lowering like a metal dish cover.'[8] This lament was prompted by comparisons with the youthfully vigorous and now increasingly culturally dominant America. The influence of the United States was as pervasive as it was more or less secretly resented. GIs had been sourly dismissed, through gritted teeth, as 'overpaid, oversexed, overdressed and over here', and the cultural elite deplored the threats of industrialized mass culture and a healthier yet *blander* masculinity in no uncertain terms. Evelyn Waugh was the most anti-American of the mandarins, although his satires on America's vulgarity – most prominently *The Loved One* – also expressed a mood of depression and defeat; a deep-seated fear of the world to come, a mass culture that would erode the dandy with a gum-chewing smile. The twin fears of emasculation and cultural annihilation were best expressed by the medium that was also the most immediately influential carrier of threatening iconography and role models: the cinema.

Two of the most successful British films of the post-war period were *Spring in Park Lane* (1948) and *Maytime in Mayfair* (1949). Their hugely popular star was a mildly dandified Michael Wilding, displaying all the marks of an affluent pre-war gentility that was more than a little phoney in an era of rationing and demob suits (his image of vigorous and modern masculinity was further not helped by his toupee, chosen for him by his former lover Marlene Dietrich). While the successful American films of the early 1950s still featured stars for whom, at a stretch, British equivalents could be found – including 'the ambivalent morality and brooding sexuality of Robert Mitchum and James Mason; the solid, mature trustworthiness of Gary Cooper and Jack Hawkins',[9] and of course the all-encompassing mid-Atlantic charm of the homegrown Archibald Alexander Leach, aka Cary Grant – the later 1950s saw the emergence of an icon who offered no possibility of equality, but only of imitation: Elvis Presley (who would certainly have aroused the ire of Waugh had he deigned to comment). Presley personified not only American cultural hegemony over Britain, through mass culture in the form of rock'n'roll, but also the asset the dandies of between-the-wars now no longer possessed: youth. But while the British resented any hints of intimate familiarity with the Americans they implicitly allowed them to usurp all notions of normality and masculinity: 'English films and novels came to rely on the American Young Man, the Sonnenkind visiting England, to provide a hero valuable enough to recompense the heroine for her sufferings.'[10] Some of the dandies suffered quite directly from the general wish to appease the Americans and therefore to project a more 'proletarian' image. Cecil Beaton, keen to achieve some kind of official position in New York in the course of immediate post-war cultural diplomacy, was told by one of his friends in the British intelligence services: 'You give the impression of being a Beau, and the office wants to show that the British are really very like the Americans.'

The reaction to these disconcerting cultural developments was one that defined an essential part of the dandies' temperament, as well as their position on the cusp of decadence and modernity: nostalgia. After the Second World War, this nostalgia took the form of a melancholic hankering for a time of unchallenged upper-class privilege, the brief golden period that formed 'the link between Victorian bourgeois society and the febrile modernity that was to follow it'.[11] The nine years of Edward VII's reign, from 1901 to 1910, were not only the period into which the Bright Young Things were born, but are also generally regarded as the heyday of British male elegance and of a confident Britishness freed from the moral hypocrisy and turgid pomposity of the Victorian age. 'More money was spent on clothes, more food was consumed, more infidelities were committed, more birds were shot, more yachts were commissioned, more late hours were kept than ever before'[12] in that short decade, and not surprisingly the next period of excess, the 1960s, frequently referred back to the Edwardian era. Arbiters of taste often return for their inspiration to the prevailing aesthetic of their childhood, but rarely can this have been done in a more melancholy spirit of resistance than in the period after the Second World War. Beaton, who in his set designs and costumes for *My Fair Lady* would famously draw on Edwardian memories, wrote in *The Glass of Fashion*, an aesthetic memoir dedicated largely to the actresses and grand cocottes he admired in his childhood years: 'Philosophers tell us that as we grow older we come closer to childhood. I was still a child when King Edward's death closed the covers of the book of opulence, if not forever, at any rate for my lifetime. I am glad that my early roots

were Edwardian, for that period gave me a sense of solidity and discipline and helped to crystallize a number of homely virtues and tastes by which, consciously or unconsciously, I have been influenced in my life.'[13]

Nostalgia for this glorious period, so cruelly cut short by the First World War, started almost as soon as it was over. Beaton described 'Black Ascot', a real social event that in terms of its morbid decadence was reminiscent of Des Esseintes' all-black dinner party in Huysmans' *À Rebours*, with a nostalgic eye that always seems to regard change as a form of death: 'At the first Ascot racing season after the popular monarch's death, society appeared dressed from head to foot in black. The men wore black silk top hats with morning or frock coats, black trousers, black waistcoats, black ties, while in their black-gloved hands they carried tightly rolled black umbrellas. Their funereal ladies must have seemed like strange giant crows or morbid birds of paradise strutting at some gothic entertainment… The vast picture hats, perhaps set on one side of the head and piled high with black ostrich feathers mixed with osprey or black paradise feathers combined with black tulle, were worn not only in mourning for a king but for a glory that had gone forever.'[14]

The part Beaton played in the struggle to keep English-ness alive in a world of mass culture and Americana cannot be over-estimated. Despite his initial nostalgia, he was also one of the few Bright Young Things who was adaptable enough to manage the transition into the 1960s. He was not alone, however. Cyril Connolly sought to hold on to the qualities he saw disappearing around him – meaning and style – through his intellectual writings. While the *Unquiet*

Grave of his book title of 1944 referred to classicism itself, he made extensive use of philosophical quotations, mostly from French writers of the Enlightenment or the early nineteenth century, to carry his point. Connolly was not prone to an excessive *nostalgie de la boue*, however. Having neatly translated his innate classicism into modernism, he soon found himself 'unable to be polite to young men with bowler hats and rolled umbrellas'.[15] The stubborn persistence of class distinctions meant that classicism as a yardstick of 'good taste' proved to be far more resilient in Britain than in Germany or France. More virulently snobbish as well as more subtly perceptive than most, in his travel book *Labels* of 1930, Evelyn Waugh channelled an almost Loosian spirit when he speaks of his dislike of the William Morris tradition as the 'detestation of quaintness and picturesque bits, which is felt by every decently constituted Englishman'.[16] A mysticism of classical form saved Anthony Blunt, Keeper of the Queen's Pictures and Soviet spy who refused to go into the cold, when Marxist dialectics lost their power for him: an intellectual dandy with an ambivalent relationship with reality, he found in Poussin's classicism the superior position he sought which Marxism, having been demystified by the test of hateful reality, had failed to provide. When Blunt made his public confession on BBC television in 1979 George Steiner spoke of 'cold sophistries and eyes as chill and flat as glass'. It was only when the cameras had stopped rolling that the mask of imperturbability fell, and Blunt broke down in tears. Taste had yet again proved to be more real than any other kind of discourse to the dandyistic mind.

In *Labels*, Waugh had also paired this confidence in his

absolute authority on matters of taste with a sense of period that he believed was exclusive to the product of an English public school education: 'It consists of a vague knowledge of history, literature and art, an amateurish interest in architecture and costume, of social, religious, and political institutions, of drama, of the biographies of the chief characters of each century, of a few memorable anecdotes and jokes, scraps and diaries and correspondence and family history. All these snacks and titbits of scholarship become fused together into a more or less homogenous and consistent whole, so that the cultured Englishman has a sense of the past, in a continuous series of clear and pretty tableaux vivants. This sense of the past lies at the back of most intelligent conversation and of the more respectable and worse-paid genre of weekly journalism. It also clouds our outlook on our own age.'[17] At Oxford in the 1920s, this sense of period had taken the form of a contempt for all things Victorian, even resulting in a mock revival of the style by the aesthetes Robert Byron and Harold Acton in the mid-1920s. The Victorians were perceived as vulgar and hypocritical, character faults that were reflected in their tastes in architecture and interior design, namely Gothick and other Revivalisms. Osbert Lancaster and John Betjeman, who became lifelong friends around this time, collabourated on many a humourous anti-Victorian tract – an obsession with stylistic periods that they were to pursue in prolific fashion into the post-war era. Lancaster published several volumes of 'architectural cartoons', depicting exteriors and interiors of buildings going back to antiquity. He also coined names for some more recent styles, such as 'Curzon Street Baroque' or 'Stockbrokers Tudor'. Of all the architectural movements that influenced English taste, his preference was very markedly first for classical Greek and then for the classical Renaissance; writing of a Greek arch, he praised 'its apparent simplicity, its actual complexity and the rigidly intellectual basis on which it rests'.[18] However Betjeman, for one, was not inclined to follow classicism into modernism, as indicated in unequivocal fashion in the title of his book *Ghastly Good Taste* (1933, expanded 1970). After the war, his enthusiasm for Englishness in all its shapes was inevitably to lead him to the more eccentric end of the architectural spectrum. Like Osbert Sitwell in the first tome of his five-volume autobiography *Left Hand, Right Hand* (1945), Betjeman was in quest of 'the fantasy of England'. This led him not only to the follies and grottoes created by 'gentleman-architects' over the centuries, but even to a reappraisal of the Gothick. One of the last of the gentleman-architect breed, a survivor into the twentieth century, was Clough Williams-Ellis, who in the 1920s had started the building of the village of Portmeirion, his Italianate *paradis artificiel* in the rugged climate of Wales. The construction process continued into the 1960s, when it became the location for the cult television series *The Prisoner*.

But it was not just the upper classes and dandies who cherished Englishness; 'ordinary' people did so too. Returning servicemen-and-women rediscovered their own country with a kind of infatuation. After years of austerity and utility, they longed for ornament, gaiety and pattern, and they found all these in folk art. The dominant motifs – which included the circus, fairgrounds, gypsy caravans, and painted canal barges – found their expression not only in crockery and textile designs but also in the quirkier examples of British seaside architecture. Nowhere was this celebration of the indigenous vernacular more evident than at the Festival of Britain, which opened (less than a month before the defection of Burgess and Maclean) on 3 May 1951. On the surface, the Festival leaned towards a Scandinavian version of modernity – seemingly purged of the more baroque and decadent tendencies of dandyism – which appeared appropriate to the mood of serious democratic responsibility advocated by the post-war Labour government. Yet underneath it all, British modernism proved equally idiosyncratic and parochial, the result of a spirit of 'healthy' compromise that went hand in glove with the deep-seated ambivalence of what J. B. Priestley had described as a 'Socialist Monarchy that is really the last monument of Liberalism'.[19] Though staunch and proudly reactionary classicists such as Waugh were predictably horrified by all that the century of the common man in general, and the Festival of Britain in particular, had in store for them, there were inevitably elements that had been touched upon by more recent expressions of dandyism, including notably eccentricity, the cult of the amateur, and what the architectural critic Reyner Banham called 'the English picturesque'.[20] There were elabourate tea pavilions inspired by the work of Osbert Lancaster and the artist John Piper; there were bamboo vistas and arcades; and last but not least there was the 'Lion and Unicorn Pavilion'. The Lion and the Unicorn, modelled in straw like corn dollies, bore the legend: 'We are twin Symbols of the Briton's character. As a Lion I give him solidity and strength. With the Unicorn he lets himself go' – not a wholly inaccurate description of the man who gilded the period from 1945 to 1956, which was arguably the death rattle of dandyism in its purest form.

Neil Munro Roger, forever to be known as 'Bunny' after his nanny exclaimed shortly after his birth that he was, 'like a dear little bunny rabbit', was born in London to Scottish parents. His father and mother were born to stationmasters in neighbouring villages on the railway line from Perth to Inverness. Yet by the time Bunny was born, his father Alexander Roger, who was possessed of great entrepreneurial spirit, had already become something of a tycoon through a telecommunications company he founded and other worldwide business interests. He was knighted in 1916 – when Bunny was five – but remained proud of his roots. The same could hardly have been expected of his three sons, who assimilated their social position to the affluence they were born into. Bunny would later make ironic reference to his 'humble' origins; asked by Cecil Beaton, who was photographing him, to step down from the pavement, he quipped: 'We are only one generation out of the gutter and I am not about to step back into it.' His mother Helen, who seemed to have been a highly elegant woman and something of a wit herself, adored and pampered her three sons. A formidable character, she was the dominant influence on her sons' upbringing, effortlessly usurping the more down-to-earth personality of Sir Alexander. She was closest to Bunny, who also cared for her in later life. Sir Alexander wanted Bunny and his brothers Alan and Alexander to have a 'rigorous' Scottish education and they attended Loretto School outside Edinburgh before going on to Oxford. Having spent his childhood under the influence of a mother who was interested primarily in his aesthetic edification and a father who furnished him with all the trappings of wealth and the freedom to do and be whatever he pleased, Bunny found public school life something of a rude shock. Years later on the battlefields of Italy, when, as he put it, 'there were pieces of people flying past my nose', he thought to himself, 'this is perfectly awful but not so bad as being at school'. Despite being diametrically opposed to Bunny in temperament, his father seems nevertheless to have been happy enough to indulge his son's tastes, provided he showed a certain degree of physical fortitude. On being offered a reward for being selected for the 'nippers' rugby team, Bunny promptly asked for a dolls' house, which his father equally promptly provided.

The aesthetic initiation Bunny received more or less from birth was furthered by his contemporaries at Oxford. The crucial moment of yielding to the temptation of joining the aesthetes on arrival at the University has been described in many novels, and probably most famously in Waugh's *Brideshead Revisited*. In Bunny's case the cards were already stacked high in favour of the aesthetic set. His contemporary Osbert Lancaster, for instance, a great admirer of Max Beerbohm, was already a dandy of some note as a student, affecting pinstripes and checks, pink shirts and wide ties, sometimes a monocle and always a well-tended neo-Edwardian moustache. The academically gifted Bunny read modern history at Balliol, but was unfortunately sent down for 'corrupting homosexual practices' before he could finish his degree. It was his custom, it appears, to go to parties dressed as one of his favourite film stars – Gloria Swanson or Pola Negri – and to seduce other undergraduates, not all of whom were aesthetes. He made an impressive pinup: on being presented with a photograph of Bunny as Norma Desmond, taken by Angus McBean, it is said that Gloria Swanson graciously admitted: 'He was far more beautiful than I ever was.'[21] After flirting briefly with the idea of launching a career in Hollywood – greatly to his chagrin, a casting director compared him with the character actor George Arliss rather than Marlene Dietrich – he enrolled at the Ruskin School of Art with a view to becoming a dress designer, and in 1937 opened a salon in Great Newport Street, which he decorated with some rather elabourate Regency pieces.

It was notably during the war years that Bunny appeared as living proof that when the Lion lies down with the Unicorn, it brings forth the dandy. Fighting in the Rifle Brigade, the smart regiment for those of an artistic bent, he was allowed some indulgences. As a captain during the Italian campaign, he lined his tent in mauve and furnished it with gilt chairs. Yet on many occasions he showed that a slender physique and flamboyant appearance were no bar to cool physical courage. Loitering in no man's land at Anzio in order to touch up his make-up, he heard a voice calling from the battlefield for help. Although the order for immediate retreat had been given, Bunny stayed behind, picked the man up and brought him back to the lines. With characteristic diffidence, he later claimed to have spent the war wearing a chiffon scarf and brandishing a copy of *Vogue*. Bunny retained a fearless streak throughout his life, and was invariably the first to jump into the breach when there was any sign of trouble. Unlike many of his contemporaries, he was also a fierce patriot – he would knock off the hats of gentlemen who omitted to lift them when passing the Cenotaph – and somewhat patrician in his values. His view on his own homosexuality was equally arch. He refused to use the word 'gay', which entered common parlance when homosexuals adopted it for themselves in the 1960s (although its double meaning had existed since the late nineteenth century): 'You can't call a queer man gay. Apart from anything else they're all so miserable. The Greeks were more accurate when they called the Furies the "Kindly Ones".' His outlook was the very Edwardian one that his generation had rebelled against, and after the war he matched his suits to his soul.

Men's fashion in the immediate post-war era was still crippled by the belt-tightening that had characterized the war years. The demob suit issued to servicemen returning to civilian life in 1945 was a dullish version of pre-war fashions, and during the war civilian trade had been severely restricted by the introduction of the British Utility suit, made of brown, grey or navy cloth with a low wool content in a government-enforced economy cut – narrow, single-breasted and two-piece, with no pleats or turn-ups and a minimum of buttons. The first notable post-war fashion was the Drape or Bold look. Inspired by American *film noir* of the late 1930s and early 1940s, it was brought over to Britain by the retailer Cecil Gee and adopted by 'lesser' tailors in order to cock a snook at Savile Row orthodoxy. At its most extreme, it took the form of the zoot suit, the garb of ghetto rebellion in the United States that was quickly adopted by British spivs and 'wide boys'. With its extreme accentuation of the shoulders and negation of the existence of anything as feminine as a waist, the 'Bold look' was a visual translation of all that

British aesthetes resented about the invasion of transatlantic modes of masculinity. Looking back on the look in 1955, the magazine *Man about Town* described it thus: 'Immediately after the war there was the era of phoney muscles. Jackets were extended to give a Henry VIII look and shoulders were draped the Broadway. Lapels were long and swept to low button fastenings. Shirt collars were long and widely spaced with a gargantuan tie-knot between. Hats were flat and wide-brimmed. Shoes were wide-toed and heavy-soled.'

It was partly out of a haughty disdain for this look that the Neo-Edwardian style was born. It was also driven by a spirit of rebellion against the enforced austerity of the post-war years. Indeed, the records of Savile Row show that the prototype of the New Edwardian look had been made by a Conduit Street tailor for a young Scots Fusilier (in all likelihood Bunny Roger), who ordered it in the depths of the war 'as a protest against austerity'. The delivery date for this historic garment was January 19, 1942. After the war, it was young Guards officers who espoused the style. Tracing its origins in 1954, the fashion historian James Laver offered a psychological profile of the prototype Neo-Edwardian: 'The young man who wore it longed, at least subconsciously, to return to the days of Gentility Triumphant, when life for the Upper Classes was one perpetual party, when investments brought in dividends, and when a young man with four or five hundred a year could have chambers in Jermyn Street, two or three good clubs, and the possibility of spending most of his weekends in the great houses of the land.' While Neo-Edwardian suits were not identical to their fore-bears from the golden age of the stylish British gentleman,

they were certainly sufficiently reminiscent of them to reek of nostalgia. The look featured natural, sloping shoulders (though certainly wider than in the original Edwardian or later 1960s versions), a slim-waisted, full-skirted and flared jacket, a waistcoat often of contrasting material, and narrow trousers, ideally worn with boots rather than shoes. A bowler hat (or, as the original makers Lock & Co. of St James's still call it, a 'town coke'), crowned the whole ensemble. Worn noticeably small, it sat jauntily on the top of the head.

On 20 April 1951, the letters page of the *Tailor and Cutter* featured an interesting contretemps between the magazine, which promoted the look, and a Scandinavian (appropriately enough) reader. Advocating modernity, Mr Fritz W. Eriksson of Falun pointed out that today's man was far more of a man of action than his Edwardian counterpart, and so required more loose-fitting garments. His indignation was directed particularly at the 'womanly' aspects of the Edwardian style: its narrow shoulders, tight waist, and flared skirt. These he contrasted with the heroic proportions of the Drape look, which he perceived as accentuating the beauty of the male physique rather than masking it. The *Tailor and Cutter*, ever on the side of the gentler type of man, responded by pointing out the closeness of the Edwardian silhouette to that of the uniforms of Army and RAF officers – surely 'men of action' – which after all 'have successfully influenced the shape and style of almost every military uniform in the world'. After a lengthy defence of naturalness as more manly than exaggeration, the editor concluded that the now rechristened Military look should especially be welcomed by tailors 'if only because its advent has caused interest, comment and controversy among men in the street which had not existed with regard to men's clothes for more than a hundred years'.

Defending the 'manliness' of the Edwardian style on account of its closeness to military fashions seems at the very least a touch ironic, as the military is blessed with a history of male vanity and camp stretching further back than any other known profession. Down the centuries, camp behaviour has rarely been considered incompatible with good soldiering, and the very word 'camp' itself is thought to have derived (in one of many theories) from the process of setting up military camp (*se camper*) in seventeenth-century France. Needless to say, tents were somewhat more opulent at that time than standard-issue modern camouflage versions. Wellington himself was considered as much a dandy as a soldier, and we are told that, 'all Paris marvelled at his personal distinction, and at his peculiarly Regency blending of the austere and the eccentric'.[22] These traditions remained alive into the 1950s and even beyond. As late as 1977, Martin Green pointed out: 'The crack regiments were, and are, centres of social snobbery in the most ordinary sense. They are communities of men from great families and the great public schools, and usually with large incomes; and they allow themselves many freedoms from bourgeois prudence and decency, in matters like gambling, extravagance, and homosexuality. Their traditions maintain a connection with the world of Brummell, a connection that still seems strong.'[23] Cecil Beaton further traced this connection: with his impeccable eye for detail, in *The Glass of Fashion* he presented some evidence that it was the historical influence of the Dragoons that kept London a world centre of men's elegance. Not only are the overcoats worn by the Guards even today cut in the taste initiated by the Beau, but so are the interiors of two of the most exclusive London clubs, White's and Boodle's.

The Guards and Household Cavalry regiments are known for the strictures of their dress regulations, not only in uniform but also in 'mufti'. Even into the 1960s, an off-duty Guards officer in London was required to wear a dark suit and bowler hat and carry an umbrella. Through the Military/Edwardian look, Guards officers were thus able to transfer the tight-fitting martial glamour of their uniforms into civilian life, thereby making a virtue out of a necessity. The prime purpose of the regimented precision of military tailoring is of course to express rank. While uniform is a clear and conscious expression of hierarchy, the adaptation of these signifiers for civilian suits works more subtly, with 'rank' indicated by nuances of tailoring rather than by badges and gold braid.

The Military/Edwardian look was doubly loaded with class signifiers, expressing high rank through its waisted and flared silhouette, and nostalgia for privilege in its flapped pocket details and velvet collars (first worn by English aristocrats during the French Revolution in sympathy with their Gallic counterparts who were perishing on the guillotine, the female equivalent being a thread-thin blood-red choker). The adoption of the look by aesthetes such as Beaton, the ballet critic Richard 'Dickie' Buckle, and most eloquently Bunny Roger added to this *haut goût* mixture of privilege and nostalgia the all-important ingredient of desire.

Interviewed in 1955 by an Italian magazine, his face by now *dolcemente sciupato* (gently dissipated), Bunny related

the origins of his personal appropriation of the Edwardian look in ingeniously empirical fashion: 'In 1942, my Uncle Jeremiah gave me a wonderful watch chain. Now, first of all, I needed a pocket watch. Once I had acquired that, I found I needed a waistcoat, in order to show the ensemble off appropriately. I ordered a waistcoat from my tailor, but still the chain wasn't on display, nor could I reach it easily under my double-breasted coat; so I decided to have a single-breasted coat made in a style that pre-dated the invention of the wristwatch, just to err on the side of caution.' The story goes on in a similar vein. Once the dedicated Messrs Watson, Fargerstrom & Hughes, the tailors to whom Bunny had been introduced by his father and with whom he remained all his life, had come up with a resplendently long Edwardian jacket, it was found that narrow trousers were needed to go with it. The young trouser-maker refused to make them to the exiguous measurements he was given, for fear they would rip on delivery. Bunny came to the rescue with a pair of his grandfather's trews, and carried the day. According to his travelling companion John Blarney, he experienced similar difficulties when ordering trousers from local tailors in Capri in 1948: through countless fittings Bunny repeated the instructions 'stretta, stretta', until the requisite pencil-thin silhouette had been achieved.

Bunny Roger's tenacity in the creation of the *Gesamtkunstwerk* that is the dandy did not stop at the perfect suit. He understood like few others that true elegance lies in a unity of manners, dress sense and lifestyle. In the beginning, he achieved this unity through stringent historical accuracy. 'In the manner of Edward VII', he told the Italian interviewer,

who marvelled at his pink drawing-room, 'everything had to
be adjusted in order to complement my suits.' In a way that
was both literate and tangible, Bunny Roger had re-created
his *temps perdu*, the period just beyond his memory. But to
remain alive in a world of mass communication, which by
the 1950s was starting to democratize imagery and style,
dandyism also had to change. A distinct weariness with mere
nostalgia was already showing through: 'It is neither easy
nor pleasant to constantly be the last dandy, nor a dandy of
fifty years ago. I can't take the Underground; I'd feel slightly
ridiculous. What I mean to say is, I prefer the bus. But still,
somebody who dresses like I do really needs a valet to help
him into an ancient car with a ball horn, or better yet a horse-
drawn carriage. The world has changed. For a while I was
under the illusion that I was rewinding the clock by dressing
like my grandfather. But you can't change the world with the
same ease that it takes to change a suit.' Bunny Roger would
be only a footnote in the history of dandyism had he not
managed to transcend mere historical accuracy – to regain
time, indeed. For him, the Neo-Edwardian style proved to
be less a means of conjuring up a more decorous age than a
possibility of realizing his very own, fundamentally frivolous
idea of elegance. He used the Edwardian era as a visual vocabulary with which to express his individuality and desires. He
spelt this out in conversation with Nicholas Haslam, telling
him that the suit he perfected was the ultimate version of
the clothing he found attractive on other men, and adding
fatalistically, 'Such a mistake, one never gets anyone.'[24]

Bunny pushed the Edwardian suit's buttoned-up sobriety
to almost fetishistic proportions. Being blessed with broad

shoulders, a twenty-nine-inch waist even into his sixties, and enviably long legs, he possessed natural advantages which he showed off in the cut of his coats – what might be described as a masculine version of the trapeze-line. In many ways his silhouette mirrored the proportions of the New Look, where the wasp waist was achieved through corseting. Bunny pulled off a similar effect through over-cutting the shoulders, and wearing his trousers high and his waistcoats short, in the 'postboy' fashion. His trousers, usually cut with cross pockets (sometimes known as 'go-to-hell' pockets) to emphasize the hips, were largely free of pleats and turn-ups, and tapered to a breathtakingly tight hem of fourteen inches (undercutting the minimum width recommended by tailors by two inches). But it was particularly in his choice of colours that he went against Edwardian sombreness. While in 1955 his fourteen suits (by the mid-1960s he would be ordering that number on an annual basis) were still confined to shades of charcoal and midnight blue in order to cope with the effects of the London smog, soon a wondrous range of colours would enter his wardrobe. From lemon-yellow summer suits to velvet dinner jackets in a range of jewel colours, from candy-coloured shirts to tweeds in his favourite 'menopausal mauve', Bunny abstained from little.

After the war, Bunny first reopened his couture business in Bruton Street, and then took a fashion franchise at Fortnum & Mason, the department store that carries on in a quaint notion of Regency Englishness to this day. When pictures of one of his annual New Year's Eve parties appeared in *Picture Post*, he was politely asked to take his business elsewhere, however. The theme was 'Fetish', and more or less respectable figures from public life were pictured being paraded on dog leashes by their wives. On perusing the pictures, Lady Roger wondered, without turning a hair: 'How did these men manage to walk in such high heels?' Bunny then invested in his friend Hardy Amies's dressmaking house, and worked out of his premises for twenty years until he retired. Bunny's couture business sprang from a deep admiration of the elabourate gowns worn by Dietrich, Swanson and their ilk, which he initially sought to emulate – occasionally to devastating effect, as we have seen. His favourite colour, mauve, crops up frequently in Cecil Beaton's childhood memories of grand Edwardian ladies, and glamorous actresses such as Gaby Deslys, a French performer known more for the exuberance of her costumes than for her acting talent. When presented with a musical written especially for her by J. M. Barrie she memorably declared: 'I can't act, I can't dance, I can't sing, but I can do it!'[25] In Edwardian days, mauve furthermore carried somewhat risqué connotations, for during the trial of Oscar Wilde it had become associated with decadent aesthetics in general and homosexuality in particular. After the notorious fetish party at his London house, Bunny would celebrate New Year's Eve at Dundonnell, the Scottish estate the Roger brothers had acquired. There he would not only guide his guests through some of the more arcane reels, but would also revel in the opportunity to sport kilts, or shawl-collared dinner jackets in the Roger tartan, which conveniently happens to be pale yellow and mauve.

Bunny did however continue to give balls to mark every passing decade of his life at his London house in Addison Road, naming them after precious stones. On the occasion of the Amethyst Ball to celebrate his seventieth birthday, he commissioned a catsuit embroidered with mauve bugle beads, which he wore with a mauve organza cape trimmed with lilac fur and topped off with a feathered headdress. By this stage, however, he had learned not to cross the line into full transvestism: he always wore trousers or culottes, never frocks. With a true understanding of the art of camp, he appropriated femininity without ever impersonating it. His instinct for sartorial propriety was unfailing: nearing his destination in a taxi on one occasion, he discreetly adjusted his make-up. As he alighted, the driver shouted after him, 'You dropped your diamond necklace, love', to which Bunny firmly replied: 'Never with tweeds.' Bunny Roger was never anything but a gentleman, no matter how heavily made up his face might be, nor how often it was lifted – so often, indeed, that he quipped that he might soon have to shave behind his ears. If his suits were conspicuously exaggerated, this was made to appear natural by the perfection of his manners. Indeed anything less pronounced would have appeared as false modesty. Where the line between art and life blurs, camp is often a useful negotiating strategy. Bunny employed camp as a subtle inversion of 'good taste', replacing the self-regarding earnestness of 'high taste' with what can only be called high camp. At his meticulously orchestrated parties Bunny played host to a cross-section of people, from dustmen to duchesses: a mixture of classes that would have been unthinkable before the war. Among the many figures of complex ambiguity in the Proustian canon, only the most intriguing of them all, Baron Charlus, can compare with Bunny Roger's ingenious blending of the outrageous and the thoroughly proper. As with Charlus, Bunny's camp complexity grew out of his involvement with diametrically opposed milieux and the effortless blending of attitudes associated with them; out of the snobbery associated with his elevated social rank and the inverted snobbery associated with his marginal sexuality. Like Charlus, Bunny acted according to the principle of *parcere subjectis et debellare superbos*. On receiving her invitation to the Amethyst ball, the Duchess of Argyll objected that she disliked the colour mauve. Bunny's answer was simple: 'Don't come then!'

How revolutionary the concept of class appropriation still was in the 1950s is demonstrated by the phenomenon of the Teddy Boy ('Teddy' being a shortened form of 'Edwardian'), which emerged around 1954. The first 'Teds' were groups of teenage boys who drifted around the fringes of the South London working classes in search of a sartorial identity, equipped for the first time with the spending power to make it happen. If their coup d'état was their requisition of the Edwardian style, their new order was a quite different look. In a brilliant mixture of cultural motifs, they took elements of the Edwardian look and fused them with its binary opposite, the Drape look, so creating the first British subcultural style. The Teddy Boy outfit consisted of a broad-shouldered, loose-cut drape coat, drainpipe trousers, fancy waistcoat, brightly-coloured socks, crepe-soled brothel creepers and bootlace tie. Where the Neo-Edwardians wore their hair slightly longer around the edges and raised it to a nascent quiff in front, to differentiate it from the clean-cut skullcap of the 1930s, the Teds went to town with enormous pompadours, long sideburns and a DA (duck's arse) at the back.

The hybrid of Edwardian gentleman and rock'n'roll rebel ended up somewhere in the region of the Deep South riverboat gambler (the Confederate flag later became an element of Teddy Boy iconography), but was a cultural expression all of its own.

Savile Row and the breeding ground of the Edwardian style were prompt to issue warnings. The costume historian James Laver admonished: 'The "Teddy Boys" have no golden age to look back to; and therefore their clothes are only superficially Edwardian, and they destroy the whole effect of Edwardianism by the exaggerated width of the shoulders. "Teddy Boy" clothes say "I am a man!" whereas Edwardian clothes say "I am a gentleman", which is a very different thing.'[26] To the notoriously conservative tailors of the Row themselves, the emergence of these sartorial parvenus was an occasion for lavish self-flagellation for having become involved in anything as adventurous as a new look in the first place. Where sartorial appropriation had once taken a generation or two, with the durable Savile Row suit passing down to the valet and thence to the second-hand trade only after the death of its original owner, it could now happen almost overnight. Where their customers feared the erosion of sartorial class distinctions, the tailors feared the need for constant restyling in order to keep one step ahead. Their common enemy was the new technologies that made these unsettling events possible.

If the Teddy Boys were blatantly trespassing on proscribed territory in order to appropriate and violate upper-class dress codes, the fact that their emergence was of concern at all proves that the superiority of these codes could no longer

be taken for granted. In 1956, Nancy Mitford, daughter of Lord Redesdale and sister-in-law of British Fascist leader Oswald Mosley, edited a collection of essays entitled *Noblesse Oblige*, which discussed the terms 'U' and 'non-U' (upper class and non-upper class) that she had introduced in an article published the previous year, in which she had laid bare for public consumption characteristics of aristocratic speech and manner that had hitherto been used intuitively. As Nik Cohn points out in his history of post-war fashion, *Today There are No Gentlemen*, where habits of dress were concerned these codes went back to Beau Brummell. Before Brummell, clothes were judged by their impact; after Brummell, they were valued firstly for their propriety and secondly for their quality. Too much impact was immediately suspect: 'Very spruce,' said *The Times* of Rex Harrison, intending it as a put-down. Yet within these parameters were countless nuances, which acted as indicators of the wearer's precise position in the class system, sexual orientation, and – even more generally – temperament and ambition. In the 1950s, a variety of styles would qualify as acceptable in U-circles, as long as identity and nuance were in harmony. The undoubtedly homosexual connotations of the Edwardian look were permissible in upper-class terms by an extension of the same logic that tolerated homosexuality in the higher echelons of the army. By 1960, elements of its Teddy Boy appropriation had crept back into the original style, facilitated by the classlessness of homosexual desire. James Fox, author of *White Mischief,* describes a meeting with the notoriously predatory Bobbie Shaw and his mother, the politician Nancy Astor. A former officer in the Royal Horse Guards, Shaw had also

served a prison sentence for 'importuning a guardsman' of lower rank: 'Podgy and creased-looking, he was dressed in a sub-Teddy-boy mix: a long jacket, thick crepe suede shoes, narrow trousers, his hair slicked back and dyed jet black, his fingers covered in rings, a Cartier watch on his wrist. He smoked Woodbines, the cheapest cigarette one could obtain, which he kept in a Fabergé cigarette case.'[27] Bobbie Shaw committed suicide in 1964, shortly after the death of his mother.

According to the more conventional bourgeois standards of propriety, the exaggerated detail of undiluted Neo-Edwardianism were already signs of a dangerous otherness. A clear example of this may be found in the character of James Bond, who despite the indubitably U credentials of its author was conceived very much as a middle-class hero. The obsessive interest in labels that marks Fleming's novels invariably concentrated on the masculine quality of the accessory rather than on the detail of dress. It would have been unthinkable for Bond to remark on a flattering waistline, or to wax lyrical about an elegantly flared cuff. In the short story 'The Property of a Lady', Bond offers a wary assessment of a Neo-Edwardian: 'The stranger was middle-aged, rosy, well fed and clothed rather foppishly in the neo-Edwardian fashion – turnback cuffs to his dark blue, four-buttoned jacket, a pearl pin in a heavy silk cravat, spotless wing collar, cuff links formed from what appeared to be antique coins, pince-nez on a thick black ribbon. Bond summed him up as something literary, a critic perhaps, a bachelor – possibly with homosexual tendencies.' The progress of spies in fact and fiction indeed holds up a clear mirror to class developments in men's clothing, as well as in the secret services. Although Guy Burgess was notoriously slovenly, even grubby, in his appearance, he still seemed to place an emphasis on quality that was somewhat at odds with the clothing available in the Soviet Russian domicile of his twilight years. Even after his flight to Moscow, he continued to order his suits from Savile Row and his shoes from John Lobb. When questioned about the patriotism of supplying such a client, Eric Lobb, who ran the exclusive bootmakers at the time, would reply: 'He might be a traitor but he is still a gentleman.' Burgess's bequest to Kim Philby, who arrived in Moscow the year before he died of alcoholism, was a number of books, including first editions signed by Evelyn Waugh, some Savile Row suits and a few of the Eton ties that he always wore: the estate of a dying dandy. The next fictional spy of significance after James Bond was John Le Carré's Alec Leamas, *The Spy Who Came in from the Cold*, a rather dour if suitably cynical man, whose 'suits were of artificial fibre, none of them had waistcoats'.[28]

As the conflict between the Drape look and the Edwardian look indicates, one of the criteria of bespoke gentlemen's clothing is a cut that is a natural, if idealized, version of the wearer's body. A circumspect man will only appropriate the Grecian ideal of the naked male body in as far as his physique allows. In the original Edwardian suit, this meant that shoulders were not exaggerated, the natural waist was indicated and trousers were cut fairly close to the leg. The suits pioneered by the Duke of Windsor in the 1920s and 1930s offered an interpretation of the male body that was more abstract, but that still respected the ideal proportions as reestablished by Brummell quite as solemnly as he had done himself, thereby mirroring Modernist architecture's debt to Greek temples and other buildings. The Neo-Edwardians then exaggerated Edwardian proportions, adding an element of decadence, thereby arguably violating the very architecture of the suit. They also indulged in detailing that might be considered merely decorative and therefore excessive, including multiple-flapped pockets, lapelled waistcoats, turnback-cuffs and covered buttons – a solecism that risked opening the style up for appropriation by 'less desirable elements of society',[29] as the Duke of Windsor saw it. Indeed, the look had not only travelled all the way down to the working classes, but intermittently also infiltrated the ready-made suits worn by the middle classes. In his autobiography *Skip All That*, the broadcaster Robert Robinson described his own flirtation with the Edwardian look: 'I dressed like a prat in those days, and it was nice of Godfrey not to mention the cuffs on the sleeves of my jackets, and the revers on the waistcoats: the bowler hat seems to have been a special error, and I remember the man in Scott's of Piccadilly handing it down beneath the counter to his colleague in the basement who steamed the brims, saying, "Set this one up very smart, Mr Phipps."'[30] What technology started increasingly to erode in the late 1950s was the hitherto all too visible difference between the bespoke suit and the off-the-peg product, which at that stage started vastly to improve. Before the arrival of ready-to-wear men's fashion, the multiple versions of the gentleman produced by mass-market tailors such as Burton were already quite at odds with the dandy.

There was also a need to distinguish between matters of class and of fashion. In an open letter to Nancy Mitford in 1956, Evelyn Waugh used the example of fish knives to illuminate this point. While John Betjeman had famously cited fish knives as being 'non-U' in his poem 'How to Get On in Society', Waugh refuted this commonly held opinion: 'Higher in the social scale, at some (I am told at many) of the really august stately homes fish-knives have been in use for nearly a hundred years. They were a Victorian invention in pretty general use in polite society in the 60s [1860s]. Certain old-fashioned people, of the kind who today eschew the telephone, derided the gadgets, which soon began to appear among the wedding presents of professional persons. The old-fashioned people scratched away with two forks and also picked their teeth at table, which was considered low by smart Londoners... But it has all been a matter of fashion not of class.'[31] Waugh went so far as to deny the existence of a class system in England, preferring to call it a system of precedence, embracing countless minute gradations in rank rather than three broad categories. It is true that at no point would there have been a standard gentleman's suit, and what qualified as such was subject to variations in identity and fashion: differences expressed through nuances rather than bold statements. For all that the menswear revolution of the 1960s gained a great deal in terms of 'freedom of expression', it lost the definitiveness of these nuances for ever.

While the U and non-U debate was raging, there emerged in the arts a new type of masculinity, constructed in direct opposition to pre-war gentility. In May 1956, John Osborne's *Look Back in Anger* was first performed at the Royal Court Theatre in Sloane Square, to be hailed by the young theatre critic Kenneth Tynan as portraying 'post-war youth as it really is... The Porters [Jimmy Porter was the protagonist of the piece] deplore the tyranny of good taste... they are classless.' The same month also saw the publication of Colin Wilson's *The Outsider*, a digest of mainly French and German existentialist philosophy that proved to be a surprise success. Osborne and Wilson, with their distinctive polo-neck sweaters and corduroy trousers, were labelled as Angry Young Men, soon to be joined by others including Kingsley Amis, whose *Lucky Jim* was also published in 1956. That *annus mirabilis* of cultural shift also saw the unmasking of the third man in the Cambridge spy ring, Kim Philby, and in November the Suez crisis, bungled by the supremely elegant Anthony Eden, whose main achievement seems in retrospect to have been the revival of the Homburg hat. In *Look Back in Anger*, Jimmy Porter's wife Alison solemnly muses about the generation gap to her 'Edwardian' father: 'You're hurt because everything is changed and [Jimmy's] hurt because everything's the same.' From another culture and another hierarchy, Giuseppe di Lampedusa's *The Leopard*, published in 1967, commented sagely on the eternal ambiguity of change: 'Everything has to change, so everything can stay the same.' A few decades on, Kingsley Amis was propping up the bar in White's and John Osborne had become (according to the title of his autobiography) *Almost a Gentleman*.

If 1956 was to sound the belated death knell for the Bright Young Things, it did not presage the demise of the dandy per se. Modernity, aided by technology, was on the march, and new 'industrialized' dandies now took the helm. The 'Mods' who started to appear around 1958 were the first original dressers to be entirely disconnected from the upper class, emerging largely from a petit-bourgeois suburban background. Unlike the Teddy Boys, the Mods were not originally a group movement but were influenced by individual avant-garde dressers such as Bernard Coutts and Mark Feld (later Marc Bolan). But the peculiar energy that dandyism had derived from the opposite poles of modernity and decadence was weakened by its split into different factions. While modernity was carried on by the Mods, others resigned themselves to being purely retrospective. For masculinity, the 1960s meant above all a loss of fixed identity. All classes, professions and sexual orientations appropriated the dress codes of all classes, professions and sexual orientations. On the surface, the least affluent of men could afford to be dandies. Yet the inevitable sacrifice entailed by this democratization of style was the loss of coherence between form and content. The image began to be detached from the complexity of its creation, thereby calling into doubt the dandy's *raison d'être*. Ultimately, the result was the plethora of hollow styles that we see today.

If most of the fashions of the 1960s were homosexual in their influences, the message had now changed. Camp, which to the Duke of Windsor and Bunny Roger had been the grammar of their very individual vocabulary, had shaken off the largely homosexual connotations it had acquired in the early part of the century and entered common parlance. Where dandyism had originated on the cusp of aristocracy and democracy, Bunny Roger was both pioneer and last mohican, surveying the dissolution of his own art. Velvet suits and flowing silk scarves do not make a dandy. Bunny Roger's greatest achievement lay not in his indubitably significant contribution to men's fashion, nor in his defence of

a very English mode of masculinity against the American onslaught, but rather in demonstrating once again the degree of courage, sensitivity and practical cultural knowledge that true elegance ultimately requires. Two decades after Bunny had forged his identity, there emerged a fictional figure who superimposed all the cultural phenomena of the swinging sixties on to the style that Bunny had made his own. John Steed, the male protagonist of *The Avengers*, was Bunny Roger refashioned for a mass audience. Steed had an eye for the ladies, while the fetishistic aspects of Bunny's persona were neatly offloaded on to the special agent's impressive female assistants (a partnership beautifully acknowledged in the French title, *Chapeau melon et bottes de cuir*). An early press release for the television series described Steed as 'well-to-do, with an Old Etonian background, a sophisticated taste in living, a flair for clothes, an eye for a comely wench and a not too fastidious ruthlessness in getting his own way. A Regency buck, in fact, twentieth-century style.' The character assimilated elements of the actor Patrick Macnee's own upper-class/bohemian background, and initially the clothes were designed by Macnee himself, incorporating what he described as 'the eighteenth- and nineteenth-century influences' that had shaped his aesthetic sensibility.

Later, in a curious twist, the costumes were supplied by Pierre Cardin, who in 1960 had made a splash with his Edwardian-inspired *Style Anglais*. The results of this exercise in anglophilia were – needless to say – *plus anglais que les anglais*, and set the tone for a series laced with such ironies. As Toby Miller points out in his study of *The Avengers*, the prevailing Pop Art aesthetic was 'always leavened by Steed's

ability to breach the space between old and new'. What Steed, variously described as a proto-Mod and a high Edwardian, had learned from Bunny was the juxtaposition of the ambiguities of modernity and decadence in such a way that they appeared homogenous. One of Miller's sources describes this process as the capacity to be 'in age and dress and manners the hallmark of the establishment, yet still so chic and always ethically on side with the counter-culture' – a precise pinpointing of the dandy's ambiguous socio-geographic position in appropriately 1960s terminology.

On 30 January 1998, Bunny Roger's ample wardrobe was auctioned off in its entirety by Sotheby's, London. Despite the excitement surrounding having these mystical objects, 'the last dandy's' suits, on tangible display and available to try on, it soon became clear that they were but empty vessels without the man to whose individuality they had been so closely tailored. Like the pharaohs of ancient Egypt, so often referenced in his Regency furniture, Bunny should have taken his earthly goods with him to the grave. He had of course understood this. Feeling *un peu faible* on the eve of one of his last balls, he asked to be laid out in his party outfit so his guests could admire it, lest he should die before they arrived. He finally did so on 27 April 1997.

d.

QUENTIN CRISP

L'Étranger

She is an eighteenth-century woman, whose emotions
turn instantaneously to wit.

REYNALDO HAHN ON MME DE CHEVIGNÉ

When all masks have fallen the true mystery begins.

JEAN COCTEAU

It is remarkable how every image of Quentin Crisp, even
the most incidental, has something of an iconic quality.
There are few others of whom this can be said, including
perhaps William Burroughs and certainly that other self-
created being, Andy Warhol. It is a quality that goes beyond
great beauty or sexual attractiveness. Cartoon characters
have it and film stars of Hollywood's golden age in the 1920s,
1930s and 1940s had it. It is the art of always looking the
same. Cartoon characters are drawn that way, and the stars
of the golden age had an army of people making sure that
the image stayed intact, even in supposedly private snaps.
Quentin Crisp devoted a lifetime – almost literally – to
perfecting this image of himself by himself, and not only did
ensure that this image he presented to the world was perfect,

but he also took great care – and herein lies an even more cogent reason for the striking quality of every single one of these portraits – that it was the most accurate depiction possible of the being underneath. Quite early on in a long life the two became inseparable. Quentin Crisp tampered with his personal appearance until it 'unified' him, and once he had adopted his 'uniform', the rest of his life 'solidified' around him 'like a plaster cast'.[1] Not for him the habit of 'trying out a whole new image' that is so prevalent among people in the worlds of fashion and popular culture. From that point on, Quentin Crisp remained impervious to fashion – indeed to change of any sort. His friend John Haggarty, whom he met in the 1940s, decided early on in their friendship that Crisp was 'all of a piece, the front very formidable but bonded, like rubber and metal can be bonded, to the inner self which nobody knew'.[2] While everyone is judged to a degree by how they look, this judgement will rarely be accurate. Creating this accuracy forms the groundwork of the dandy, and its successful results are the essence of his dandyism.

Quentin Crisp was born Denis Charles Pratt on Christmas Day 1908 in Sutton, Surrey, the youngest of four children. As so often, the original impulse that fostered the development of dandyism was a feeling of inadequacy. 'I had two brothers and a sister and they were only semi-hopeless, but I couldn't do any of it... I couldn't cope with the world,' he was to say of his childhood when looking back late in life.[3] Contracting pneumonia as an infant left him with a taste for the attention that was heaped upon him at the expense of his siblings (he later claimed that 'a fair share of everything is a starvation diet for an egomaniac),'[4] as well as for the lifestyle that went

with it: 'At a time when my two brothers aspired to be splendid icons of manliness such as firemen or ships' captains,
all I wanted was to be a chronic invalid. For this vocation
I had a certain flair.'⁵ Other factors that contributed to the
flowering of his extreme individualism were an indifferent to
occasionally resentful father (a solicitor who was seemingly
rather pallid in character) and a mother who acted out her
frustrated social ambitions through a penchant for stylish
theatricality: 'My mother was middle-class and middle-brow
but she rightly regarded the suburbia in which we were compelled to live as a sort of purgatory of style. She had her own
way of improving the lustreless hour. There was a moment,
when, as a child, I stood beside her in a butcher's shop. She
was just about to place an order with the man behind the
counter when another customer darted into the place and
interrupted my mother in order to say, "Mr. Jennings, I
simply must tell you that I ate the pork chop you sold me yes-
terday at ten o'clock at night and slept like an angel." "You'll
pardon me," my mother began slowly, "but the angels never
sleep. They cry continually day and night – though whether
because of the late eating of pork chops the *Book of Revela-*
tion doesn't say."'⁶ She was indulgent of young Denis's own
feebleness and flights of fancy, letting him use his wardrobe
as the prop department for his fantasies, and allowing him
to appear as a fairy in *A Midsummer Night's Dream* in green
tulle and a wreath of roses.

The four years he spent at boarding school in Stafford-
shire were dominated by feelings of fear and hatred for
his masters and fellow pupils alike. He took little part in
the ersatz sex games popular with boarding school boys,

on account of his then naturally peculiar looks, which he described as a 'formidable natural chastity belt': 'My rich mouse hair was straight but my teeth were not. I wore tin-rimmed glasses.'[7] A photograph taken at this time shows a stern-looking but elfin creature. It was also during his time at boarding school that he discovered what would remain a cherished habit for life: 'Masturbation is not only an expression of self-regard: it is also the natural emotional outlet of those who, before anything has reared its ugly head, have already accepted as inevitable the wide gulf between their real futures and the expectations of their fantasies.'[8] Though rather good at exams, he took no real interest in any of the subjects taught, achieving good results by feats of memorizing. His greatest gift and desire were already for complete idleness. Aware of this, his father wrote to his classics master in his last term to ask what on earth could be done with the boy. The master suggested that although young Denis did not have the makings of a scholar – clearly lacking as he did the application required by academia – he had a talent for writing, and should try his hand at journalism. Though he found himself completely unsuited to this field, on account of his inability – fostered at boarding school – to get on with strangers, he found himself taking a course in journalism at King's College London at the age of eighteen: 'I did not protest at the absurdity of this. I dared not. I had nothing to suggest in its place and I knew that while I sat dreaming through the lectures, at least I was putting off for another two years my terrible confrontation with the outer world.'[9]

He was still living with his parents, who had now decamped to Battersea, and he stayed there for a while after he had left

King's without a diploma, 'finding no better occupation than sitting at home getting on my parents' nerves'.[10] An advantage of being in London, however, was that he found others who were 'like him'. In the 1920s, when homosexuality was by and large still displayed through such subtle signifiers as suede shoes (these were not deemed acceptable until well into the 1930s, making the Prince of Wales's penchant for them all the more daring), those who espoused the love that dare not speak its name were rather hard to spot in the provinces. Not only did signifiers of distinction and allegiances of any kind tend to be extremely subtle until the late 1950s, but in this case the inclination in question was in fact illegal (and was to remain so until 1967). In London, however, there were men whose effeminacy was so obvious as to suggest that they couldn't help themselves. Even if they had ordinary day jobs, many of these men spent their evenings working as male prostitutes and playing cat-and-mouse with the police. Quentin (he changed his name in his twenties) was soon to join their ranks, less from desperation than out of a wish to embrace fully the first milieu to which he seemed vaguely acceptable. The extra money also came in handy.

More significantly, soon Crisp decided to be more than somebody who 'can't help himself': 'I wanted it to be known that I was not ashamed and therefore had to display symptoms that could not be thought to be accidental. I began to wear make-up.'[11] So began his one-man campaign for what at the time he thought to be the right to be homosexual. It was only much later that he realized that what he sought to present accurately to the world was in fact nothing other than himself. Indeed, looking more like himself proved to be an obstacle when it came to living out his sexuality: not only did he not want people to think that he had adopted an effeminate appearance merely in order to solicit custom, but men also stopped approaching him, as they found it too risky or distasteful to go with such an obvious homosexual. Through trying to avoid at all costs giving the impression that this was his intention, he began to develop also another characteristic that is central to the dandy personality: distance. At this stage, distance had of necessity to be literal. Walking faster and never looking strangers in the eye, he sometimes either inadvertently or deliberately, in order not to embarrass them, swept past or cut people he knew quite well: 'Without knowing it, I was acquiring the haughty bearing which is characteristic of so many eccentrics. What other expression would you expect to find on the face of anyone who knows that if he turns his head too quickly, he will see on the faces of others glares of stark terror or grimaces of hatred? Aloofness is the posture of self-defence, but even people who quite liked me said that I felt superior to the rest of the world.'[12] While his true education continued thus, his parents made another attempt to prepare their now twenty-one-year-old son for the 'real' world, sending him to do a course in commercial art at an art school in High Wycombe, where they now lived.

The first inklings of happiness came on finally having a room by himself in Pimlico, after a depressing interlude of sharing with a friend in Barons Court and King's Cross. Crisp at last realized 'that the future was now'.[13] After a surprisingly non-confrontational talk with his father, he had promised to move out by Christmas. His father died soon after. A first job as a tracer with a firm of electrical engineers proved shortlived, but lasted just long enough to entitle him to receive unemployment benefit. From then on, the paltry sum of 15s 3d changed his impoverished status from living off pocket money from his parents to 'Soho' poverty, which he explained 'comes from having the airs and graces of genius but no talent'.[14] He learned ways of 'ducking and diving' to make do. One thing he found he could exploit was the snobbery of the times: he discovered a restaurant where you could eat for a shilling whose owner viewed him not as an effeminate homosexual but rather a gentleman 'of high degree but at low ebb'[15] – fallen grandeur being of course one of the masks of the dandy. She therefore made sure he was given triple portions, which she watched him eat with great satisfaction. Another 'type' the lesser-known species of the dandy is often mistaken for is that of the artist, the reverence for which amongst 'ordinary' people Quentin found also worked to his advantage. Meanwhile his appearance became increasingly bizarre. 'Blind with mascara and dumb with lipstick,'[16] he walked or rather minced everywhere, partly out of poverty but mostly because of his heightened exhibitionism – an exhibitionism that was soon to earn him hostile attention, to the point of slaps in the face from complete strangers and beatings from yobs with mixed motives. These incidents did not diminish his evangelical zeal, but rather enhanced it. But at just twenty-two, his happiness still lay in expectations of the future rather than in the dandy state of mere being. He dabbled in writing plays and librettos, and dreamed of one day being a famous writer, actor or painter. Only later was he to formulate his definitive mantra of happiness: 'The essence

of happiness is its absoluteness. It is automatically the state
of being of those who live in the continuous present all over
their bodies. No effort is required to define or even attain
happiness, but enormous concentration is needed to abandon
everything else.'[17]

After a succession of jobs in the art departments of advertising agencies (still a seedy business in those days), from which
he was inevitably sacked – each time feeling the mixture of
indignation and relief known to all with 'higher things' on
their minds – he made his first great step towards achieving
the dandy state of being: he gave up gainful employment. 'I
cannot claim that from this moment I was always happy, but
from the age of twenty-eight I never did for long anything that
I didn't want to do – except grow old.'[18] He did however continue to make a paltry living as a freelance commercial artist,
as well as managing to write a book about window-dressing,
a subject that he claimed to know absolutely nothing about.
Yet writing did not develop into the second career he had
hoped it would be: he remained a dilettante in every field he
tried his hand at, albeit with far more success than he would
have ever been willing to admit. It was to be another thirty
years before he settled on writing about the subject that was
compatible with his innate dandyism: himself. Despite his
relief at finding himself living alone in Pimlico, this happy
state was not to last. Periodically destitute, Crisp had also
not yet arrived at the state of emotional and existential self-
sufficiency that he was later to achieve: 'My choice of room
was never dictated by taste or convenience. I gravitated only
towards the greatest opportunity for putting myself at the
mercy of other people, and moved into a succession of places

let to me by friends, and in some instances by mere acquaintances, who wished to lighten the burden of their rent but had no accommodation that they would have dared to offer to a stranger. When the discomfort and sometimes downright degradation became too much for me, I moved on to fresh pits and pendulums new.'[19] In fact it took another eleven moves before he was able to settle into permanent bedsit bliss, a momentous event that was preceded by a few months by the outbreak of the Second World War. This event he marked by safeguarding the continuity of his image, taking the precaution of having two pounds of henna sent from France.

It was in the summer of 1940 that Crisp took up residence at 129 Beaufort Street, Chelsea, where he was to remain for forty-one years until 13 September 1981: 'I finally gave up trying to disguise from myself my deep-seated indifference to the fate of others, settled into a room by myself and admitted that solitude was one of my essential needs.'[20] In fact it was the very way in which he related to other people that made it necessary for him to live alone. Always a work of art on show, he felt compelled to entertain his friends – and to put on a complete cabaret turn for strangers – whenever he was confronted with them in anything approaching a domestic setting. In order to keep up this constant level of performance, he needed a private space to retreat to, where he could prepare and relax: he needed a 'dressing room'. At Beaufort Street he was also free to fully put into practice his by now famous philosophy on housework. Despite his appropriation of femininity in appearance and manner, he was utterly averse to domesticity, at this time still very much a female realm: 'Squalor rapidly became my natural setting.

I felt it was only by a series of unfortunate accidents that till now I had always lived in the captivity of hygiene... I changed the bed linen once a week... About cleaning the rest of the room I did nothing at all. Except that after a while it became necessary to jump in the air while putting on my trousers so as to avoid trailing them in the dust, I never found that this omission brought in its filthy wake any disadvantages whatsoever. As the years went whizzing by, I was able to formulate a law: it stated that there was no need to do any housework at all. After the first four years the dirt doesn't get any worse. Later... I was given a chance to deliver this message of hope to a drudging world.'[21]

Viewing active service in the armed forces as a welcome means of avoiding ever-impending penury, as well as embracing the possibility of a glorious and convenient death, Crisp hoped to be called up and eagerly awaited his appearance before the Army medical board. When it finally came, he was exempted from any kind of war effort on the grounds of suffering from sexual perversion. But the war did bring him the first job that approached his desired state of being, as opposed to doing. First of all, yet another episode of dire poverty presented him with what might be called the classic depressive's dilemma – being bereft of both the will and energy for life and the resolve necessary for death: 'When a third wave of poverty overwhelmed me, I knew with even greater certitude... that the only complete solution to my problem was suicide. I never brought it off. I was afraid. A lifetime of never making positive decisions, accepting instead the least of the evils presented to me, had atrophied my will. It was not so much that I longed for death as that I didn't long for life. Emptiness, though, was not a sufficiently definite feeling to lead to a violent act. Instead of sitting in my room and balancing the relative convenience of various ways of ending it all, I ought to have been busy trying to summon up a reasonable amount of despair. Hopelessness was thinly spread like drizzle over my whole outlook. But, in an emergency, I could not find a puddle of despondency deep enough to drown in.'[22] In this plaintive state of mind, a glimmer of hope was offered by a Chelsea artist who wanted to paint him and reluctantly agreed to pay him as well. These sittings, which resulted in three portraits, were merely a foretaste of the career to come.

Some time in 1942, Crisp received a phone call from an artists' model he had known some years earlier, imploring him to stand in for her at an art class the following evening. After agreeing, he quickly cobbled together an outfit for this assignment, knowing that in England male life models were never entirely naked: he made a posing pouch out of an old pair of underpants. Having survived the first session, he quickly decided that being paid to be looked at presented a singularly apt way to make a living, for 'it required no aptitude, no education, no references and no previous experience'.[23] Despite its apparently passive nature, it did however require a great deal of endurance. Discovering that this was the first job of which he had some innate understanding, he decided to re-create the whole process of life drawing in his own image. Ever the classicist, he tried to imbue his poses – and with luck the work that resulted from them – with the quality he so admired in Michelangelo. A quality which in essence is the integration of form and contents in the image of man: 'I was an avowed enemy of culture but I admired his work unconditionally. Of all the paintings from the nude that I ever saw, only his appeared to me to be not merely of living people but of what it is like to be alive. The drawings of Ingres, continually held before the lustreless eyes of students as an example for them to follow, always seemed to me to be seen from the outside – to display a lascivious preoccupation with surfaces – with the convexities and concavities of the body. Michelangelo worked from within. He described not the delights of touching or seeing a man but the excitement of being Man. Every stroke he made spoke of the pleasure of exerting, restraining and putting to the utmost use the divine gravity-resisting machine.'[24] Deciding to bypass the obvious obstacle of his body being somewhat less Michelangelo-like in its proportions – 'I was undersized in all respects except for a huge head and a pigeon chest'[25] – he strove to create by pose alone what Brummell had achieved with clothes: the appearance of an antique sculpture: 'I twisted and turned, climbed up the walls of life rooms and rolled on their paint-daubed floors, morning, nude and night.'[26] The exertion required by these poses presented and the importance of line in their depiction soon led him to model mainly for life drawing: 'Drawing is a science; painting is just something for the long winter evenings.'[27]

One day when he was posing at Goldsmiths College a German bomb fell nearby, shattering the windows of the life drawing room. Crisp held his pose as immovably as the statue he was trying to portray would have done. In addition to displaying a *sang froid* bordering on *sang congelé*, this episode also typified Crisp's attitude to the war per se, an attitude he would later describe as the possibility of 'death made easy'.[28] He was in the country with an actress friend when he heard that the bombing of London had started, and his reaction was to rush home to Chelsea immediately – partly out of a fear of missing any of the drama, and partly out of a genuine desire to embrace disaster. Being *un homme sans immediateté*, as in Sartre's description of Baudelaire, somebody so distanced from his own feelings (or as the modern expression goes, out of touch with his emotions) that he could never be sure whether he was feeling them or just feeling that he ought to feel them (a state of alienation that he naturally cultivated as a self-defence mechanism, of which more later), he occasionally longed for the one emotion of unquestionable immediacy, fear: 'As soon as the bombardment of London began I was totally engaged.'[29] The determination of Londoners to 'keep calm and carry on', ignoring the dangers of the Blitz as far as they possibly could, has since become something of a truism. Quentin Crisp took this spirit to its logical conclusion, however. Remaining an inveterate flâneur when even policemen were sheltering in doorways, he 'ceased to go out only when it was necessary and started to search London for my own true bomb'.[30] But there was another aspect of the 'spirit of the Blitz', much sentimentalized since, from which Crisp realized he could profit: the levelling of differences between people in order to unite against the common enemy: 'As soon as bombs started to fall the city became like a paved double bed.'[31] Not only was he introduced by a fellow model to the truly bohemian night cafés of Charlotte Street, where his sexuality simply was of no consequence and he was thus able to move from crusading to entertaining, but he also found that the general sense of camaraderie amongst Londoners at times extended to embrace even him. Apart from becoming the more or less compliant object of black-out fumblings, along with many others, he experienced a renaissance of his sexuality as soon as GIs arrived on British soil. What appealed to him especially was the immediacy and friendliness with which these complete strangers approached him. As their propositions were made without spite and rejections were accepted gracefully, Crisp was able to deploy all the feminine coquetry he desired. These experiences appeared to him a significant landmark in his pursuit of the holy grail of happiness: 'To the rest of the world happiness was a suspiciously regarded byproduct of some other pursuit (preferably noble). Americans and homosexuals sought it for its own sake.'[32]

When this golden period was cruelly curtailed by the declaration of peace, Crisp also found himself gradually being weighed down by a particularly dandyistic form of midlife crisis: 'My failures to win true love, to stay in the movie industry, to write books that anyone would publish were not a series of unconnected accidents to which I was prone because of my exposed position in society. They were the expression of my character – the built-in concomitant of a morbid nature to which dreams were more vivid than reality. The infinitesimally small success that I had known had been achieved inevitably in terms of being rather than of doing. I had gained what I had aimed for when I first got control of my own life. But in middle-age physical well-being faded. Money, fame, wisdom, which are the booby prizes of the elderly, I had never been able to win. My preoccupation with happiness had been total. I would not yet have described myself as miserable but I was deflated. I realized that the future was past. Whatever I could hope to do or say or be, I had done and said and been. This state of affairs occurred prematurely because I had subjected a shallow and horribly articulate personality to a lifetime of unflagging scrutiny. Even a marriage with oneself may not last forever.'[33] On the outside, this change manifested itself through a change in hair colour. Ever brutally truthful, he did not want it to be thought that he hennaed his hair in order to hide the grey. So on his fortieth birthday he began to replace red with a blue rinse. Feeling that he also needed a change from the physical agonies of modelling, he found employment first in a publishing house and then with a manufacturer of display units. He even wrote a rather Firbankian[34] novel called *Love Made Easy*, the main originality of which lay in its lack of a conventional love story. A comment by a close friend offered a poignant reminder of the dandy's tragedy: 'I wish you hadn't made every line funny. It's so depressing.'[35]

Bored with working for a living after a few years, as usual, he realized once more that 'for me no job could ever be more than a seaside romance with respectability'.[36] And so he eventually went back to modelling. Yet by this stage – when as he said, 'the time for having a career was far behind me'[37] – these setbacks no longer had the power to upset him. Alongside the physical decline of middle age, he also experienced one of its melancholy mercies, that of things ceasing to matter so much: 'Each unsuccessful attempt to win fame brought me nearer to the time when triumph would be useless even if it came.'[38] In his social life, he discovered a truth that eventually hits everybody condemned by their nature to a life of eternal bohemianism – that most fellow travellers eventually fall by the wayside: 'The daily routine of back-breaking idleness proves too much for certain novices. The self-inflicted orgies that are the inevitable punishment for the slightest deviation into the bourgeois way of life are more than their frail flesh can stand. Many discover to their shame that they have scruples; they have roots and, greatest disadvantage of all, they have hope.'[39] Some die, some get married and move to the suburbs. Although the 1950s are now held up as the golden age of Soho, nostalgic spirits were already glancing backwards at the glory days of Fitzrovia in the previous decade. The 1960s presented Crisp with a different predicament. While a hitherto unprecedented degree of tolerance now prevailed – 'the utopia, dreamed of by me and the friends of my youth, was here'[40] – he found that his once outrageous attire had become the norm for the very young, which ironically had the effect of making him look like a middle-aged man trying to appear younger: 'I inadvertently gave the impression of trying to gatecrash a King's Road party for people two generations younger than I.'[41] Approaching his sixtieth year and finding the work of art he had made of himself long ago completed, but with the finishing touch of death remaining irritatingly unforthcoming, Crisp now directed his lifelong habit of unrelenting self-scrutiny towards a final assessment. As mercilessly self-deprecating as always, he ended the autobiography that resulted, *The Naked Civil Servant*, by questioning the value of self-scrutiny itself, so making the serpent eat its own tail: 'Even a monotonously undeviating path of self-examination does not necessarily lead to a mountain of self-knowledge. I stumble towards my grave confused and hurt and angry...'[42]

The Naked Civil Servant was published in 1968. Little could Crisp have suspected that there still lay in front of him not only another thirty-one years of life, but also fame and self-realization as a dandy-dilettante in its fullest form. At this point it seems appropriate to take a brief look at *The Naked Civil Servant* as a text in its own right. In his textual analysis in *The Stately Homo*, Paul Robinson has accused Crisp of being 'the classic unreliable narrator, whose passion to entertain is forever sabotaging his duty to inform',[43] of 'leaving us tied in epistemological knots',[44] and his book of being 'the last word in indecipherability, that supreme postmodern virtue'.[45] He concludes that 'no autobiographer in my experience is more elusive'.[46] The literary/lifestyle devices Crisp actually employs include: irony that is sometimes bitter to the point of sarcasm, paradoxes that reveal a truth, self-deprecation and the occasional pun. All of these seem no more than what 'one would expect from any cultured gentleman'. In their extreme profusion and intensity in *The Naked Civil Servant*, they display the dandyistic quality of pushing the convention to its ultimate extreme in order to transcend it. Crisp's book is classically modernist in adopting complexity and ambiguity as a formal device for arriving at the truth. Janus-faced like the dandy, it is also so radically forward-looking and revealing in its contents that its publication would have been barely thinkable, and certainly not advisable, in the climate of intolerance before 1968. Apart from the fact that homosexuality was not legalized in Britain until 1967, its degree of revealing self-scrutiny regarding psycho-sexual and bodily matters would have seemed alarming outside the pages of a Freudian academic text.

Despite his later protests that he did not hold with culture, especially the high variety, it is quite apparent that Crisp was extremely well read. He seems to have been especially knowledgeable about Marcel Proust, referring to him several times in his writings and describing *À la recherche du temps perdu* as an 'almost perfect work of art'.[47] Although Proust's work admittedly does not claim to be a straightforward auto- biography, it does rather put Robinson's remarks concerning the elusiveness and multi-layered meanings of Crisp's auto- biography into perspective. When it comes to 'postmodern indecipherability' *The Naked Civil Servant* can hardly touch *In Search of Lost Time*, the very definition of Modernism in literature whose meaning has been dissected ad infinitum. Significantly, when the performance artist Penny Arcade asked him, 'Do you believe in Postmodernism?' Crisp replied, 'No. I believe that once there was modernism, then it ended, now there is only decline and decay'.[48] In a small way, *The Naked Civil Servant* is Crisp's *Recherche*, though for Proust's fugal reflectiveness he substitutes a very British empiricism, while also lending a distinctly British sense of humour to the qualities of irony and ambiguity that are present in Proust. In *Le temps retrouvé*, Proust describes the essential qualities that form the rounded social persona of Robert de Saint-Loup: 'Accustomed by his impeccable breed- ing to avoid defensiveness, refrain from vituperation and empty phrases'.[49] This is the quality that springs to mind when Crisp is accused – as he often was retrospectively – of reflecting 'internalized homophobia' by apparently expressing a high degree of self-loathing, sexual and otherwise. Yet given that his whole persona was formed around the notion that he did not want anyone to think that he was ashamed, a sentence such as 'I regarded all heterosexuals, however low, as superior to any homosexual, however noble' can only appear as biting sarcasm, designed to disarm and at the same time ridicule the bigots. Why indeed should he stoop to defending who he is and can't help being, thereby tacitly accepting that it needs defending? Crisp is Proustian and not Wildean. Not only did he loathe Oscar Wilde – once describing him as a gross human being trying to enter English society[50] – but he could also justify this position convincingly, *en passant* expressing his own dandyism and negating Wilde's: 'Mr Oscar Wilde, considered by some the great expert on this subject, said that, in matters of importance, it was not sincerity that mattered but style. To the true stylist [read dandy] they are the same thing.'[51] But of course Crisp's discourse does not arrive at the deep truth it ultimately conveys by means of plain sincerity. Indeed, to anyone as finely tuned to posturing and self-deception as he was, mere sincerity would ultimately appear dishonest, as he explained in *Manners from Heaven*: 'There is a nursery school of thought which advocates that people should be sincere: that they should be constantly expressing what's on their minds. Creeping sloppiness, the philosophy of the unruly class, holds "sincerity", "spontaneity" and "candour" in great esteem; but in fact the usual results of practising these pseudo-virtues are confusion, misunderstanding and hurt feelings. In my experience most so-called "truths" are emotional in their base and far more unreliable than a lie.'[52] Yet there is one sense in which

Crisp does deceive us, if only to the degree that he wishes to deceive himself, which is to say ultimately unsuccessfully. This concerns his opinions on emotional matters: 'To have feelings is a weakness; to give expression to them is disgusting,' he advises us in his guide to dandyistic living *How to Have a Life-Style*.[53] Yet as his description of his early life tells us, he was not only guilty of both these sins, he was also by nature so thin-skinned and prone to sentiment that he would constantly have been in floods of tears, had he not exerted the supreme self-control that he had learned over the years. Similarly, it hardly needs saying that his definition of love has been arrived at through the hurts and disappointments, which are inevitably suffered by one who has exalted expectations of it: 'The message that "love" will solve all our problems is repeated incessantly in contemporary culture – like a philosophical tom-tom. It would be closer to the truth to say that love is a contagious and virulent disease which leaves a victim in a state of imbecility, paralysis, profound melancholia and sometimes culminates in death.'[54] The fact that we can trace the way these maxims were formed in no way detracts from them, however. It is indeed advisable to reach a high degree of self-sufficiency in order to avert disappointment, and it is indeed salutary to realize that there is 'no salvation, only laughter in the dark'.[55] In one sense, the formation of the dandy-persona as a whole can be explained by a banal truism: behind every cynic lies a disappointed romantic. Yet once this persona has been successfully forged, through all the painstaking processes described in these pages, it would be hard to deny that it stands up fully and in its own right.

Another aspect of Crisp's persona that is significant in this context is his resolve to stay on the bottom rung of society, whatever the circumstances. By the end of his life he had in fact amassed a substantial fortune, yet he continued to live in a filthy bedsit with a shared bathroom. This was more than the mere fear of impoverishment, of one day having not enough to eat, that apparently afflicts even billionaires. Brummell had started with a small fortune and had created the parameters of perfection that he wanted to achieve in his life within the bounds of that fortune – before exceeding them, to his peril. For most of his life, Quentin Crisp lived from hand to mouth, never expecting to amass any significant amount of money. He set the material bounds of his life accordingly, keeping the necessary outgoings to a minimum. This asceticism can also be seen in his attitude towards the more conventional indulgences of decadence; as he remarked, 'Even in depravity I lacked stamina.'[56] He never took drugs and never drank to excess. Indeed the puritan part of his personality derived as much satisfaction from forgoing a pleasure as from indulging in it. He created the artificial paradises he inhabited by the power of his imagination alone. When he became – in all likelihood – quite rich, he saw no reason to adjust the parameters he had set, preferring instead to give away his surplus and leave most of the rest in his will. Part of his enormous success in terms of dandyism is precisely this sense of containment bordering on claustrophilia that guaranteed control of his style. Style to him was not wealth, or even elegance, but continuity. An anecdote Paul Bailey recalls in *The Stately Homo* illustrates this point perfectly: 'He was very admiring... of a woman known to the "hooligans" of Soho and Fitzrovia as the Countess. She was honoured with this sobriquet by reason of the fact that she acted in the grand manner, although her home was a trunk in the graveyard of the bombed St Paul's Church in Wardour Street (like Beckett's Winnie in *Happy Days*, up to her neck in sand). It was thought the Countess had come from a prosperous family, since the battered leather trunk with its gold handles was the kind that used to be taken on ocean liners. The countess was small enough to fit into it snugly. She had a change of clothes, a kettle, teacups and saucers and a portable stove, but what really impressed Quentin was that she entertained visitors, who had to employ the broken gravestones as chairs. But woe betide them if they turned up on the wrong day or came unexpectedly. He was there one afternoon when an acquaintance knocked on the trunk. The lid shot up and the Countess emerged. "You have not made an appointment," she snapped. "I am seeing no one today." Whereupon she pulled the lid down on her.'[57]

Quentin Crisp's beliefs and the way he lived them have all the makings of his own brand of existentialism. In Albert Camus' *The Outsider*, Meursault says on the eve of his execution 'And I gave myself up completely to the tender indifference of the universe.'[58] When Crisp says he likes 'nothing better than a luxurious wallow in indifference'[59] the seeming paradox indicates the very relief of being able to face life and death with equanimity, of being liberated from slavery to one's emotions. Though he claimed never to have made a decision in his life, he exercised his free will in a way few other public figures of the twentieth century could have claimed. His life exemplifies the uniqueness of fundamental moral choices, the impossibility of reducing them to a general principle. Among other things, in his definition of style, Crisp asserted that the moral choices that define any-one's life are creative, in the same way that a work of art is the creative expression of the artist's personality. Once, at the beginning of his career as a model, he was asked for his opinion of modern art: 'I said I never understood art of any kind and I meant it. Whereupon one of the masters said, "That's no answer, because you have made yourself a work of art – maybe a bad work of art – but all the same, you are a conscious creation and have thought not only about your appearance but also your entire way of life, your mode of speaking, your gestures, the way you live. You've done all this exactly like someone standing in front of a canvas, saying, 'The pink is too bright, I'll tone it down a little.' You have rearranged yourself until you are the best you can do with the poor materials available." (He didn't actually say that but that's what he meant.) It was then that I realized that I had indeed become my own creation – not merely noticed by others but recognized for what I was. I was suffused with a feeling of relief, as if at last I had crossed a bridge from muddled youth to self-confident maturity.'[60]

Commenting on Sartre's description of Jean Genet as an existentialist saint, Crisp remarked: 'If existentialism is the philosophy that decrees that you can exercise your free will only by swimming with the tide but faster, then it is the creed of style.'[61] To existentialists, freedom is of course not only an irreducible but also an inescapable feature of human exis-tence; as Sartre put it, man is not only free, but 'condemned to be free'. Crisp certainly felt this keenly, especially during the early, painful stages in the process of finding his style. Yet part of the forging of his persona was a decision to embrace the alienation that is the concomitant of true freedom, particularly the freedom from conventional, romantic and sexual love, from loving *les autres*. In defence of his preferred sexual activity Crisp remarked: 'In an incorrigible fantasist, auto-eroticism soon ceases to be what it is for most people – an admitted substitute for sexual intercourse. It is sexual intercourse that becomes a substitute – and a poor one – for masturbation. If this is evil then Baden-Powell, instead of urging the male adolescents of the world to take colder and colder baths and make wilder and wilder assumptions about the stuffiness of their mothers' view on puberty, should have found some way of warning boy scouts that alienation was the probable result of the habit. I regard this alienated state as good. It grants the intellect some freedom from the body. It saves a person from judging others by the confused standards of male, female, old, young, beautiful, hideous, in a way that can never be achieved by eating vegetables or sitting cross-legged in the middle of California or wearing purple on Wednesdays.'[62] 'Each of her dresses appeared to me as something that enveloped her quite naturally and inevitably, as if it were merely the projection of a particular manifestation of the soul inherent to her.'[63] Thus Marcel describes Mme de Guermantes' dress sense in *Le côté de Guermantes*. The soul Quentin Crisp sought to project initially was that of a femme fatale.

As *The Naked Civil Servant* offers us mere glimpses of bright shirts and gold sandals rather than a whole outfit, we have to piece together an impression from the few pictures that survive from the time before he was famous. A

studio portrait taken by Angus McBean in 1940 is of his head
only, and apart from a generous helping of mascara displays
mostly a hairstyle that is not so much a woman's style as
a very grown-out and elabourately bouffant (presumably
permed as his hair was naturally straight) and coiffed men's
style (it is still shortish at the back, though hardly the mere
bristle thought appropriate at the time). What renders it feminine is largely the way in which all the hair to the left of the
parting tumbles sensuously over the forehead. Although the
photo is black and white, we know that the hair was bright
red. Another photo taken in 1948 shows Crisp sitting on his
bed, wearing what appears to be a conventional 1940s cut
suit, with wide-bottomed trousers and equally wide shoulders, made flamboyant by the addition of the long silk scarf
that he wears knotted around his throat instead of a tie. His
features – which one observer would much later describe
as 'both male and female, noble and ignoble, depraved and
imperious'[64] – still have a boyish prettiness that is remarkable in a man of forty. Elabourately decorated sandals have
been discarded to allow a view of painted toenails. Crisp's
relationship to footwear is revealing of the dandy's search
for his ideal set of measurements: 'My feet were smaller than
any ordinary mortal's and I wanted everyone to know this.
As time went by I wore shorter and shorter shoes, not because
the length of my feet decreased but because the amount of
discomfort I could bear became greater.'[65] The whole look is
one that nowadays might be described as 'boy-drag', a woman
wearing men's clothing in a feminine way. Indeed the writer
Patrick O'Connor described coming across both Bunny Roger
and Quentin Crisp in 1960s London: 'What was strangely

appealing about them both, by then, was that they looked like male impersonators from the music hall, like elderly women dressed as men.'[66]

By this time Crisp was of course on his way from notoriety to fame, and his look had come into its own. The plethora of photographs from the late 1960s on show us that his style remained fundamentally the same with subtle adjustments, but reveals more of its variety. In the street he always wore a wide-brimmed hat (fedora or beyond) perched at an extravagant angle, beneath which the architecture of his hair grew ever more labyrinthine, owing to his wish not only to appear feminine but also to cover up what towards the end of his life became almost complete baldness. As he had neither the money nor the desire to go to a bespoke tailor, his outfits were literally concocted from clothes he'd been given, making the continuity and singularity of style that he achieved all the more astonishing. In some photographs he has even replaced the scarf with an ordinary tie, and wears a classic combination of sports jacket and trousers with just the slightest flare – he did employ the services of a woman he described as 'the best trouser taperer in London'[67] – and a pocket handkerchief arranged in such a way that it just crosses the line from discreet adornment to flamboyant limpness. Leaning on his umbrella, he creates a visual impact that is as poignant as ever. By the late 1960s, mainstream masculinity had of course caught up with Crisp. Cultural protagonists such as Mick Jagger adopted what had hitherto been viewed as effeminate – long hair, tight-fitting shirts and jackets, flowing scarves, flared (skirt-like) trousers and high heels – and turned it into the insignia of a liberated sexuality that made

the male the object of the sexual gaze, just as the female had always been. In the same way that Bunny Roger had anticipated the look of the late 1950s and 1960s, Quentin Crisp was decades ahead of the late 1960s and 1970s.

Yet before men went effeminate, women had gone butch, if only for the duration of the war: 'At all ages and on every social level, they had taken to uniforms – or near uniforms. They wore jackets, trousers and sensible shoes. I could now buy easily the footwear that I had always favoured – black lace-up shoes with firm, medium heels. I became indistinguishable from a woman.'[68] Despite the increased problems this caused with the police and the indignant public Crisp of course stuck with his style, just as he was to do thirty years later when it was appropriated by heterosexuals. The third period when his persona caused him trouble for what might be called the wrong reasons was in the late 1970s and 1980s, when gay men started to adopt an image of almost caricature masculinity, leaving him once more ostracized by those he had long ago given up regarding as his natural allies: 'When I was young a homosexual man was thought to be effeminate… This tradition has been brought to an abrupt end in America by political correctness. The gay community… parade an egregious masculine image, wearing crew-cut hair, a kitchen tablecloth shirt, pre-ruined jeans, tractor boots and a small moustache, if not a full beard.'[69] Particularly distasteful to the dandy was what he saw as the vast disparity between form and content that these new images entailed: 'Young men who had never seen a horse began to wear full Western gear; boys who couldn't even catch a fly – let alone hurt one – donned stormtroopers' uniforms. I have never understood how these disguises can hold up for more than ten minutes... Moreover, what is the use of desire provoked by or admiration bestowed upon someone you are not?'[70]

At one of his live shows, *An Audience with Quentin Crisp* from 1980, he wears a black velvet suit with flared trousers, a white shirt and a black scarf, and uses a monocle to read out questions from the audience, looking more like a theatrical Regency fop than anything else. This appearance, together with his pronouncements on homosexuality, rendered him a reactionary in the eyes of the politically correct, who had now replaced the bigots in showering opprobrium on him. Despite his claims that effeminacy was the style of homosexuality (two things he tended to confuse) up to the 1970s, Crisp never conformed to any stereotype. Having learned early to suppress his real emotions with a steely resolve, he never indulged in the displays of false emotion that are associated with the 'queeny' variety of camp. À propos of an acquaintance indulging in pat phrases like 'a woman's work is never done' he remarks in *The Naked Civil Servant* 'About camp, with its strong element of self-mockery, there seemed to me something undignified – even hypocritical.' His delivery was as tightly controlled and rehearsed as his wit, and neither seems ever to have descended to the level of bitchiness, which tends to be the expression of spiteful emotion (bringing Saint-Loup's impeccable breeding to mind again). The writer Andrew Barrow, who met him several times, confirms this: 'There was never anything pathetic about him, and in spite of his stagey movements, cinematic delivery and theatrical declarations he was not in the least bit camp. He was far removed from the grand old queens of high society and their tempestuous, finnicky ways.'[71] This lack of spontaneity also had its drawbacks: with one's character virtually set in stone, and constant repetition of the same sayings more or less inevitable, after a while one is unlikely to bring surprise or wonder to one's own life or to those who know one well. The dandy's perennial problem of having perfected himself assailed Crisp many times after he first became aware of it in middle age: 'I've exhausted all the potentialities of my character.'[72] Yet even at the very end of his life, he was certain that the choice he had made was the right one. Asked in 1998 about his habit of consciously curtailing his emotions, he answered: 'I don't want to be someone who says, "I hope I shan't make a fool of myself," as if they weren't certain of what they were going to do. I'd like to feel certain, that I knew what I was.'[73]

Crisp had originally wanted to call his autobiography *My Reign in Hell*, since like Lucifer he had refused to serve in heaven (in his case respectable society); the eventual title, *The Naked Civil Servant*, was a reference to the fact that life models were paid by the Department of Education. Even though it would ultimately be another seven years until the fame, for which in some way he had been preparing for sixty-five years would envelop him, the writing of his autobiography must be seen as the spark that lit the fire to come (the book itself had grown out of a radio interview the writer/fellow bohemian Philip O'Connor had done with Crisp in 1964). In July 1970, Granada television broadcast a documentary about him by Denis Mitchell in its *World in Action* strand. But it was the film of *The Naked Civil Servant*, made for Thames Television by Philip Mackie and Jack Gold with John Hurt as Crisp ('my representative on earth'), that suddenly catapulted him (and Hurt) to fame and made him a household name. Broadcast in 1975, it was universally lauded by the critics and well received by the public, making his image recognizable to everyone from schoolboys to taxi drivers. Partly owing to the increasingly liberal climate of the seventies and partly to merely having been on television, Crisp found that recognizability also meant an increased degree of acceptance. He was now a sought-after public speaker, having started to tour with his one-man show *An Evening with Quentin Crisp*, and he discovered that fame itself was an instrument in his self-realization as a dandy: 'To be identified with our publicity is simply yet another way of merging our outward and inward selves.'[74] Yet, never prone to reckless optimism, he still continued to do his art school modelling.

Soon fame took Crisp across the Atlantic and even further afield, first to Canada and Australia, then to America. On his second visit to New York, the impresario Hillard Elkins signed him up, promoting him incessantly and ensuring his one-man show toured all over America. He was now in what he called 'the smiling and nodding racket',[75] and his former expression of haughty disdain while cruising the streets of London was replaced by one of permanent 'fatuous affability'.[76] His first visit to New York had brought back some happy memories: 'The moment I caught sight of it, I wanted it and stretched my arms through the car window towards the skyscrapers like a child beholding a Christmas tree. Every street along which we drove brought back the memory of some long dead movie seen when life was dreary and only the world of celluloid was rich and full, every person on the sidewalks reminded me of the soldiers who invaded London during the happy time.'[77] At that time he had declared that he was 'by nature American'.[78] This is ironic, as despite the resentment he would protest over and over again at the treatment he had received in England in his early years, it would be hard to think of a character more formed by Englishness than Quentin Crisp. He could hardly be accused of sharing the qualities of boundless optimism, spontaneity and immediacy that he so admired in the GIs. But when he finally moved to New York in 1981, the almost unreserved acceptance and celebration he received allowed him a share of what he regarded as the American talent for happiness for probably the longest period in his life. Self-aware as ever, he was under no illusions on this score, however: 'Wherever I am on this earth, I am and shall always be only a resident alien'.[79] His need for material goods remained just as frugal in the New York years, but he was finally free to indulge shamelessly in events and people. For eighteen years he now lived the life of a dandy-dilettante that he had always desired, sharing his aphorisms and his company with absolutely everybody who wanted, constantly being invited to parties and events where he could speak and be seen, and never turning down an invitation. He also – like Andy Warhol, whom he admired – loved to be photographed ad infinitum, never caring whether the result was flattering or not.

Apart from acting in various movies, notably playing Queen Elizabeth I in Sally Potter's *Orlando* in 1992, he now also took to writing film reviews for a gay magazine called *Christopher Street*. Having always been an avid movie-goer – he claimed to have spent a large part of his midlife crisis in the 'forgetting chamber' – he took to this new profession like a duck to water. Having earlier declared the cinema the 'richest mine of style',[80] he was still unflaggingly aware that in the movies, as in every other art form, style must never be divorced from substance. Commenting on what he perceived as the decline in Alfred Hitchcock's career from around the time of *Psycho* he remarked: 'if style has become distinct from and more important than content, things are going badly'.[81] Though never vitriolic in his criticism, he was rarely enamoured of 1980s cinema, observing of Louis Malle's *My Dinner with André* that it was 'as boring as being alive'.[82] Though not in favour of realism, he insisted that the illusion should be convincing, taking issue with improbabilities and obvious inaccuracies on the grounds that 'Life is under no obligation to obey the laws of probability, but the movies are another matter.'[83] He was nostalgic for the perfect illusions the Hollywood films of his youth created; and not surprisingly, much of his thinking about movies centred on the notion of the star. For the star as for the dandy, the secret is to project an innate personality through an identifiable style and to stick to it for evermore. In this respect, stars are the polar opposite of actors, as acting implies the ability to inhabit a character different from the actor's own. This was a course of action that Crisp actively discouraged: 'Not only is it fatal for a star to act, it is unwise for her to be known ever to have acted in her entire life.'[84]

Although his New York years were probably his most fulfilling, Quentin Crisp's fame had come very late in life, if not too late. While his mind never faltered, his body was becoming frailer, and his thoughts eventually returned to

death with the relish that he had always reserved for the subject. Crisp was unusual among dandies in living to such a ripe old age, a fact that he attributed to 'bad luck'.[85] Among his many *bons mots* about the desirability of death from his last years, it is the briefest that sums up this 'shabby dandy'[86] most succinctly: 'I've outlived my wardrobe (I'm ready to die).'[87] Although he regarded suicide as 'the last graceful gesture of someone whose style has been completely mastered',[88] he found that after a lifetime of romanticizing it he still lacked the stamina. The dandy's flair for tragedy was not lacking though and he now hoped for a 'significant death' in the form of murder. In a neat reversal of his belief that dying is the surest way of avoiding one's obligations, death came to Quentin Crisp when he was fulfilling his. At the age of ninety and in frail health, he found himself unable to turn down the tour of England his manager had arranged for him. He died in his sleep on 21 November 1999, a month before his ninety-first birthday and the end of his century. Ironically, he died in Chorlton-cum-Hardy near Manchester, the very place that Brummell had left the army to avoid. Despite Crisp's self-proclaimed aloofness from the human race, the lessons this 'self-aware solipsist'[89] learned from a life of intense self-scrutiny quite often contain a good deal of what might reluctantly be called common sense. This he imparted to the world with imperious humility. The essence of dandyism, he suggested, is not lost on any life: 'Dressing as I did did not make me "happy" necessarily, but it unified me – and that is what we must all do with our lives. There are always penalties up to any age for presenting the world with a highly individualized image, but if it is the genuine you and not some affectation (a distinction which, I realize, may take years to sort out) then you must be what you are, honestly and bravely, with all the taste and intelligence you can muster. Life will be more difficult if you try to fulfil yourself, but avoiding this difficulty renders life meaningless. To arrive at the end of your life thinking, I never did anything I really wanted to do... must be one of the most profound miseries the human soul is capable of feeling – and one for which there is no last-minute cure or consolation.'[90]

JEAN-PIERRE MELVILLE

To Become Immortal
and Then Die

Jacques Becker died of haemochromatosis. The organs of
his body made iron which it could not eliminate. When
he died, he was transformed into a statue of iron. He was
handsome, so handsome on his deathbed, Jacques Becker.
Those who saw him will never forget.

JEAN-PIERRE MELVILLE, INTERVIEW BY RUI NOGUEIRA

Consider; for a smile is the chosen vehicle for all
ambiguities, Pierre. When we would deceive, we smile;
when we are hatching any nice little artifice, Pierre; only
just a little gratifying our own sweet little appetites,
Pierre; then watch us, and out comes the odd little smile.

HERMAN MELVILLE, *PIERRE OR THE AMBIGUITIES*

The characters in Jean-Pierre Melville's films do not
smile. They wear the Baudelairean mask of melancholy
immovability that was attributed to the actor Alain Delon
on his seventieth birthday: *'Je trône dans l'azur comme un
sphinx incompris; J'unis un cœur de neige à la blancheur des
cygnes; Je hais le mouvement qui déplace les lignes, Et jamais*

je ne pleure et jamais je ne ris (I am enthroned in the skies, an inscrutable sphinx; My heart is of snow with the whiteness of swans; I abhor movement which disrupts line, And I never weep and I never laugh).'[1] Yet Melville had filmed an alternative ending to his and Delon's best-known film, *Le Samouraï* (The Samurai), in which the killer Jef Costello, who has orchestrated his suicide at the hands of the police, laughs as he dies. Faced with the eternal and inescapable ambiguity of life and death – 'You can either laugh or cry,' as the painter Francis Bacon famously (and not as callously as it might appear) said on hearing of the suicide of his long-term lover. Or you can do neither, which is not only the mask of ambiguity but also that of the despairing absence of feeling that is pathological melancholy.

The stylization of melancholy, often with a beautiful face, has a tradition in France that is inextricably linked to the reception of dandyism. Before Baudelaire, Barbey d'Aurevilly had written: 'On rereading Rancé, I find in Chateaubriand a virtue that was unknown to me: He makes you love death… You understand the enchantment of this silent contempt which is poisoned like every enchantment. I'll be damned! To learn to love death is a fine aim in life.'[2] Jules-Amédée Barbey d'Aurevilly was born in Normandy in 1808, the son of a minor aristocrat. While studying law in Caen, he one day spotted the dishevelled figure of Brummell. It was a sight that was to stay with him, and that was one of the reasons why, after completing his degree, Barbey decided not to practise the law but to settle in Paris and make a living as a writer and journalist – a decision that did not preclude the expression of a clear (if somewhat theatrical) leaning towards dandyism.

Barbey wrote a handful of novels that are counted among the works of French decadence, his most notorious work being *Les Diaboliques* (The She-Devils), a collection of short stories published in 1874. His most significant work in the context of intellectual reception of dandyism was the essay *Du Dandysme et de George Brummell* (Of Dandyism and George Brummell), published in 1845. Intended as a vanity publication for a few friends, this developed into the first theoretical discussion of the ideal of dandyism, adding a metaphysical dimension that had so far eluded the empirically inclined English. Put simply, what the English had invented, the French now explained to them.

Setting aside an epilogue describing the seduction of Mlle de Montpensier by the Duc de Lauzun, the essay can be divided roughly into five parts. Barbey starts out with an apologia for vanity, in which he identifies dandyism as the incarnation of vanity most appropriate to the English character. According to Barbey, the English are 'lymphatic and pale, cold as the sea of which they are the sons', and they need alcohol to relax their temperament. This he contrasts with the vanity of the 'highly-strung and hot-blooded French',[3] which satisfies itself in amorous adventures and the seduction of women. By the time we reach the book's conclusion, we can be in no doubt as to which form of vanity Barbey prefers. He seals his eulogy on dandyism with the declaration that dandies have 'dual and multiple natures' and are of 'ambivalent intellectual sexuality', their 'grace is heightened by their power, and their power by grace'. He closes with a clue to dandyism's classical roots: 'They are the androgynous beings of history rather than fable, of whom Alcibiades was the most supreme example in the most beautiful of nations.'[4]

In the second part of his essay, Barbey endeavours to reach a definition of dandyism. In contrast to British approaches – whether positive, as in Captain William Jesse's biography of Brummell, or negative, as in Thomas Carlyle's *Sartor Resartus* – Barbey argues that the quintessence of dandyism is not reached through perfection of clothing alone. Rather, dandyism is informed by the spirit on whose mortal form the clothes are displayed: 'Dandyism is a whole way of being – a way of being composed entirely of nuances.'[5] In the third part, Barbey sets out to draw up a genealogy of dandyism, concluding that despite some antecedents on both sides of the Channel, the founding spirit of dandyism *propre* can be none other than George Bryan Brummell, to whose life and influence the extensive fourth part is dedicated.

After presenting the reader with the great man's biographical details, Barbey goes on to outline the characteristics that predestined Brummell for his career. While he dismisses the possibility of any hint of homosexuality fostering the rapidly developing friendship between the latter and the Prince Regent, he nevertheless maintains that a friendship between men can also be founded upon impulses that are aesthetic and verging on the sensual: 'for are there not friendships that originate in physical things, in external grace, just as there is love that springs from the secret, intangible charms of the soul?'[6] Later on, Barbey returns to Brummell's asexuality, which he identifies as part of his mask of invulnerability. Underlying Brummell's eschewing of libertinage were compelling psychological factors. It seems he never consummated the female admiration that he excited – according to Barbey women and priests always side with those in power – as: 'to love means to desire, which means being dependent, a slave to one's desire'.[7] Brummell's armoury included one weapon in particular that made it impossible for his vanity to be rendered ridiculous: irony, 'the gift that dispenses with all others'.[8] After all, the conversational equivalent of ambiguity is irony.

It is also in this part that Barbey diverges from previous accounts of dandyism and establishes his quintessentially French view of Brummell. For Barbey, the perfection of Brummell's dress, its refinement to the point of total simplicity, is merely the starting point of his significance as a dandy. Barbey defines the dandy as a kind of holy man who transcends mere clothing in order to reach a non-religious form of spirituality; he is *un homme qui porte en lui quelque chose de supérieure au monde visible* (a man who carries within him a certain something that is superior to the visible world').[9] Brummell's art lay not in his dress but in his life; his greatness lay in his presence. Hence the last part of the essay might easily be read as the obituary of a film star: Brummell ruled through his aura more than through words, his effect depended on a look, a gesture, a silence. He was destined to his fame by a *'Je ne sais quoi'*, in the phrase coined by Montesquieu in a fit of pique – as Barbey had pointed out in his earlier essay 'On Elegance' – when he failed to formulate a definition of taste.[10]

Jean-Pierre Melville would later reiterate this when he described a film star as an ordinary human 'with something else extra'. Barbey describes the beginning of Brummell's decline, his flight to the Continent, in terms that would be fitting to an actor taking his leave from the stage: 'His ruin was final, and he knew it. With the impassiveness of the dandy, he had calculated, watch in hand, the precise length of time that it was wise to remain on the battle scene, the scene of the most admirable successes a man of fashion had ever enjoyed.'[11] With the love of the gambler for letting fate decide, Brummell had played, lost and left. Yet to paraphrase Norma Desmond in *Sunset Boulevard*, he had not really lost; it was life that had become smaller.

Charles Baudelaire read *Du Dandysme et de George Brummell* soon after it was published, and was to spend much of his life engaging (and in his own way also identifying) with dandyism. Indeed the year 1845 was to prove a turning point in Baudelaire's life (and in the development of his brand of dandyism). Born in Paris in 1821, Baudelaire came into his inheritance on coming of age, as his father had died when Charles was still a child. This fortune gave him a brief lease of freedom in which to cultivate his burgeoning dandyism, during which he lived with his mistress Jeanne Duval in the sumptuous Hôtel de Lauzun on the Ile Saint-Louis, employed a valet, bought quantities of antique furniture, works of art and books, and became one of the better clients of his tailor. In 1845, his mother and stepfather – Mme Baudelaire had remarried – discovered that young Charles had already squandered half of his inheritance, and promptly put the remainder in trust. Although the benevolent lawyer who administered the trust gave Baudelaire a handsome annual allowance, he was to suffer from financial problems for the rest of his life. Despite his writings on the subject, he was in thrall to the idea that a dandy needed to be a man of wealth:

it was the gulf between this sense of entitlement and the reality of his financial position that was to drive Baudelaire to make one latent element of dandyism entirely his own: despair.

In the second half of the nineteenth century, dandyism started to weave itself into the structure of the city. The dandy became a flâneur, stepping out of the club into the street. This was particularly the case in Paris, where a more heterogeneous bourgeoisie had grown up, engendering specifically French variants of dandyism in the form of the artist-dandy, the *bohème*-dandy and the *ecrivain*-dandy (as both Barbey and Baudelaire styled themselves). And of course the boulevards of Paris offered a spectacle in themselves, an exterior *mise en scène* as a substitute for the interiors of the salon. And it was in the back rooms of the boulevards, their cafés and bars that the flâneur lived out his social life. Baudelaire set little store by the approval of the aristocracy, but discerned a noble pedigree – independent of blood or title – in the metropolitan dandy: 'The observer', he noted, 'is a prince who everywhere enjoys his incognito.'[12] In the city, the mask of the gentleman, formulated by Wilde and invoked by Loos, might conceal a multitude of types: dandies, homosexuals, gangsters. Proust's Baron de Charlus barely hid at least two of these metropolitan types behind his mask: 'But however hermetically Monsieur de Charlus tried to seal this face, to which a light dusting of powder lent a mask-like air, his eyes remained like two crevices, the only loopholes that he had failed to close.'[13] For Baudelaire, the dandy's mask of impassiveness served to hide his despair. It was specifically the gentleman's coat on his back that isolated him not only from

the establishment he had disavowed, but also from his bohemian peers: 'In the Bohemian world the very cleanliness of
his linen, the presence of a rug on the floor of his apartment,
the formality of his speech and the old-fashioned politeness
of his manner were conscious anomalies. They expressed his
belief in an aristocracy of spirit, which disassociated itself
equally from extravagant affectations and negligent dis-
array.'[14] Baudelaire shared Brummell's preference for dark
colours, not only for their functional elegance but also as an
appropriate expression of contemporary melancholia, specifically his own: 'But all the same, has not this much-abused
suit [the black one] its own beauty and its inherent charm?
Is it not the necessary suit for our suffering age, which wears
the symbol of a perpetual mourning even upon its thin black
shoulders?... We are each of us celebrating some funeral.'[15]

As Baudelaire lacked role models in life for his dandyism,
he developed most of his attitudes – like other aspiring French
dandies – from literature. His anglophilia, for instance, manifested itself not in the equestrian interests that prompted the
founding of the Jockey Club, but in a preference for books
of Anglo-American provenance. His particular passion was
reserved for Edgar Allan Poe, in whom he spotted a kindred
spirit and whose works he translated into French. Like Poe's,
Baudelaire's existence also alternated between brief spells
of creativity and long phases of poverty-induced desperation
and alcoholic excess. Baudelaire can scarcely have known
how right he was – only later did he become familiar with
Poe's biography – when he noted in his self-admonitions
to mental hygiene: 'De Maistre and Edgar Poe taught me to
think.'[16] Edgar Allan Poe – who since being translated by

Baudelaire has enjoyed a far higher reputation in France than in the anglophone world – was a defining influence in the literary education of another young Frenchman: 'Three American writers shaped my youth: Edgar Allan Poe, Jack London and Herman Melville.'[17] Jean-Pierre Grumbach, to become better known as Jean-Pierre Melville, was born in Paris in 1917, the son of a wholesaler; his family were of East European Jewish extraction but had been living in Alsace for generations, and had moved to Paris just before Jean-Pierre's birth. He grew up there in a cultured bourgeois environment, with a tendency towards bohemianism. He would later attach particular importance to a childhood experience that not only convinced him that he possessed impeccable aesthetic judgement, but also sowed the seeds of a virtual cult of taste in his life: 'My uncle was an important Parisian antique dealer. One day, he taught me to discern between beautiful and less beautiful things. Prompted by my asking him the reason for the enormous price difference between two very similar objects in his shop, he took two seemingly identical Louis XV chairs and said to me: "You see, here are two more or less similar armchairs. Yet one is worth more than the other. Look at them carefully so you make no mistake, then tell me which is the more beautiful and therefore the more expensive." I looked at them carefully, I thought hard, and I made no mistake. Pleased, my uncle then added: "From now on, throughout your life, you will always know the difference between what is beautiful and what is not."'[18] Luis Buñuel would later caricature this dualistic aspect of *haut bourgeois* aesthetic sensibility – the desire to distinguish between virtually identical objects – in the film *Tristana* (1969).

Another defining moment in the young Jean-Pierre's life was the gift of a Pathé Baby-Ciné camera and projector when he was six. Initially eager to use the camera, he soon lost interest in the amateurish products of his labours and transferred his fascination to the projector, which enabled him to watch other people's movies. Thanks to Pathé's comprehensive lending catalogue, which embraced the whole of American silent cinema from Chaplin to Westerns, Melville's passion for film was born, and he was transported by an *amour fou* for the cinema: 'I started my day at nine o'clock in the morning in the cinema and finished it there at three o'clock the next morning. It was stronger than everything. I could not control this all consuming desire to devour films again and again.'[19] Virtually at the dawn of the new medium, the adolescent Melville was ineluctably drawn in by the escapism that is still at the heart of cinema's attraction today. To the dandy's four modes of flight from the constraints of time – suicide, illness, travel and debauchery – the twentieth century had added the possibility of a combination of all of them. Intriguingly, Melville was later to claim that the first words ever spoken on the silver screen were 'Civilization! Civilization!'[20] Even when he had become a highly respected director, he would spend his nights watching his favourite films over and over again in his private projection room. He never entirely detached himself from the persona of the anonymous observer (even though he was no longer 'alone in the crowd', an essential part of the modernist quality of the cinematic experience): 'What is it after all that I do in my films? I make the films that I'd like to see. If I see a film that resembles one of mine a little, I am pleased. I try to create stories and characters that are similar to the ones in the films I like... Remember that first and foremost I'm still a spectator, and that being a spectator is the most wonderful profession there is.'[21] Right up to his early death, Jean-Pierre Melville never stopped chasing the aesthetic phantoms he had glimpsed in the darkened temples of his adolescence.

Young Jean-Pierre went to the Lycée Condorcet, the respected school for children of the *haute bourgeoisie* in central Paris, which he would later immortalize in his film of Jean Cocteau's *Les Enfants Terribles* (1950). He was one of the *lycéens* who made up the Gare-Saint-Lazare gang of *petits gangsters*, whose members would go on to become police inspectors and lawyers. After leaving school he drifted for a while, taking a variety of jobs until he was called up for military service in 1937. Still in the army when war broke out, he fought at Dunkirk. From Dunkirk he was evacuated to England, where he spent a few days in London, the city he was later to mythologize in his own mind and by proxy in *L'Armée des ombres* (Army of Shadows, 1969). In London he experienced one of a handful of magical coincidences in his life (which he was prone to interpret as signs), when by chance, just a few days after seeing *Gone with the Wind*, he ran into Clark Gable in a shirtmaker's in Jermyn Street. In 1940 he returned to France, where he worked with the Resistance. It was at this point that Grumbach became Melville. While a *nom de guerre* was a necessity in the Resistance, Melville – inspired by his unbounded admiration for the author of *Moby-Dick* and inventor of the naysayer Bartleby – decided to keep his for the rest of his life. In 1943, Melville arrived in Tunisia and joined the *Forces Françaises Libres*.

After taking part in the French and Italian liberation campaigns, he was demobilized in 1945. Although he would later play down his wartime exploits, saying that 'being in the Resistance if you're a Jew is infinitely less heroic than if you're not', his courage is beyond doubt. What should also not be underestimated is the impact that the experience of the war and the German occupation had on post-war French culture in general, and on Melville's work in particular. The director-dandy, who sought to live in his own hermetically sealed aesthetic and intellectual world, would later recall this time of action, of engagement with an intense reality: 'I am part of a generation who went through the war or took part in it, and who – I know this sounds bad, but that's how it is – feels a certain nostalgia for that time. What I witnessed in the war was direct action. The war finished for me in 44/45 and that's a long time ago. Since then I have only been able to take action in flights of the imagination. I can write scripts and make films which describe a certain type of action. Not primary action, but a type of action that is a little more complex, more reflected, maybe even a little intellectual.' For his definitive film about the Resistance, *L'Armée des ombres*, he chose an epigraph from Georges Courteline: 'Welcome, unhappy memories, for you are my distant youth.'[22]

As soon as he was demobilized, Melville set about realizing his childhood dream of becoming a film-maker. As early as November 1945, he founded his own production company; in 1946 he made the short film *Vingt-quatre heures de la vie d'un clown* (Twenty-four Hours in the Life of a Clown) about the clown Béby – a man who lives behind a mask – which he later considered embarrassingly amateurish. Taking his lead from his pre-war Hollywood idols, Melville was an *auteur* a decade before the term was applied to a select group of film-makers by the critics of *Cahiers du Cinéma*. He remained an independent throughout his career, making sure every one of his films spoke in his own authorial voice. Even though he tried to distance himself from some of his films to the point of disowning them – the pathological perfectionist was all too aware of the impossibility of perfection – he still hoped that his first and his last film would have something in common, that they would share his signature: 'The tragic thing, for me, is when a creator suddenly makes a radical change in his way of talking about things, because this means that one of his two formulas – maybe the new one, maybe the old – is wrong.'[23] One of the few directors to have his own studio, Melville carried out most functions in the course of his film-making career: he was his own producer, scriptwriter, cinematographer, set decorator, cutter, actor and of course director. Initially, the *jeunes loups* of the *Nouvelle Vague* regarded him as a father figure. In homage, Jean-Luc Godard gave Melville the role of the writer Parvulesco in *À bout de souffle* (Breathless, 1959), which in turn offered Melville the opportunity to comment implicitly on the paradox of the dandy. Asked by Patricia, played by Jean Seberg, 'What is your greatest ambition in life?', Parvulesco/Melville answers: 'To become immortal and then die.' With the increasing politicization of Godard, Truffaut *et al.*, the paths of Melville and the *Nouvelle Vague* diverged. In the build-up to 1968 and afterwards, *Cahiers du Cinéma* labelled Melville a reactionary stylist, and mistakenly dismissed his most abstract and personal films – such as *Le Deuxième*

Souffle (Second Breath, 1966) and *Le Samouraï* (1967) – as conventional. After finishing his most artistically refined and critically under-appreciated film, *Un Flic* (Dirty Money, 1973), Melville died from a heart attack in a Japanese restaurant. He was fifty-five.

In her memoir *Paris France* (1940), Gertrude Stein boldly claimed that 'Between 1900 and 1939 Paris was where the 20th century was at.' Cultural pre-eminence had of course been claimed for Paris much earlier, although mostly by Frenchmen such as Marivaux, who in 1734 declared: 'Paris is the world; the rest of the earth is nothing but its suburbs.' Paris in the eighteenth century could certainly claim to lead the world in cultivated living, not only setting the template for modernity but also reaching a pinnacle that has scarcely been attained since. Before Brummell simplified and abstracted the cultivated urbanite into a prototype for modern man, in his poem 'Le Mondain' Voltaire had already described a creature so defined by his tastes in day-to-day living that they constituted his identity. The mythologization of nineteenth-century Paris as the modern city *par excellence* was begun by Baudelaire and continued (with ample reference to him) by Walter Benjamin. The city's aura was further enhanced when it became the focus of Louis Aragon's notion of the *merveilleux quotidien* in 'Le Paysan de Paris' (Paris Peasant, 1926). But for Jean-Pierre Melville, it was the pre-war Paris of his childhood and adolescence that he nostalgically sought to recapture when he was barely forty.

Bob le Flambeur (Bob the Gambler, 1956) starts with a tracking shot that begins at Sacré Cœur, *'le ciel de Montmartre'*, and ends down in the 'hell' of its gambling dens, '*l'enfer de Montmartre*' in Melville's own voiceover. It is dawn, and as Paris awakes the film's protagonist Bob Montagné is postponing going home to sleep through the day. In Albert Simonin's *roman noir, Touchez Pas au Grisbi*, the main character describes how his day ceases to be divided into day and night; instead he lives in slices of the twenty-four hours, sleeping whenever it suits him. Melville himself was notoriously nocturnal, preferring to write undisturbed in the stillness of the night. Rarely photographed without sunglasses, he believed sensory deprivation to be the most receptive state for the *créateur*. His one-time assistant Volker Schlöndorff also describes how Melville would drive around Paris at night, 'cruising' at a snail's pace in his Ford Galaxy, looking for locations or spotting starlets amongst the prostitutes at La Madeleine. Melville would later say: '*Bob le Flambeur* is my declaration of love for Paris. Declarations of love are written at night.'[24] Bob is a nocturnal flâneur, and Paris (or rather his microcosm of Montmartre, to him 'still the only place to live')[25] is the setting for his promenades. The opening sequence has little narrative significance: it is *temps mort*, reflecting the flâneur's empty existence and serving only to showcase the city. Walter Benjamin viewed the flâneur as a precursor to the detective, whose indolence is merely a mask for the intense concentration of the professional observer (whimsically portrayed by Jean-Pierre Léaud in Truffaut's *Baisers Volés*, or Stolen Kisses, of 1968). Bob is the other side of the coin, however. As we gather not only from the *sang froid* with which he approaches his idle pursuits – as a flâneur, gambler and chainsmoker – but also, and chiefly, from the way he dresses.

Bob wears a soft, belted raincoat and a trilby with a medium brim: an outfit – recalling Bogart of the early 1940s – that was retro *avant la lettre* and would have looked quite out of place in mid-1950s Paris. While clothes nostalgia became a variant of fashion in the late twentieth century, in earlier periods it was a peculiarity unique to dandyism. In a display of yearning not only for his own prime but also for that of Brummell before it, Barbey d'Aurevilly wore the tight redingotes and strapped pantaloons of his youth into the 1880s, by which time he appeared as a bizarre anachronism to his contemporaries. Melville's nostalgic reconstruction is also a complex one. On the one hand, he was nostalgic for his own self, before and during the war. When Melville had lived in Montmartre before the war – his addresses including the evocatively named rue de L'Armée-d'Orient – he had been a different person: a man of action, even an *homme à femmes*, according to his friend and actor in his films Pierre Grasset.[26] Melville would later also make oblique reference to his familiarity if not his involvement with the *milieu* (the French *mob*). The war had tainted the dubious glamour of the 1930s gangster, particularly as large sections of the Corsican mafia had collabourated with the Gestapo. Melville's personal nostalgia therefore goes hand in hand with a nostalgia for a pre-war golden age of 'honest' gangsters that he was quite well aware had never really existed: 'There is nothing more boring and idiotic than the life of a French gangster... the milieu is as rotten as the bourgeoisie. Why should it be any better?'[27] As Ginette Vincendeau points out, Melville's interest lies in the phenomenology of the gangster rather than in his psychology. The gangster is the fitting protagonist for modern tragedy since he is tragic a priori. Viewed in this light, the phenomenological gangster is an over-determined version of the tragic aspect of the Baudelairean dandy, whose role at the centre of modernity is also one of ultimate failure. The analogy between dandyism and criminality of course also had its literal antecedents, for example in the person of the English serial killer Thomas Wainewright, who viewed his crimes as a legitimate extension of his dandyism.

Melville's extreme americanophilia had at its centre the notion of a rather more tangible golden era, that of 'classic' pre-war Hollywood. Melville drew up a list of sixty-three pre-war directors whose films he considered as potential classics of this comparatively young medium. The style of dress adopted by French gangsters before the war had of course been heavily influenced by their American counterparts, both in real life and in the Hollywood studios. If Hollywood stars like Cagney and Bogart wore chalk-stripe on charcoal double-breasted suits and grey hats with very broad bands, French gangsters soon started sporting the same – not forgetting the obligatory dinner-jacketed bodyguards, as pointed out by Farid Chenoune. In both there was an element of caricature of the well-dressed businessman of the time. Like the dandy, the gangster could – to the untrained eye – quite closely resemble his legitimate counterpart. Yet, as we know not least from the writings of Jean Genet, there was also a fetishism in the details that – although it again mirrored the dress of the daytime world – had a gangsterish flavour all its own. While the *Guys and Dolls* combination of light tie on dark shirt is rather too broad a cliché, in *Notre-Dame de Fleurs* Genet mentions suede belts, for example, as being

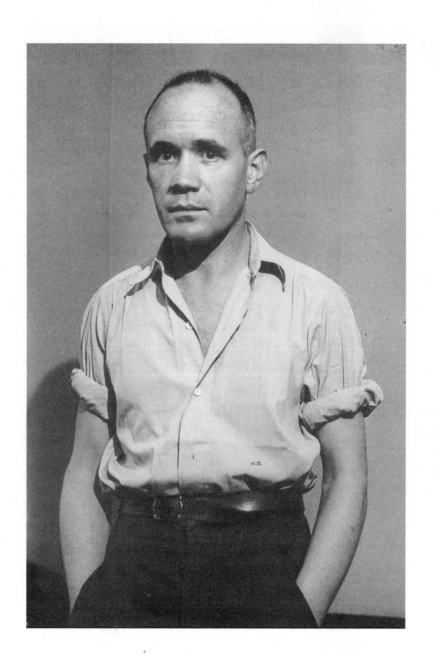

de rigueur. A familiar photograph of Genet himself (albeit taken after the war) shows him wearing a 1930s-style tennis collar shirt open two buttons too far at the neck, with the sleeves rolled up and without a coat or tie. Despite Genet's clear aim of conveying casual sexiness through this state of *semi-déshabillé*, what really fixes the image in the mind is the monogram, discreet in both size and position, just above the waist. Melville himself did not merely sign his films metaphorically with his distinctive authorial style. In one instance he quite literally added his monogram: after Jansen has shot out the alarm in *Le Cercle Rouge* (The Red Circle, 1970), we see that the bullet has penetrated just beside the maker's name: initials J. P. M.

There was also a specifically French style of over-dressing, however, which already in the 1930s centred around trousers that were very wide at the bottom and worn long, giving a flared appearance although they were in fact uniformly wide. With these statement strides went a short, often double-breasted jacket with very marked shoulders. Naturally this gangster look was soon coveted by ordinary adolescents, not least style-conscious bourgeois teenagers: 'Boys from prestigious secondary schools were even seen wearing short, bum freezer jackets, outrageously checked vests, banner-like pocket handkerchiefs, shoe-masking trousers and dust-sweeping overcoats.'[28] We may fondly imagine the teenage Jean-Pierre Grumbach got up like this and affecting argot, before leaving such youthful 'lapses of taste' behind.

Closer inspection of Bob's wardrobe reveals that it is not entirely anachronistic: while they are American-influenced, the suits and sports jackets worn by him and the rest of the male cast are in fact Paris 1956, designed by Ted Lapidus. But for the viewer, it is the hat and coat in which he first appears that establish the archetypal silhouette of the Hollywood gangster. Melville himself adopted two recognizably American accessories as his visual trademarks: Ray-Ban Aviator sunglasses and Stetson hats (initially the 'Large Metal' model and the trilby, followed from 1963 by the 'Caravan' and an off-white cowboy hat). He also invariably wore the black knitted tie seen in countless American movies of the 1940s and 1950s.

Bob le Flambeur is part of a Franco-American dialogue: the iconic American gangster on the realistically filmed streets of Paris.[29] France was of course engaged in just such a dialogue in the post-war period. Since Baudelaire's translation of Poe, an appreciation of American culture was widespread among French intellectuals. As in England, jazz and cocktails had appeared in Paris in the 1920s, merging with European cultural phenomena to signify modernity. After the Second World War, American influence grew in response to America's contribution to freeing France from occupation and subsequent domination of Europe, both politically and economically. Culturally, this exchange encouraged the creation of Franco-American hybrids, most particularly in the fields of crime literature and film. The term *film noir*, denoting American crime thrillers of the 1930s and 1940s, itself derives from Gallimard's Série Noire imprint, translations of hard-boiled authors such as Chandler and Hammett, founded just after the war. Inspired by the Série Noire, French authors were soon writing about French gangsters. The distinctively French characteristics of novels such as *Touchez pas au grisbi* and Auguste Le Breton's

Du Rififi chez les hommes (both published in 1953) were the use of argot, the incestuous relationship between gangsters and flics and the central importance of Paris to the narrative. This atmospheric geography of the city followed in the tradition of Eugène Sue's *Les Mystères de Paris* and had long been a feature of George Simenon's writing. Both *Rififi* and *Grisbi* were very successful, and were soon filmed by Jules Dassin and Jacques Becker respectively. They were to usher in the most popular cinematic genre in post-war France: the *policier* or *polar*. What distinguishes the best *policiers* from their American models is a quality that is often seen as peculiarly French: the whole is more than the sum of its parts. A quality that is also a good analogy for dandyism, certainly as defined by Barbey d'Aurevilly.

Melville had read Hammett's *The Glass Key* in an earlier translation when he was twelve, long before the inception of the Série Noire. But his literary sensibility soon evolved into a cinematic one, a phenomenon that by 1967 he claimed was widespread: 'Today the cinema is the ideal form of literary creation, and young people no longer have a literary culture but a filmic one. This would have seemed impossible fifteen years ago.'[30] In his next gangster film, *Le Doulos* (1962), based on a novel by the contemporary French author Pierre Lesou, Melville took one step further on a journey that was ultimately to transcend the genre. It was also his first film to emphasize quite distinctly the central significance of clothes in the gangster/dandy universe, as is already apparent in the title. As Chenoune explains, French gangsters began to fetishize certain items of clothing to such a degree that they invented new names for them: 'a shirt was not a *chemise* it was a *limace*; trousers were not *pantalon* but *falzars* or *fendarts*; hats were not simply *chapeaux* but *doulos* or *bitos*'.[31] The *doulos* sported throughout the movie by Silien, played by Jean-Paul Belmondo, is indeed a fine one, its very broad band and snap brim nodding towards American phenomena of the late 1950s such as Frank Sinatra and Madison Avenue. These contemporary references to popular culture and the neat proportions of the hat also serve to complement Belmondo's youthful star persona and muscular build. But whatever its proportions, and however serious or frivolous it might be, Silien's hat clearly signals and visualizes the character's identity. While the model might be of its time, Silien's attachment to it recalls Melville's imaginary golden age: before the war a guy would never think of going out without a hat. The hat also symbolizes the inevitability of Silien's tragedy: when he visits the Cotton Club and checks it in at the cloakroom he receives a ticket with the number 13. And when mortally wounded at the end of the film, he adjusts his image in the Louis XIV sun-burst mirror at his house in his desire to make a beautiful (or rather perfect) corpse, only to lose his *doulos* when he tumbles into death.

But *doulos* also has another meaning in argot: it also means a police informer. While this refers to the ambiguity of Belmondo's character in the film – until the end the viewer does not know which side Silien is on – the ambiguity of the title itself holds the key to Melville's moral universe. The first work by Herman Melville that the young Jean-Pierre Grumbach read was *Pierre, or The Ambiguities* (1852), a book that he claimed formed him for ever. Ambiguity, the consistent unity of the disparate, reflects the dandy's Janus-like character in history, as well as his elusive nature, hovering between materiality and transcendence and between triviality and complexity. Melville himself claimed: 'Faith, be it in God or Marx, for me that is now over.'[32] This expression of faithlessness forms part of a refusal to see any single path or ideology as the way to salvation. *Pas d'espoir* leaves the dandy unable to view things other than in aesthetic terms, a cult of taste that is so reliant on nuances for its legitimization that within it ambiguity itself becomes a virtue rather than a vice. For Melville, the logical consequence of his dystopianism was a retreat into complete privacy – itself a paradox for a public figure – hiding away in his ivory tower on rue Jenner, where he created his studio and lived as an '*ermite à cinq*' with his wife Flo and his three cats Griffaulait, Fiorello and Aufrène. Echoing des Esseintes's exile in the suburbs, Melville explained: 'The 13th arrondissement has absolutely nothing in common with me, therefore I could build my fortress here and instal my observation post without disturbances.'[33] Never inclined to take himself too seriously, he ironically acknowledged that according to the Marxist thinking that was omnipresent around 1968 his attitude made him a reactionary. Asked whether he was a man of the right, Melville answered: 'Well, it amuses me to say so, because everyone else claims to be left-wing, and that irritates me. I hate following the crowd, and in any case to say that one is wholly right- or left-wing is ridiculous... I don't think it's possible. Philosophically speaking, my position in life is extremely anarchistic: I am an extreme individualist, and to tell you the truth I don't wish to be either of the right or the left. But I certainly live as a man of the right. I'm a right-wing anarchist – though I suppose that's a barbarism and that no such thing really exists. Let's say that I'm an anarcho-feudalist.'[34] A century earlier, Barbey d'Aurevilly had called himself a conservative anarchist.

In contrast to the novel, which like its predecessors by Simonin and Le Breton was written in 'gangster slang', the title is the only word of argot in *Le Doulos*. Though romantically inclined towards argot in his youth, rather in the way the Duke of Windsor affected a cockney accent, Melville couldn't stand argot in the cinema. Its abandonment in the film also works further towards turning his characters into abstract *hommes melvilliens* rather than members of an actual *milieu*. Melville, who professed to love abstraction, aimed to create archetypes, men who are not defined by their personal history, their class, their origins. Where Brummell divested himself of his background by rejecting his family, Melville's fictional characters are stripped of their history by a lack of concrete facts in the narrative. Though they have a 'past' – referred to only in the mythical terms Melville used when talking about his own life – they have no back story, unlike Hollywood gangsters. They are defined only by their essential humanity within an overarching system that consists at one end of abstract ideas of self-realization such as loyalty, professionalism and correct form, and at the other of an overriding death drive. They are aristocrats without either title or pedigree. Melville's desire for abstraction as a form of cultural idealization mirrors modernist architecture – as in Le Corbusier's Modulor Man – as well as post-war high culture: Existentialism, Samuel Beckett and the nouveau roman. In the 1940s and 1950s, Melville had lived in St Germain-des-Prés, within the orbit of these concepts. Yet he admitted no hierarchy between the things he loved (modernist literature and American popular culture), and knew how to merge high cultural ideas with more populist forms.

In his next gangster film, *Le deuxième souffle* (1966), Melville shifts the balance yet further in favour of high cultural ideas. The film's protagonist, Gustave 'Gu' Minda, is a man out of his time. His true achievements lie behind him, and while he tries to walk forward his face is turned towards the past. It is suggested that he was on the verge of suicide ten years before the action begins, and that although he failed to act on this impulse, he is only on reprieve. There is no question of him succeeding: his attempt to relive the past, playing by rules that are now meaningless, is doomed. His ultimate failure is inevitable, and – in a world that is no longer his own, that appears vulgar and indecent to him – he implicitly longs for it. Gu is beyond good and evil; the crimes he commits, as well as his acts of friendship and loyalty, exist within a system that might mirror the real world to some degree, but that is quite clearly beyond it and outside it. The mythical quality of Gu's character and those of some of the gangsters around him – Orloff, who remains a sketch, a one-letter haiku, is nonetheless the ultimate *homme Melvillien* – is that of classical tragedy, and it is as a tragedy (not least through its length of two and a half hours) that *Le deuxième souffle* plays out. The atmosphere of tragedy is intensified by the austerity of the *mise en scène*. Most of the time, the action forms the only soundtrack. But *Le deuxième souffle* abounds with fine hats signifying tragic masculinity. A particularly striking 1940s-style pearl-grey fedora turns out to be the head of a Trojan horse and leads ultimately to Gu's death. It is worn by a policeman disguised as a gangster, who deceives Gu into betraying his accomplices: 'I had him powdered and made up like the Neapolitans so that he'd look like an old-time gangster – because before the war some crooks used make-up, though it had nothing to do with homosexuality.'[35] The quick temper and competitiveness of Petit Antoine, a 'modern gangster', are suggested by his fancy waistcoat. The signifiers of Gu's own gangster status, on the other hand, are far from obvious: he wears a more discreet contemporary trilby and a charcoal suit. When he tries to disguise his identity by adding steel-rimmed glasses, he gains an intensely cerebral, almost spiritual quality, like a priest without religion or morals: neither good nor bad.

Melville's last three gangster films share the same leading actor, Alain Delon. The choice of Delon for these three movies creates an unusually intense correlation between star and movie: while Melville chose Delon for these films, Delon's physical appearance and his star persona – which Melville consciously used – were also defining elements. Delon was thirty-two when he starred in *Le Samouraï* (1967), which established the character he would play with only minor variations in the majority of his subsequent roles. Delon's androgynous beauty had been displayed in his earlier films to a degree that was unusual for a male star. Melville gave this narcissistic quality its full pathological expression by linking it to the melancholy which is its natural realm. To the youthful amorality that Delon had brought to films such as *Plein Soleil* (Purple Noon, 1959) he had also been cast originally for Visconti's film of Albert Camus' *L'Étranger*, Melville added the depth of abstract existentialist concepts. With the Delon trilogy he brought the application of these concepts to generic movies to their pinnacle; virtually encapsulating this added depth in Delon's features. Delon was to use this abstract quality to great effect in later films such as Joseph Losey's *Mr Klein* (1976).

Alain Delon's on-screen persona before *Le Samouraï* has been described as an *homme fatal*. As well as playing the male lead, he had also usurped the role generally played by the female lead, the object of desire, of aesthetic contemplation. While women are liberally seduced, in accordance with the French convention, in most of Delon's early films, the character of Tom Ripley in *Plein Soleil* (and even more so in his original conception by Patricia Highsmith, who thought Delon an ideal Ripley) is one of peculiar sexual self-sufficiency: this is a man who 'conscious of his own seductiveness doesn't find it necessary to seduce'.[36] In the context of the 1960s, intense celebration of consumerism, Alain Delon himself signified the commodities his characters desired: women, languid idleness, and of course clothes. The aura of the pre-war Hollywood star was updated and intensified by Delon: the clothes he wore in his movies achieved an overwhelming significance and desirability and came to embody 1960s and 1970s modernity. This update first took the form of the *tricheur*, who enters into a dangerous flirtation with the more vulgar aspects of self-objectification; and, post-Melville, that of the philosophically and tragically enhanced amoralist. While the temperament Delon displays is without doubt a very masculine one – verging on unwitting parody, in his lesser films – his is an internalized masculinity. Delon is the 'strong, silent type', yet he is no action hero; his untouchability lies in an inner resolve expressed in gestures and aura. The rare acts of violence he commits owe their chilling impact to the surprise of their emanating from such a controlled and elegant physical presence. The minimalist modernity of his acting and his epicene features lend him a darkly angelic quality: the horror that lies within his glamour is the comforting horror of a death that he brings to others as though it were a gift, so intensely does he desire it himself. Delon's screen deaths – and it is hard to recall a Delon film of any significance that does not end in his death or the kind of glorious failure that is almost equivalent – are among the most celebrated rituals of nihilistic beauty to be found in post-war cinema.

The narcissistic persona that Melville projects in the Delon trilogy displays two mutually dependent characteristics: pathological nostalgia and sexual abstinence. Freud describes the brief period of infantile self-sufficiency as the narcissistic phase: 'What [the narcissist] projects as his ideal is the substitution of the lost narcissism of his childhood, in which he was his own ideal.'[37] While the innate narcissism of every human can thus be taken as a given, the pathological narcissist fails to successfully transfer his desire on to a human object, but is more likely to attach it to objects from an idealized past. As fulfilment is located in the past, the narcissist's desire is necessarily thwarted, and the only domain in which he can comfortably identify himself is that of melancholia. The concomitant loss of libido allows him to appear wholly self-possessed, or cool. But 'Narcissus is not completely without object. The object of Narcissus is psychic

space; it is representation itself, fantasy. But he does not know it and he dies. If he knew it he would be an intellectual, a creator of speculative fictions, an artist, writer, psychologist, psychoanalyst.'[38] He would be Proust or Melville.

Art and artifice, the creation of a 'beautiful world' as a successful sublimation of the depressive's death wish was written about extensively by Freud and subsequently by Julia Kristeva. What Melville shared with Proust in this regard is clarity of thought. The dandy invents nothing. It is reality that is rendered artificial. Abstract dreams inspired by memory unfold from a position that seems already to be impervious to time. The dandy has a past but no future. Like Proust, Melville was an analyst who composed the fictional personas in his work from several real-life models and in the fusing created new characters. Despite (or because of) its ephemeral and elusive nature, beauty assumes a supreme value in the melancholic's world: it is his other domain. While the dandy per se confines himself within the tragic world of Narcissus when he employs his aesthetic memory in the culti-vation of his own person, the writer-dandy and by extension the director-dandy are arguably in a privileged position as they can apply their ideals to the limitless realm of fiction. The latter even has the potential to fulfil the depressive's ultimate dream, the creation of a hermetic, artificial and complete world in accordance with his own highly individ-ual ideal of beauty, his specific tastes. The dandy's essential narcissism will however ensure that this world remains a melancholic one. In his quest for the person to act out his dreams, Melville could hardly overlook a star persona of such emphatic ambiguity and narcissism as Alain Delon's.

By using Delon in his place, Melville – corpulent, bald and marked by the sedentary nature of melancholic passions – comes close to creating an embodiment of his intellectual and aesthetic ideals, something the dandy can generally only achieve through his clothes and gestures. To bring Delon closer to his own age – middle age – Melville made him grow a moustache in *Le cercle rouge* and put on weight in *Un flic.*

Le Samouraï abounds with the motifs of melancholia, depicted by Melville in such a way that they might become the equivalent of Proust's *temps perdu* for subsequent generations of melancholics: unconsummated sexuality, interiors of shabby austerity, and permanently dark or rain-lashed exteriors. Walter Benjamin wrote of a rainy day in Paris, the kind that Melville professed to love: 'Urban rain with its sly lure to dream oneself back into days of early childhood, can only be fathomed by the child of the metropolis. Rain masks more everywhere, turns the days not only grey but homogenous. From morning to evening one can do the same, play chess, read, [watch movies], while sun shadows the hours quite differently and doesn't bode well for the dreamer. Hence he has to elude the bright days with guile [sleep].'[39] The first ten minutes of *Le Samouraï*, in which not a word is spoken, feature all three of the above motifs. The film opens with an extended shot of Jef Costello lying in a darkened room, smoking. His bedroom is sparse, shabby and virtually monochrome. Behind the sash windows is a black-and-white back projection of Bronx-like cityscape. A quotation appears on the screen, attributed to *The Book of Bushido* (although Melville in fact made it up): 'There is no solitude greater than the samurai's, unless perhaps it be that of a tiger in the jungle.'

Delon gets up already wearing a suit. In front of the mirror, one of the very few pieces of furniture in the flat, he assembles his identity: a mid-grey fedora with a broad band and a trench-coat, *un imperméable*, a neat signifier of his hermetic and urbane nature: 'I think the virile hero needs a horse, boots and saddle. As you've probably noticed, they're not exactly common on the streets of Paris, but at least you can give him a hat, a raincoat with a belt and a collar that can be turned up, and a button to do up when it rains.'[40] Jef identifies completely with an image that is constructed from these totems, and fails to acknowledge any reality that does not fit with the myth he inhabits. Though the mythical world in which the dandy lives is fragile – hence failure is a necessary part of the myth – its fragility is relative to its complexity. The more complex the myth, the harder it is for banality to reach and corrode it. So when Jef adjusts the brim of his hat – a gesture that Delon copied from Melville – it becomes clear that the act of dressing is highly significant to him, a ritual. Jef's melancholia has progressed to the next stage: he is a schizophrenic. Melville 'heightens' his protagonist into the realm of mental illness: Jef is abstracted from reality even in his own mind. He is an innocent in the sense that a schizophrenic may not know he is committing a crime. Melville himself was naturally still aware of everything, real or unreal, his minimalism always the essence of complexity: '*Le Samouraï* is the analysis of a schizophrenic by a paranoiac, because all creators are paranoiacs.'[41] Jef goes out into the Paris streets. It is pouring with rain. As he steals a DS, a lingering frontal shot of him through the windscreen blurs his mask of imperturbability with the rain, lending it a liquid quality that centres around

his pale blue eyes – windows behind a window. Although he is rendered vulnerable at this point, the rain cannot touch him as it does Alain Leroy in *Le Feu Follet*. At a traffic light a young woman in the next car smiles at him. He notices her gesture but does not acknowledge or return it; nothing can deflect him from his fate.

In apparent opposition to this soothing *grisaille* is a modernity that has rarely been documented so accurately on film, with the exception of Godard's *Alphaville* (1965) and particularly Jacques Tati's *Playtime*, also made in 1967. While Melville's transposed Americana are as present as before – the hitman employed to kill Jef drives a huge American car (a Cadillac Fleetwood 75 from 1963) of the kind Melville favoured himself – Continental modernity and popular culture contrast starkly with Jef's drab apartment and other features of his world, such as the suburban garage to which he delivers the stolen cars. The cars Jef steals are both Citroën DSs, that pinnacle of innovative French engineering mythologized by Roland Barthes along with other phenomena of post-war Continental cool, such as 'Roman' haircuts. Jef's enigmatic client's flat is furnished with a mixture of classical-style antiques, exotica echoing Delon's 'japanesque' features and vocation and highly contemporary Pop Art on the walls. Martey's nightclub, with its Harry Bertoia wire-mesh chairs, is furnished in the 1960s taste of a modernity that optimistically envisioned a brighter future expressed by the sleek and silvery space-age fittings. A more timeless modernity is pictured in the Metro, through the functionalist beauty of its illuminated map, a literal representation of the emotive topography of Paris in which Jef is hunted by a police

inspector played by François Périer with a bourgeois articulacy and open cynicism worthy of a 1960s Talleyrand (he even carries a rolled umbrella, to Cyril Connolly the badge of the reactionary). To Melville, modernity is intoxicating. But while he depicts its rapture he also watches it with a distance and wariness, an awareness of the dangers of alienation. It is hardly a safe distance, however, as Melville's point of view is at the centre of modernity itself. His characters are already living the alienation implicit in modernity, having reduced it to its idealized form. His romanticizing of the city tells of this dream-like rapture that wants to keep on the move, to see the next street corner, to move further along the labyrinthine map, the mystery of which lies on the surface and the prerequisite of which is night. Like its apparent opposite, love, alienation is its own reward. It was this intoxication that Melville was seeking on his nightly cruises, his little bit of delirious New York in Paris.

The women in Melville's films wear clothes that are not modern but are fashionable, which is its opposite in the Loosian sense. While this echoes a familiar perception of the ephemeral nature of woman, it also represents the intensity of Melville's obsession with male clothing. A decade earlier, Melville had abandoned a film that he had already started shooting after an argument with the actor Pierre Grasset over the width of a hat brim: 'I'm very prone to clothes fetishism: the clothing of men plays a decisive role in my films, while women's clothing alas concerns me less. When an actress has to be dressed an assistant usually takes care of it.'[42] Modern man wanders through the decades of modernity with his costume relatively unchanged, modest adjustments of detail only serving to maintain an apparently eternal look. The price of eternity is tragedy, however, and the fulfilment of his paradoxical fate is the dandy's driving force. Neither of the two women Jef is involved with has any influence on his decision to commit suicide. He merely uses them as instruments, Jeanne in his quest to play his death game to perfection, and Valerie in the very act of dying. Although Jef pursues Valerie, he is merely projecting his death wish on to her. He carries his tragedy within himself.

While the dandy is clearly at home in a context of stylized melancholy, he is also an integral feature of modernity. He walks through the literature and films of modernity, and while he does not progress, he walks with confidence. His very melancholy makes him the man of modernity: man's failure in its face is there in his own. On the subject of modern beauty, Baudelaire had claimed that the dandy's features bore traces of 'one of the most interesting characteristics of beauty, of mystery, and last of all (let me have the courage to admit the point to which I feel I am modern in my aesthetics) of unhappiness'.[43] To Baudelaire, melancholy is the very essence of modern male beauty. The figure of the *Samouraï* unites all three aspects of the Baudelairean equation. Where Maurice Ronet had been the face of melancholia *quand le masque tombe* in *Le Feu Follet*, Delon's is the hermetic face of melancholia. Similarly, it is with the *Samouraï* that the cinematic myth of the gangster or cop began to be fused with that of modern man in the person of Delon, an identity that only began to disintegrate with the disintegration of modernity itself in the 1980s.

The suit Delon wears has attained mythical status.

Melville has imbued it with the supernatural qualities that Aragon saw in the clothes in shop windows as night fell. The sartorial dream is dependent on the right *mise en scène*. What appears magical in Paris can be rendered listless in Berlin. Banality turns the dream into a nightmare, and the dandy finds himself in the wrong movie. To protect its fragility he must 'make his dream his address'. In an interview, the English singer Lloyd Cole chose the suit worn by the Samurai as the item of dress he most coveted, but mistakenly remembered it as a black three-button – thereby assimilating it with his own ideal. There are actually two suits. While the initial suit Jef wears is mid-grey, he changes into a charcoal one of identical cut when he exchanges his damaged trenchcoat for a black Crombie. The change of suits is paralleled by the DSs he steals: first grey then black, the latter marking the beginning of his journey towards death. The cut is a hybrid of the Italian/Continental style and the later English-influenced Minet style. The coat has two buttons and squarish shoulders. It is slightly shaped at the waist but has no vents. The trousers are low-rise and beltless with one shallow pleat. They are tapered and worn short with a narrow turn-up. Jef wears a matt black tie that seems to be wool and which apparently – though we never see it – has a pin-up girl painted on the back. To Walter Benjamin, ennui was a warm grey piece of cloth with a glowing silk lining – the cloth we wrap ourselves in when we dream.

From *Le deuxième souffle* on, Jean-Pierre Melville's sartorial universe becomes distinctly more anglophile, as his dandy self truly comes into its own. The early 1960s look of boxy short jackets, very tapered trousers and pointy shoes, as sported by Jean-Paul Belmondo not only in several *Nouvelle Vague* films but also in Melville's own *L'Aîné de Ferchaux* (1962) and *Le Doulos*, carried a number of connotations from which Melville would have sought to distance himself as soon as contemporary tailoring styles made this possible. Firstly, it was Italian in origin: apart from his obvious *faible anglo-américain*, the Alsace-bred Melville's conception of Frenchness veered distinctly northwards, disowning the Mediterranean elements that make up an equal part of the national stereotype, alongside the intellectual and aesthetic rigour of the north. Secondly, the Italian look was not only *Nouvelle Vague* but also *nouveau riche*, considered vulgar for its very emphasis on newness and a sexually charged *sprezzatura*, very different from well-worn English 'bad taste', the sexiness of which lies in its very absence. The Italian look became the costume of choice for the new-style urban *dragueur*, a kind of pedestrian playboy. Not only was it the uniform recommended in Alain Ayache's 1960 *Guide du parfait dragueur*, but it was also sported, with the addition of a car-coat, by Jacques Charrier in *Les Dragueurs* (The Chasers, 1969) – the year in which Charrier had married the sex symbol Brigitte Bardot.

There are three periods of *anglomanie* in the history of French taste. The first, which started as early as 1740 with the adoption of country clothes by a handful of French aristocrats and merchants who had brought them back from visits across the Channel, established the term around 1760. Anglomania was then strengthened by the growing reputation of Brummell, and the fact that a number of officers from the Duke of Wellington's highly dandified 33rd Regiment made Paris their home after the battle of Waterloo in 1815. The second wave arrived in the 1930s, when the Prince of Wales's own excessive interest in matters of elegance drew French attention to places that were apparently dusted with sartorial stardust (such as Oxford), as well as to a whole cornucopia of tartans and regimental stripes that would shed their hierarchical significance as they crossed the Channel. The third – which began around 1963 – was instigated (like the first) by young men from affluent Parisian families. The original *Bande du Drugstore*, named after the eponymous shop on the Champs-Élysées where they gathered, consisted of teenagers from the 7th and 16th arrondissements and fashionable Neuilly – Melville himself grew up in the respectable 9th – who wore distinguished-looking English suits, with very waisted coats, worn over wide trousers with tiny turn-ups, shirts with long pointed collars, and a knitted tie or silk scarf. Other British staples were also adopted, such as double-vented sports jackets worn over crew-neck lovat sweaters, or double-breasted blazers sporting alluring if unmerited crests. Established Parisian shops selling British goods, such as Old England beside the Opéra (since 1867) and Burberry, had catered to earlier generations of anglophiles. But English styles would have also been picked up on the obligatory cross-Channel trip made by all affluent French school students in order to brush up their language skills, as portrayed in the 1976 film *À nous les petites Anglaises*.

By 1965, these cross-Channel rich kids had started to train their own tailors and had earned their own nickname: Minets. The young anglophiles originally also favoured jazz, another feature that distinguished them from their less well-bred rock'n'roll-loving contemporaries, who perhaps inevitably dubbed the Minets *pédales* (fags) or snobs. The latter term soon became a point of pride, and was divorced from its original meaning; in 1969 it was used as a noble epithet in the Minet pop star Jacques Dutronc's 'Laquelle des deux est la plus snob', a song that rather ironically struggled with nuances of taste. The most distinctive feature of the 'middle-class English look' was trousers that were wide at the bottom, not only referencing the 1930s but also reintroducing a skirt-like, feminine element into male apparel. Pleat-less wide-bottomed trousers began to appear from 1962, in marked contrast to the extremely tapered Italian-style trews, which had narrowed to just fourteen inches in 1958. Renoma, the most prestigious of Minet tailors, cut proper flares as early as 1963, and took what they perceived to be the main features of the Englishman's coat – narrow shoulders, a fitted waist and deep side vents – to extremes. The coats of these suits – cut at first with three buttons in grey flannel or blue serge for the winter and beige gabardine for the summer – became increasingly figure-hugging throughout the 1960s, allowing no extra play at the chest and shoulders, and with armholes cut painfully high.

Renoma, in alliance with some of the more trend-setting Minets, thus created the template for the surprisingly long-lived 1970s suit, which travelled back to England around 1971. In the post-1968 version of the Minet silhouette, wide trousers had adopted a definite flare, lapels had become longer and broader, and shoulders were pagoda-shaped. The pagoda shape was first sported by members of the demi-monde in the 1930s, but then with widely overcut shoulders. Inevitably, the French perception of the English cut was, like so many visual memories, an involuntary misrepresentation. While the Duke of Windsor had sported wide-bottomed trousers, they had always been wide over their full length; the probably more characteristically English Edwardian trouser of the 1900s, and then again the late 1950s and early 1960s, was very tapered, though higher-waisted than Italian models. Only hacking jackets had always been cut tight on the chest and shoulders, and were of course single-vented in order to divide elegantly over the saddle. There was a similar misapprehension concerning size with the adoption of more casual items of preppy American styles by younger Minets in the second half of the 1960s: Levi jeans were routinely shrunk in the bath in order to make them as figure-hugging as possible (taking the notion of 'shrink-to-fit' to its literal conclusion). Shetland jumpers, meanwhile, were worn small, reaching just to the waist or even above. At this point the only American with a place in the popular imagination who had worn his 501s tight (perhaps not entirely intentionally) was Marlon Brando in *The Wild One*.

'English' outfitters such as Ted Langley on the Champs-Élysées and Edward VII at Porte Maillot, resplendent with mahogany and brass fittings, started springing up all over Paris and soon in other European capitals. Even if many of these anglophile shops have now disappeared, this 1960s 'Anglo-American mania' has left a lasting aesthetic legacy. While Minets styled themselves in opposition to the 'vulgar' Italian look – which had earlier been adopted by the English Mods – they still continued in the modernist spirit that Continental cool had tried to convey. The translation from English to French involved a stripping of detail, which resulted in a less parochial appearance. The application to these clothes of modernist principles such as minimalism and abstraction was what enabled them, with slight variations, to live on right through to the dissolution of modernity in the 1980s. Button-down shirts and knitted ties (preferably black), were examples of Americana that remained very common in French films up to around 1983, having become part of a Continental modernity that was quite distinct from their New England roots. The modernist story of these garments is one of being transplanted out of their original context.

There are parallels between the homosocial structure of the Minets and *les hommes melvilliens*: the professionalism that bonds the latter together is mirrored in the knowledge of sartorial detail that unites the former. Although in Melville's films sartorial knowledge dare not speak its name, it is so obviously present that the technical virtuosity of his gangsters can almost be taken as a metaphor for it. Stella Bruzzi has commented on the peculiar interplay of nostalgia, male bonding and sartorial desire in gangster films: 'This over-identification with appearance and the open display of fetishistic interest in each other's clothes has obvious homoerotic undertones, signifying a dual attraction for a man the gangster both desires and wants to become.'[44] Significantly, though, what appears as homoeroticism is really the narcissist's desire for a mirror image of himself and his sartorial obsession: the dandy's tempestuous love affair is with 'what he himself is, what he himself was, what he himself would like to be, someone who was part of himself'.[45] Melville's penultimate film, *Le Cercle Rouge* (1970), does not feature a single woman in a speaking part. Sartorial sublimity is part of the classicist universe, and in *Le Cercle Rouge* Melville applies the rules of classic film-making distilled from his list of sixty-three American directors in virtually textbook fashion. The plot situations – it is a heist movie – are utterly conventional and basically those of a Western, beginning with Delon's release from prison at the beginning of the film. Yet there is not a single banal moment in the film's 150 minutes. Within Melville's œuvre, *Le Cercle Rouge* is the point at which he takes the dandy's art to its logical conclusion: he follows the convention to such a degree that he transcends it.

This marked adherence to the confines of the classic framework is mirrored in the active claustrophilia of Melville's *mise-en-scène*. Interior space signifies the hermeticism of his artificial world: Jef is secure only inside his apartment, his most immediate protective layer being of course his clothes. The bourgeois tradition of privacy in domestic interiors has its origins in the aristocratic preferences of the eighteenth century. Whereas in seventeenth-century residences size was an essential signifier of status, and rooms were as large and high as possible, the eighteenth century was an age of down-sizing. Smaller spaces were not only more intimate, but were also easier to light, so gaining in appeal after dark. Thus the eighteenth century gave rise to the atmospheric staging of rooms through light, a nocturnal pursuit that the twentieth century continued in the popular medium of the cinema, and nowhere more so than in *film noir*. Melville's own apartment within his studio on rue Jenner was a distillation of the atmosphere of the films he loved: intimate rooms kept permanently dark by drawn Venetian blinds, sharp pools of light beneath cylindrical lampshades, and a few pieces of neo-classical furniture.

There was also another aspect to the eighteenth century's reduction in architectural scale. For the first time, each small space was devoted to a specific activity: a writing room, a dressing room with in-built storage space, a bedroom with *en suite* bathroom. When Jansen, the alcoholic marksman played by Yves Montand, enters *le cercle rouge*, he is lying on a mattress in the throes of delirium tremens. The lizards and other animals he sees seem to present a unique moment of fantasy in Melville's œuvre, but to a man suffering from alcohol withdrawal they are a reality and as such are congruent with everything that Melville had ever shown: a completely individualized dream, or in this instance a nightmarish variation on reality. They also recall the chimeras in the precise architectural etchings of another cold romantic: Charles Meryon, the melancholic artist championed by Baudelaire. Apart from the shabby mattress, the Regency-wallpapered cell in which Jansen suffers exhibits no worldly goods except two large Louis Vuitton trunks which contain his clothes. Jansen literally lives in his wardrobe. A more precise architectural metaphor for the dandy's reductive yet complex identity could not be imagined. This understanding of intellectual space calls to mind another *rêve bourgeois* nearing its end. Days before his suicide in 1945, Pierre Drieu La Rochelle put down some thoughts on interior design in extremis: 'I contemplated all the objects in my study with a deep sensual delight; for a few months I thought more and more of Baudelaire and Poe: I remembered what they had said about the beauty of certain interiors, which are arranged entirely according to an intellectual intuition. Chair, ink-well, sofa, vases, pipes, bowls, books, all this was – as though by a scent – pervaded by my feeling of renunciation, all this seemed to be as separate from the world as myself and ready to go away with me.'[46]

With *Un Flic* (1973), Melville ventured yet deeper – if it were possible – into this arcane, poetic and artificial dream world. While, like Drieu, he had no desire other than to become one with it – which is truly to become identical with oneself – Melville once more transcended mortality by shedding light on the opaqueness of the aesthetic dream: by translating taste into art. Despite the fundamental importance of the tragic in his world, Melville ultimately emphasizes aesthetic experience over pathos: it is the knowledge of the inevitability of the tragic that inspires the dandy's cynicism, which in any case is preferable to cant. Radical disillusion, paradoxically, is the salvation of the dream. The epigraph Melville chose for *Un Flic* is a quote from Eugène-François Vidocq, the thief who founded Napoleon's secret police: 'The only feelings man can ever inspire in the police are ambiguity and derision.' Because artificiality is heightened yet again in *Un Flic* – everything is false – the dream is at its most real. Where the world of *Le Cercle Rouge* remains green in the memory – the jade of the Buddha, the US Army lovat of Delon's trench-coat – *Un Flic* inhabits a world that is entirely blue. And large parts of Melville's last film are set at dusk, *l'heure bleue*, when reality is at its most poetic and self-knowledge most acute. It is at the blue hour that Gaby emerges, the transvestite-prostitute who is also an informer to Delon's *flic*, Edouard Coleman. This fragile creature, whose whole beauty lies in his/her artificiality, is a wry comment on the ambiguity of Delon's star persona and that of the star per se. Gaby is not Coleman's lover; she is his brother and sister, whose tenderness he reciprocates in a way that is complicit rather than sexual. When Coleman hits Gaby, he is beating himself up for having failed to arrest the drug smuggler. When he says, 'You have to go as a man again', he means you have to be like me again – me, Delon, and indeed me Melville, a man willing to prostitute himself not for money but to make a dream appear real. Sadly on this last occasion he was left standing on the boulevard. *Un Flic* was a critical and commercial failure. Melville, who in accordance with Hollywood practice equated commercial and artistic success, himself described it as too hermetic.

In terms of dandyism, *Un Flic* is Melville's most revealing work, the legitimate hubris of the artist is at its peak. The dandy celebrates his pathology, thereby turning his weakness into strength. Gaby is merely the most determined in a melancholy realm of beautiful dispossessed characters. Where Hitchcock dared to express his sadistic sexuality in his last films, Melville expressed his camp imagination. Mathieu la Valise, the almost grotesquely butch-looking drug-trafficker, who sports peroxide-blond hair and takes the sleeper train equipped with a Louis Vuitton briefcase full of heroin. The aristocratic homosexual who, robbed of a Maillol-sculpture, does not want the attractive minor who stole it arrested, and answers Coleman's 'He might be a repeat offender' with 'Aren't we all?' – meaning not just homosexuals but all who inhabit this futile and ambiguous world. Cathy (played by Catherine Deneuve), who early on appears dressed as a nurse

to administer death, and whose dramaturgic value equals that of Delon's Cartier Tank, which like Melville he wears on the inside of his right wrist. The ritualized way Cathy and Coleman conduct their assignations, designed to keep the ghastly realism of sex out of their aesthetic universe. And there is Simon, Coleman's friend and antagonist, played by Richard Crenna, who for no particular reason appears at the Louvre divested of his gangster garb, carrying an umbrella and wearing a velvet-collared double-breasted coat and a homburg, echoed in the Van Gogh self-portrait behind him. In the middle of the heist he directs, Simon suddenly emerges in an immaculate silk dressing gown, and takes what seems like an eternity to put a straight parting in his hair. Yet these baroque flourishes within a framework of strict classicism never appear affected, as they so easily could in a less perfectly constructed aesthetic universe. They are entirely congruent with a modernity in which every *acte gratuit* celebrates its own futility. Melville himself declared in 1970: 'I like fruitless endeavours. Progressing towards failure is something entirely human. Man goes from success to success towards inevitable failure: his death.'[47] If *Un Flic* is a failure, it is the flamboyant failure of a dandy. It was Jacques Rigaut who remarked: 'One should not leave the stage without having comprom oneself.'[48] Or as Quentin Crisp would have said, revealed oneself. When Melville died a few months after the release of *Un Flic*, he had just been having a discussion with his dining companion about the width of his lapels.

RAINER WERNER FASSBINDER

Barbarian at the Gates

Dandyism appears especially in periods of transition,
when democracy is not yet all-powerful, and aristocracy
is only partially unsettled and depreciated... Dandyism
is a setting sun; like the star in its decline, it is superb,
without heat and full of melancholy.

CHARLES BAUDELAIRE

He often indulged in synthetic sorrow, the 'happiness of
despair', he called it.

MIRIAM J. BENKOWITZ ON RONALD FIRBANK

While Quentin Crisp had declared the cinema the
richest mine of style, referring specifically to the
pre-war films he loved, in the post-war era – and particularly
in a state of such conceptual modesty as West Germany – the
aesthetic barometer of the nation was more likely to be television. What comedy is to the British, the *Krimi* was to West
Germany and indeed the crime genre mirrored the fledgling
nation's tastes and mores most accurately. By the 1960s the
genre had started to take hold on national television, and
by the 1970s series such as *Der Kommissar, Der Alte, Tatort*

and *Derrick* were among the most popular and defining of German cultural artefacts. *Der Kommissar* was first aired in 1969, a year which, in the view of German intellectual Hans Magnus Enzensberger, saw a 'rapid acceleration of change in society'. The failed 'revolution' of the preceding year had nonetheless left its prominent mark, and nothing was as it had been in the years of the economic miracle that had preceded it. The pill, pop culture and political protest: the bourgeois restoration that had followed Nazi barbarism was under attack. In the conditions that led to the 'revolution' of 1968, dandyism played a marginal role. Yet the post-revolutionary years were marked by an atmosphere that was extraordinary in ideological and aesthetic terms, a dualistic culture – a restorative bourgeoisie on one side and the counter-culture on the other – that proved to be fruitful ground for dandyism.

Der Kommissar positions itself specifically at the crossroads of these two cultures. While hair gets longer and German youth discovers sex, drugs and rock'n'roll (jazz had by now supplanted classical music in the canon of 'good taste' to be upheld against a new kind of *Neger-Musik* [Black Music]), *Der Kommissar* and his team defend the bourgeois values of the young republic: rationalism, tailored clothes, spirits and cigarettes, against psychedelia, flowing lines and drugs. Alcohol and cigarettes are consumed as lavishly by the protectors of law and order as the effects of drugs are condemned – often by showing a young hippy girl spouting portentous irrationalities under the influence. Indeed the omnipresence of cigarettes in modernity is a constant reminder of man's ultimate failure in its face, a celebrated *memento mori* (just as the tie may be seen as a hangman's noose, another instance of modernity's glamourized fatalism). The defending team is led by Kommissar Keller himself, a soothing middle-aged presence presiding over crime and punishment with a mixture of laconic imperturbability and humanist compassion that is beyond moral judgement. Keller is an ageing existentialist more at home in the immediate post-war era (the scriptwriter Herbert Reinecker based him on Maigret). He is assisted by a team of three men, the youngest of whom is Harry Klein, who because of his youth proves the most susceptible to counter-cultural subversion. In a conscious acknowledgement of this, he also often has to play the infiltrator of the counter-culture, pretending to want to score drugs or serving as a Romeo agent to lure in 'hippy chicks'.

At the beginning of the series Harry and Keller share the same style in suits: a barely waisted soft and broad-shouldered three-button jacket worn with gently tapered trousers that sit comfortably just below the natural waist. It was this style of suit that had dominated the sartorial appearance of the 'Bonner Republik' from the late 1950s onwards, supplanting the heavily draped American styles of the late 1940s and 1950s. While clearly influenced by American drape and Italian styles, its easy-fitting appearance of democratic modernity and bourgeois restraint served also specifically to distinguish it from the sharp-shouldered and fitted lines of 1930s tailoring, inevitably associated with Nazism in the German post-war psyche.

After the war, German culture busied itself with catching up with the international developments in the arts, literature and philosophy. Nazism had been an overt reaction against

modernism and modernity, and had interrupted a development in which pre-war Germany had been dominant. If post-war Germany looked not only to America but also to French, English and Italian cultures, it was also a side glance tinged with envy at cultures that existed with incongruities but without an abyss. Abstract expressionism, existentialism *à la* Sartre and Camus, and American authors such as Faulkner, Steinbeck and Hemingway were significant cultural landmarks in 1950s Germany, and helped to suppress thoughts of the recent past and its significance for the present. From its inception around 1958, the influence of the *Nouvelle Vague* on the tastes of German youth also cannot be overestimated. Every new film by Chabrol or Godard was a momentous cultural event, a repeated 'shock of the new' of a magnitude that is significantly absent in contemporary culture. While these influences were immediately adopted by German youth, they also gradually seeped into the mainstream, where they lingered for some time: an early episode of *Der Kommissar*, entitled *Das Messer im Geldschrank* (The Knife in the Safe, 1969) has Harry Klein enter the crime scene dressed as an *homme melvillien* of the *Le Doulos* period or thereabouts, in a loose-fitting three-quarter-length trench-coat, with a black knitted tie just visible underneath.

Also in terms of other consumer-products the BRD sought to distance itself from the supposedly Germanic and *gemütliche Blut und Boden* (blood and soil) aesthetic of the brown rule. 'Good design', in a continuation of the interrupted Bauhaus tradition, was represented by institutions like the legendary Hochschule für Gestaltung Ulm (Ulm School of Design) and the products of manufacturers such as Braun.

The HfG Ulm may be regarded as the spiritual home of much of the 'romantic sterility' that characterizes the best of post-war West German modernism. Braun suggested functionalist rationality through an almost platonic simplicity. Products like the famous 'Snow White's coffin' (The SK4 record-player and radio) gained their cult status precisely by means of such high-cultural and classicist allusions, rather than pure functionalism. Straight lines and right angles also dominated the design of 1960s German cars like BMWs and the NSU RO 80, which was Kommissar Keller's own vehicle, just as they characterize the non-waisted jackets of the 'Bonner Republik' suit. At the Hochschule für Gestaltung Ulm, where classicism was embraced in every aspect of life and not without dogmatism (only Bach and the Modern Jazz Quartet were acceptable listening), the straight line in tailoring was also de rigueur among students and lecturers alike. Significantly, the Hochschule was dissolved in 1968. Of course not all the material worlds of post-war Germany could claim such high-cultural credentials. The 'Nierentisch-Baroque' that had dominated the 1950s was a far more accessible form of modernism, bastardized as it was by allusions to organic and indeed baroque forms.

In stark contrast to both these 'high' and 'low' tastes of the post-war era were the folkloristic and neo-historicist tastes of the counter-culture. An episode of *Der Kommissar* featured a drug-addled hippy derelict sporting a bandana around his head and an Afghan-style waistcoat known to his peers as 'Teekanne', on account of his only and much-treasured possession: an antique teapot. What the series amply demonstrated over the seven years of its run was how the aftermath of the 1968 revolution not only created the counter-culture that spread from its initiators but also infiltrated the very bourgeoisie it attacked. Young Harry's suits soon became more fitted, while his hair grew ever longer. The flared and low-cut trousers of his suits and sports jacket combinations were cut like the jeans of the hippies he and Keller were frequently up against.

In 1974, the character of Harry Klein migrated to the new series *Derrick*, where he increasingly dispensed with tailoring altogether and appeared in various combinations of denim and leather jackets (before 1968 no German over thirty would have dreamt of wearing jeans). 'Derrick', named after the Chief Inspector whose sidekick Harry now was, outlasted the Federal Republic of which it had been so representative by almost a decade, thereby also unwittingly documenting the demise of modernism. The figure of Stephan Derrick, though an unlikely candidate for dandyism, is nevertheless interesting in terms of anglophilia. The actor Horst Tappert had initially worn his own clothes, good-quality English-style suits and sports jackets, as well as the Burberry trenches and raincoats that remain vastly more popular on the Continent than among English gentlemen themselves. Similarly, a glimpse of Derrick's flat reveals that it is decorated in that particular 1960s/1970s continental take on English taste, with Regency-green walls and an abundance of mahogany and well-upholstered Chesterfields.

The look of the young German democracy was both modernist – continuing the interrupted Bauhaus tradition – and anglophile: a continental coupling that had existed at least since Adolf Loos. The apotheosis of Federal Republican anglophilia had unfolded earlier on the big screen: a hugely popular series of films based loosely on books by Edgar Wallace had started in 1959 and petered out in the early 1970s. While the films were supposedly set in London or various stately homes, they were largely shot in Berlin and Hamburg, with just the occasional archive shot of Piccadilly Circus adding scant authenticity. This fantasy version of Britishness involved sleuthing butlers and plenty of *Glen-check* (the German name for Glenurquhart check), but remained solidly German both in its aesthetics and in the larger-than-life theatricality of the acting. Though the films mixed a humourous approach with sometimes rather bizarre villainy (the German title of the first film in the series translates as 'The Frog with the Mask'), the usual police inspector hero tended to be a rather straitlaced civil servant, capable of the occasional sarcastic remark but hardly of irony or indeed any hint of ambiguity. Wit was also in scant supply in *Derrick* and its ilk. Yet a degree of ambiguity is communicated through the all-pervasive melancholy that imbues the genre (Lars Albaum has termed the whole genre of 1970s German crime 'Bourgeois Melancholy-TV').[1] Stephan Derrick had this melancholy written on his very face: hardly a beau, though apparently a sex symbol in Japan, he boasted the baggiest eyes ever seen on a figure of public myth. His manners were of the formal politeness that in Germany is traditionally regarded as the trait of the English gentleman. Yet earlier German hierarchies did not impress Derrick: presented with a Rittmeister in *The Man from Portofino* (1975) he shows no deference. Derrick truly believes in the democratic and rational values that the Federal Republic sought to represent. But while *Der Kommissar* carried the last cosy traces of a society with a functioning communal realm, in *Derrick* the cracks are increasingly beginning to show. Like Keller, Derrick often has a Maigret-like air of understanding the perpetrators he has brought to justice. Though neither his status nor his mindset would allow him to declare that 'Crime is just another form of life's struggle', the words so memorably uttered by Louis Calhern as Alonzo D. Emmerich in *The Asphalt Jungle* (1950), he acknowledges that these murderers have simply failed in the face of the human tragedy that he himself also inhabits.

In the 'post-revolutionary' period the *homme brummellien* of modernity is himself fighting a losing battle for classicism in the face of flowing irrationality, 'feminine form' and the disappearance of tailored individuality in men's fashion. Already the 1960s clumsily anticipated a culture of arbitrariness, which in the 1970s began to corrode unified conceptions of the world, and by the end of the decade abolished them altogether. While the years between 1968 and 1973 appear as the last stand of the dandy and modernity, the aesthetics of modernity only truly seem to have disappeared by about 1983. Around this time a popular poll in Germany forced the Derrick actor Horst Tappert to change his style of dress to more fashionable suits, and accessorize them with *nouveau riche* 1980s trappings such as Cartier glasses and a large gold Rolex. It was also at the end of the 1970s that the counter-culture lost its authenticity. While despair over the failure of the 1968 revolution had turned the hedonism of its children towards a serious drug culture, and their political activism towards terrorism, the 1970s remained the heyday

of counter-cultural activity. As the French neo-noir writer
Jean-Patrick Manchette explains, it was the dream of '68 that
kept it alive: 'From my point of view this was a special period
in time, namely the one after 1968… a period in which a re-
incarnation of the revolution of '68 still seemed possible.
This ceased to be a possibility by the end of the 1970s.'[2]

It is precisely the interplay between a bourgeoisie hanging
on to an ageing modernity and the counter-culture that
makes the 1970s the most extraordinary time in the history
of modernity, both ideologically and visually. Towards the
end of the twentieth century, the decline of the great vision
of the nineteenth became apparent, prompting the defend-
ers of bourgeois notions of ambiguity to retreat behind a
mask of gentle melancholy. In Germany especially, the contrast with the euphoria of the glory years was palpable.
Stylistically, the 1970s may be equated to the Hellenism of
modernity, rich in the baroque elements that have always
had an ambiguous relationship with modernism and specifically dandyism. Referring to the social changes that brought
about this late-flowering *richesse*, Guy Debord noted: 'The
moment of decadence of any form of social superiority is
doubtless rather more amiable than its vulgar beginnings.'[3]
In 1968, the euphoria of a new way of life rapidly gave way
to the depression that ensued after its failure, following the
processes of an accelerated modernity – as compared with
the far more gradual pace of change at the turn of the eighteenth and nineteenth centuries. Looking back, what marks
out the 1970s in terms of atmosphere, not only in German TV
series but also in the best European films, is a pervasive and
often sophisticated melancholy, prompted by the aftermath

of the failed revolution on the one hand and the slow death of modernism on the other. Today the architecture of late brutalism appears virtually as a celebration of melancholy and alienation that is still preferable to the knowing meaninglessness of 'post-modernism'. In terms of the arts, the 1970s also provide a break, an oasis between the more commercial 1960s and 1980s, in which more authentic voices could make themselves heard.

It was in the 'post-revolutionary phase' of 1968 to 1973 that public recognition in Germany first came to the man who was to say: 'The only expression of emotion I accept is despair.'[4] Ostensibly part of the counter-culture, he soon turned out not to fit into any category, neither left nor right nor high nor low. In his work embracing forty-four feature films (in addition to plays, theatre-directing and acting) over a period of thirteen years, he documented the Federal Republic through his eyes, those of an individual seeking the right to obtain his identity. On 11 June 1982, the day after his death at the age of thirty-seven, the West German news programme *Aspekte* said of his work: 'Fassbinder's films are not thinkable without the history of this republic – yet this republic is also not thinkable without Fassbinder's films.'

Rainer Werner Fassbinder was born on 31 May 1945 in Bad Wörishofen, Bavaria. His father was a doctor and his mother a translator. After being looked after by relatives in the countryside for fear the infant would not survive the conditions in the war-torn Bavarian capital, Rainer Werner was brought up in Munich. When his parents divorced in 1951, he remained with his mother. In the immediate post-war conditions, various family members lived in the flat, and Fassbinder later claimed that he didn't relate to his mother any more closely than to the others. His many lonely hours – his mother was hospitalized with tuberculosis for a long time when he was about six – were spent with books and art, the only things present in the flat and also the only things his parents or others would give him as presents: 'I lived completely by myself very early on. There was nobody there to look after me, as my mother was ill. And there was nothing in this flat where we lived but books and art. I kind of grew up like a flower there.'[5] From the age of seven, Rainer Werner became addicted to the cinema, often going three times a day. As with Jean-Pierre Melville, this would prove to be the education on which he founded his later career as a film director. To the young Fassbinder the cinema was also an *ersatz* family, the true locus of his socialization, his feelings, and his identifications. For many people in the 1960s cinema-going to excess was a common way of structuring the day; it became an effective way of turning away from reality while simultaneously finding a 'language' for it: in cinematic gestures, in cinematic role models, in cinematic sentences.[6] Indeed cinematic socialization is the very source of the synthetic dandyism of the late twentieth century. Where the original dandy sought to become art by applying the unity of a work of art to his life and thereby becoming a *Gesamtkunstwerk*, the late dandy taps into the already existing *Gesamtkunstwerk* that film has the potential to be. His dandyism is therefore necessarily more mediated and ambivalent in terms of originality. In Oswald Wiener's phrase, it is a 'secondary dandyism'.[7]

The origins of the enjoyment of cinema were ultimately

narcissistic; within its temporal and spatial realm cinema allowed the illusion of total identification long before the unsatisfying simulations of virtual reality. In the darkness of the cinema, we can assume the place of the protagonist and watch ourselves. Hence, as the film critic Thomas Elsaesser argues, there is also a covert homosexual element to the cinematic experience: in the cinema we desire our own gender, as cinematic desire equals desire for being him/her rather than merely 'doing' him/her. As the unity of art is conspicuously absent from reality, the ecstasies of a life lived through the cinema – like those of fashion – have their counterparts in despair and existential angst. The literary chronicler of the early Federal Republic, Wolfgang Koeppen, referred to the dangers of cinematic escapism in the central part of his 'trilogy of failure', *Das Treibhaus*: 'the hell of daily visits to the cinema where the devil – in cosy darkness – exchanges life against a pseudo-life... They went to the cinema twice a week; on other days they [the teenagers of the Federal Republic, the *Halbstarken]* gathered in front of it. They waited. What were they waiting for? They were waiting for life and the life they were waiting for never came. Life failed to turn up at the cinema as arranged, and if it did turn up and stood next to them they didn't see it, and the partners who came along later and could be seen, they weren't the ones they had been waiting for.'[8]

Despite the somewhat haphazard circumstances of his upbringing, Fassbinder's background was very much a bourgeois and cultured one. From an early age Rainer reacted against this background, identifying with the underdogs he idolized on screen. No doubt his mother often took him to task for bad manners and admonished him when he spoke coarsely, using phrases picked up from dubbed Hollywood films (by the late 1970s German dubbing studios were consulting convicts to obtain the latest slang).

Throughout his short life, Fassbinder persisted in attempting to adjust his reality to the movies, wanting all of his own actions, and by extension those of the people around him who constituted part of his reality, to be 'like in a movie'. His long-time collabourator Harry Baer gave an astute analysis of the pathology behind the dream: 'Cinema as *ersatz*-life – fear of life which is immediately incarcerated by new cinematic-images.'[9] To Stan Carlisle, the anti-hero of William Lindsay Gresham's novel *Nightmare Alley*, 'fear is the key to human nature', the key with which the doomed con man in the book manipulates his victims until he himself falls prey to his fears. It is often thought that this is especially true of German nature. Churchill famously declared that 'German courage comes from fear', and the German word for fear, *Angst*, has become the universal term for existential terror. To Fassbinder even love – the opposite of and antidote to fear – had in contemporary society been subsumed and instrumentalized by fear as a means of repression: he called his first feature film *Liebe ist kälter als der Tod* (Love is Colder than Death, 1969). And angst – as a result of the manipulation of emotions – is at the centre of his œuvre and features in two of his film-titles *Angst essen Seele auf* (Fear Eats the Soul, 1974) and *Angst vor der Angst* (Fear of Fear, 1975), the latter probably the most accurate cinematic depiction of depression ever filmed. Caught as the 1970s were between trauma (the war), an unsuccessful attempt at processing this trauma (1968), and the eventual death of any kind of utopianism at the end of the decade, a sense of alienation and increasing disorientation, of existential angst in other words, became a pervasive mood. As the ever laconic and seemingly imperturbable Stephan Derrick admitted in a more than usually soul-searching episode: 'If I really think about it, I am always afraid.'

While willing other people to act as you want them to is the job of a director, Fassbinder's manipulations did not end when the camera stopped rolling. This points to a problem in terms of his dandyism: the dandy confines himself to directing his own life. As soon as he extends his dream (or perhaps his nightmare) to other people, he becomes the monster that Fassbinder of course also was. 'I learned all my emotions in the cinema,'[10] he told his one-time wife Ingrid Caven, reflecting implicitly on the absence of emotion in his childhood home. Asked whether he took the mother-and-son relationship in one of his films from the one James Cagney has with his mother in Raoul Walsh's *White Heat*, Fassbinder answered: 'No, I found my relationship to mothers while watching *White Heat*.'[11] As he was of a naturally defiant temperament, his mother's rather formulaic attempts at moulding him made him not only take against education but also question certain authoritarian values of German culture, which at the time he inevitably associated with the dark years of the not-so-distant past. The evolution of Fassbinder's dandyism conforms to Albert Camus's idea of the dandy as romanticism's most original creation (Camus viewed classicism as 'subdued' romanticism). Because the dandy/rebel feels he has been subjugated by force by the existing order, he believes himself entitled to a life of permanent defiance of 'moral and divine law'.[12] The dandy (this is where he parts ways with the revolutionary) then goes on to create 'his own unity by aesthetic means. But it is an aesthetic of negation... the dandy is by occupation always in opposition. He can only exist by defiance... The dandy rallies his forces and creates a unity for himself by the very violence of his refusal. Disoriented, like all people without a rule of life, he is coherent as a character.'[13]

As with many teenagers, Rainer Werner's insecurities centred on his appearance: other boys were more loved than he was, therefore they must be better-looking. Fassbinder of course simultaneously desired (and resented) the 'other boy' in wanting to be him. 'You are myself' – desire subsumed by identification – corresponds to Jean Genet's earliest memory of loving: he wanted to be the good-looking boy who passed by.[14] Unlike Michel Leiris, Fassbinder didn't compensate for his shortcomings with extreme elegance. While his appearance mattered to him enormously, he sought to express a personality at odds with society through it. Again Camus describes this identification as congruent with the Romantic tradition: 'Without exactly advocating crime, the Romantics insist on paying homage to a basic system of revenge which they illustrate with the conventional images of the outlaw, the criminal with the heart of gold, and the kind brigand.'[15] The proletarian or criminal characters Fassbinder identified with also informed his dress sense: the leather jacket was the item of clothing he was most frequently photographed in – an over-determined symbol of rebellion.

Later on, Fassbinder was to invest a great deal of thought, energy and money in order to achieve his unkempt

appearance: a belated protest against the hollow respectability of his upbringing. Fassbinder's is an inverted dandyism.
What he shares with the original dandy is an initial renunciation: rather than risk not being loved, he does not court love.
Yet while the dandy seeks to combine unavailability with
ultimate desirability, the negativity of Fassbinder's dandyism
seeks to make his undesirability more determined: 'I played
against the audience with a direct aggressiveness, probably
going to the limits of what was possible, which no doubt
arose from the fear that the audience might not like me. So
I showed that I didn't like them ten times over, so that it
would be all too comprehensible... if they did not like me. I
wanted to prevent anyone from being able to hurt me.'[16] Fassbinder sought ugliness in itself, as a bulwark against hurt,
and yet ultimately in order to subvert it into triumph: 'I want
to be ugly on the cover of *Time* – it'll happen and I'm glad
about it and I admit it – when ugliness has finally reclaimed
all beauty. That is luxury.'[17] Fassbinder's personal aesthetic
of celebrating ugliness would ultimately find its apotheosis
in punk. What punk shared with Fassbinder was not least
the biker jacket as basic wardrobe element. Punk was the
triumph of negativity that sought to make the ugly beautiful.
Yet the wish to be loved is only masked within the joys of
absolute negativity, a mask that Michel Houellebecq would
lift more than two decades after the emergence of punk: 'I do
not wish to be loved despite what's worst in me, but because
of what's worst in me.'[18]

While Fassbinder was frequently seen in Brando's rather
too tight jeans and rough boots, he tended to top the outfit
off with the *Samouraï*'s fedora, and tailoring remained part

of his repertoire – an important point of reference in his own wardrobe and more so in his films. In terms of Fassbinder's insecurities, making films was entirely therapeutic: he projected his identity on to glamorous men and women, who spoke his lines and followed his orders.[19] Yet his complex about his appearance also made him jealous of other people's good looks, even when these were something he could exploit in plays and films. Fassbinder liked having power over the appearance of his actors, and he was sometimes malicious in the transformations he demanded. Like that other fallen angel, Lucifer, he felt justified in his actions by his expulsion from heaven (in early Roman mythology Lucifer of course meant 'bringer of light': an appropriate analogy for a film director).

On his last film *Querelle* (1982), after the novel by Genet, Fassbinder expressed the following thoughts: 'In my opinion it's not a film about murder and homosexuality. It's a film about someone trying, with all the means that are possible in this society, to find his identity.'[20] The desire to become identical with oneself is also reflected in Fassbinder's preface to the published film script: 'Only the man who is really identical with himself can be free from fear of fear.'[21] While Fassbinder's dandyism might have been secondary in terms of its source, the true and legitimate motivation (which transcends dandyism's limitations) that underlies all his endeavour remains the same: to become identical with himself, to gain sufficient self-knowledge to be unified. A goal that lies beyond moral boundaries, that cannot be evaluated in any terms, as it is entirely original to the individual. Fear of fear, existential angst: the opposite of identity, is the central conflict of Fassbinder's œuvre. If Fassbinder's films are mostly concerned with the struggle of becoming identical with oneself and the failure to do so, this echoes the dysfunctional dandy's belief in the necessity of suffering to gain knowledge, as Louis-Ferdinand Céline famously wrote in *Voyage au bout de la nuit*: 'That is perhaps what we seek throughout life, that and nothing more, the greatest possible sorrow so as to become fully ourselves before dying.' To the depressive dandy, the belief in the ennobling qualities of suffering is also a coping strategy. The serious insistence on self-identification marks Fassbinder out as a classicist, in stark opposition to the emerging pop culture of the 1960s and 1970s, which was increasingly more comfortable with role play. David Bowie's forte, for example, has always been in reinventing, rather than finding, himself.

Having been rejected by the Hochschule für Film and Fernsehen in Berlin, Fassbinder studied drama at a private school in Munich. In 1967 he joined the Action-Theatre group, and soon became its dominant force. Though his intention was from the outset to make movies, he honed his skills in the theatre and continued to work in the theatre throughout his career as a film-maker. He was later to say: ' I directed plays as if they were movies, and then made movies as if they were theatre.'[22] This is certainly true of the language used in his films. While most of his early films are set in a proletarian or petit bourgeois milieu, the specific Fassbinder-language the characters speak abstracts them from the apparent mundaneness of their reality into something entirely artificial. Even when Bavarian argot – as in *Katzelmacher* (1969) – is used, it is spoken with a high-German accent, which turns it into a language all of its own.

Curiously, this wilful unnaturalness of dramatic dialogue is something that Fassbinder's early films have in common – along with an atmosphere of underlying melancholy – with contemporary crime series on German television, many of which were scripted by Reinecker (although in that context it is less successful: while Reinecker's language is often jarringly theatrical and portentous, Fassbinder achieves quite different levels of linguistic abstraction). Fassbinder's ambivalent relationship with reality echoes Camus's thoughts on the rebel as artist: 'Art is an activity which exalts and denies simultaneously. "No artist tolerates reality," says Nietzsche. That is true, but no artist can ignore reality. Artistic creation is a demand for unity and a rejection of the world. But it rejects the world on account of what it lacks and in the name of what it sometimes is. Rebellion can be observed here in its pure state and in its original complexities.'[25] While Fassbinder was in declared opposition to the reality of the Federal Republic and saw film-making as an instrument of rebellion – of his film *Die dritte Generation* (The Third Generation, 1979) he declared, 'I don't throw bombs, I make films' – he was really in the business of creating beauty. Fassbinder created beauty by thematizing his own pathological experience of reality and abstracting it into the unified realm of art. Ostensibly, Fassbinder was searching for a utopian society beyond the exploitation of emotions. But not once does he show this truly altered reality. In the only work which is set in the future, *Welt am Draht* (World on a Wire, 1973), society has perfected the deception that to Fassbinder is the worst sin of both art and society 'to pass off spectres as humans'. This phrase from

Theodor Fontane is the epigraph to Fassbinder's film *Effie Briest* (1974), after Fontane's novel. Avatars of existing humans are produced by technology, and act in a virtual reality that hardly differs from the 'real' one, a comparatively novel idea at the time. The impossibility of showing Fassbinder's utopia is rooted in its origin: this is an artificial utopia conceived in the kino-womb of his adolescence. Its unattainability defines the dream. Despair necessarily remains Fassbinder's *raison d'être*, his means of defining himself aesthetically, a necessity that Camus had also seen: 'If they all were able to talk of unhappiness it is because they despaired of ever being able to conquer it, except in futile comedies, and because they instinctively felt that it remained their sole excuse and their real claim to nobility.'[24] Rather than reaching out into the communal realm, Fassbinder's universe becomes increasingly personal and indeed claustrophiliac as he goes on.

A hothouse atmosphere is even more constituent for Fassbinder than for Melville. Fassbinder is decidedly uncomfortable with outside space, to the point of agoraphobia. A letter to a friend by the German writer Gottfried Benn echoes dandyism's mistrust of nature, as well as its implicit misogyny – a connection already made by Baudelaire: 'Nature is empty and desolate, only the petit-bourgeois can find meaning in it... Flee from nature, she muddles your thoughts and notoriously cramps your style! Natura is feminine of course! She's always intent on syphoning off man's seed, sleeping with him and wearing him out.'[25] In Fassbinder's *Fear of Fear* we mostly see outside space framed by the windows of the protagonist's flat. While this suggests the claustrophobic life of the main character Margot – whose viewpoint we share – the discomfort we are made to feel towards the outside world is even more intense. Fassbinder's own flat in Munich – the only one he had professionally designed, tellingly by his set designer Kurt Raab – was a womb-like dream/nightmare of dark brown and mirrored walls. The most claustrophobic film in his œuvre is without doubt his television series of Döblin's *Berlin Alexanderplatz* (1980): fifteen and a half hours of barely lit interiors, making the viewing experience akin to surviving a morphine overdose. Over and over again, Fassbinder celebrates the horrors of the melancholy he depicts (to the point of fetishizing the angst-relieving drug Valium in close-ups in *Faustrecht der Freiheit* or Fox and His Friends, 1975 and *Martha*, 1974). That claustrophobia is really claustrophilia emerges with crystal clarity in his last film, *Querelle* (1982). The exteriors are quite obviously a Potemkin village built in the safety of the studio and bathed in a permanently amber light, rendering the nightmarish events in the port of Brest a sublime dream.

When he met Andy Warhol, who had gone to the next stage of the synthetic (an avatar of himself in his own body), Fassbinder, who had remained at the previous stage (an image off the silver screen), was horrified by the golden mask that managed to hide the terrors of the void. Yet Fassbinder's deeply ambivalent relationship with the 'wrong life' (he made frequent reference to Theodor Adorno's famous dictum, 'There is no right life in the wrong one') was also revealed when he was questioned by the critic Wolfram Schütte about the realism of the appearance of his gangster figures in films such as *Götter der Pest* (Gods of the Plague, 1970) or *Der amerikanische Soldat* (The American Soldier, 1970), which he

made partly under the influence of the films of Jean-Pierre Melville: 'Yes, especially amongst people who fancy themselves to be gangsters... they dress like that, they stylize themselves in this way. They are people who, to live the life they consider worth living, adapt roles, which is naturally quite sad or also quite beautiful, depending on how you look at it.'[26]

Despair (1977) starts with a scene that exposes the alienated character of its protagonist from the outset: Hermann Hermann is trying to make love to his wife, while simultaneously sitting in a chair and watching himself. Like Quentin Crisp he is an *homme sans immediateté*, a man unable to experience reality unless it is mediated by cultural reference. The scene is repeated half an hour into the film, when it becomes clear that Hermann is really the spectator. He is impotent, his impotence masked by Herman Melville's character Bartleby the scrivener's 'I prefer not to'. There is a similar scene in the French film *Mr Klein* by Joseph Losey: Klein is sitting at his desk, his back turned to his scantily clad girlfriend, who lies on the bed. He makes her read a passage from a pornographic book, while remaining apparently impassive. Both Hermann and Klein appear to the outside world as 'masterful' characters through their manner and dress: impeccable three-piece suits in a variety of different cloths.

Yet both films are about a breakdown of cultural identity: Klein's as an 'Aryan' and Hermann Hermann's as an upper-middle-class dandy. While *Mr Klein* was released a few months before *Despair*, it is set a few years later, during the German Occupation of Paris. *Despair* is set in the early 1930s, just before Hitler came to power. The critical investigation of the Fascist period was a preoccupation of the 1970s that had started in the cinema with Visconti's *La caduta degli dei* (The Damned) in 1969. In parallel, sartorial trends started to be influenced by the 1930s, the very period that 1950s and early 1960s tailoring had tried to get away from. The white collars on coloured and striped shirts, knitted waistcoats and belted sports jackets of Visconti's film were soon to appear in designer menswear collections. Inevitably, films depicting the 1930s also reflected the period when they were made. For Fassbinder – as one of West Germany's most critical artistic voices – dealing with the Nazi period was of paramount importance. What he shared with the student revolutionaries of 1968 and also the later Red Army Faction/Baader-Meinhof terrorists was the belief that the opportunity for a new start

in 1945 had been missed: the Federal Republic still shared the basic structures and values of Nazism.

Hermann's split personality represents the dandy's internal ambiguity taken to its pathological extreme. *Despair* is a text about dandyism in crisis. While in his previous films Fassbinder had largely identified with the suppressed individualities of the working class and petite bourgeoisie, in *Despair* he investigates the crisis of the haute-bourgeois ego, so following in the footsteps of other European films of the 1960s and 1970s, such as *8½*, *Persona*, *Il Conformista* (The Conformist), *Morte a Venezia* (Death in Venice) and *Providence*, the last two starring Dirk Bogarde, who also starred in *Despair*. For the first time in Fassbinder's œuvre, *Despair* deals with the problematic relationship not of the individual with others but rather of the individual with himself. In filming a book by Vladimir Nabokov, Fassbinder also chose a dandy-author, an aesthete who transcended aestheticism and thematized this process in his work. A choice apparently out of character with his earlier scripts, but hardly out of character with Fassbinder himself. With *Despair*, Fassbinder also went international: this was his first internationally financed film, shot in English with a script by Tom Stoppard that transposed Nabokov's rapier-sharp wit admirably. It deals with a transnational character in the person of Hermann – like Nabokov himself a Russian émigré in Berlin – played by the Englishman of Dutch origin Dirk (van den) Bogarde. There is an amusing play on the deracinated nature of the dandy in a scene where one of Hermann's business rivals starts a conversation about contemporary politics, to which Hermann can only respond with the strictly personal. He attempts to describe his origins first in national and racial terms, and then in analogies based on colour. He ends with: 'All I am is a yellowbelly with a brown head, but I'm holding on for myself.'

Yet *Despair* also manages to comment on two periods of crisis in the German national identity: 1929–30 and 1977, which saw the dissolution of fixed German and historical identities per se. Crucially in this context, Fassbinder contrasts the dandy's narcissistic personality with the Nazi personality; as Elsaesser remarks: 'The avoidance of sexual and social obligations and living through of a schizo-paranoid dissociation of the ego, is symmetrically positioned in the film against capitalist monopolies, Fascism and Hitler.'[27] While the Nazi personality is exemplified in the film by Muller, the production manager in Hermann's chocolate factory who over-identifies with his roots and the state, an identification defined by active hatred for anything 'other', and publicly enacted by adopting the SA uniform, the dandy's crisis is largely auto-aggressive: the dandy's narcissism stems from suppressed paranoia. In *Despair*, Hermann attempts to conquer this fear, which is at once his identity and the cause of his identity crisis, by merging with the 'other'. In the hall of mirrors of a travelling fair, Hermann encounters a tramp whom he takes to be his physical *doppelgänger* but who in fact bears no resemblance to him. From this moment on, Hermann sets in motion orchestrations with the aim of exchanging identities with the tramp, who is auspiciously named Felix. As Adolf Loos had already realized, the tramp is indeed the dandy's *doppelgänger*: a heroic expression of a strong individualism, which takes the dandy's inherent reductionism to its logical conclusion by dispensing with the cultural baggage that has obviously become painful to Hermann. The exchange of identities that is ultimately achieved through the murder of Felix is a symbolic dandy-suicide. Later on, Hermann comments incognito on newspaper coverage of the murder: 'The perfect murder would be the one where the victim did it,' implying again the self-lacerating nature of the dandy: *Je suis la plaie et le couteau* (I am the wound and the knife).'[28]

Merging with the other is also the ultimate wish-fulfilment of Fassbinder's cinema-born dandyism: truly becoming the person with whom one identifies on screen. Exile from the self in another is the ultimate fictional form of the dandy's many flights from the passage of time. Short of actually committing suicide, the dandy rejects the world as it is, without accepting the necessity of escaping it. Inevitably, what keeps him alive is just as much a part of the world as what makes him want to abandon it: 'Far from always wanting to forget it, they suffer, on the contrary, from not being able to possess it completely enough, strangers to the world they live in and exiled from their own country. Except for vivid moments of fulfilment, all reality for them is incomplete.'[29] The cinema itself is a form of exile that can offer two contradictory forms of this vivid fulfilment: an escape from one's own day-to-day reality and territorial status, as well as a reassurance in the face of disappearing conventions and the increasing complexity of the world. The desire for faraway places in the German cinema of the late 1960s and 1970s also quite clearly represents a death wish: life is not possible in exile. Fassbinder saw himself in a constant state of internal emigration, and hoped that the success of *Despair* would make it possible for him to go to Hollywood. But the film was not a success, and

Fassbinder remained tied to the Federal Republic to live out his fate. The theme of exile is of course also mirrored within *Despair* itself, set as it is in a period when the best of German art was in exile.

In preparation for the exchange of identities, Hermann had already worn a vastly more elegant version of Felix's leather jacket as part of his weekend wear. Since the beginning of the 1960s, the dandy ideal had of course been threatened by less refined forms of masculinity, as exemplified by Fassbinder's own idealization of the leather-jacket-clad outlaw. When the dandy becomes rebel he might have to change his clothes, but the identity-giving significance of his clothing remains. Just before the exchange of identity/murder, Hermann addresses his desired alter ego: 'Now, Felix, the great moment has arrived: you have to change your clothes!'

The oft-repeated notion that to the rebel, especially the leftist rebel, style is irrelevant is patently absurd. In retrospect, the mood of May 1968 was more about the spirit and style of rebellion than about a concrete political agenda. The New Left had based itself on the writings of a young Marx barely out of his teens – which Marx himself had chosen not to publish – dealing with metaphysical problems such as alienation, which proved attractive to bourgeois student revolutionaries. What survives of 1968 are the slogans and graphics of the Situationists. In Paris, the revolution was fought in black shirts and red whale cords, as furnished by New Man, rue de l'Ancienne Comédie. The terrorist organizations of the 1970s such as the Red Army Faction were as inseparable from their style as were their bourgeois counterparts. Sunglasses were part of Andreas Baader's self-mythologizing, as was the fact that he tapered his own trousers. Gudrun Enslinn was arrested as she was buying a leather jacket from one of Hamburg's most expensive boutiques. The ambiguities extend further: left-wing terrorism was prevalent in the 1970s, the most consistent period of left-wing government in the post-war era. The Red Army Faction terrorists of the first generation were – like Fassbinder – from bourgeois backgrounds, and projected their desire for rebellion on to the scarcely authentically proletarian Baader. In a statement worthy of a Melvillian chief of police, Horst Herold, head of the BKA (the German national investigative police agency), later declared: 'Nobody has understood me as well as Baader, nor have I understood anyone as well.'

Hermann's wish to dispense with his dandy personality, to free himself of his neuroses by embracing a more archaic/anarchic identity, alas leaves him with little more than mental illness. Unadorned by cultural references, the identity crisis of the haute bourgeoisie is simple madness. If Fassbinder has called *Despair* his 'most hopeful film', this is because he saw madness, like Antonin Artaud (to whom the film is dedicated), as utopian in itself. Fassbinder had earlier shown a similar cultural dissembling in *Die bitteren Tränen der Petra von Kant* (The Bitter Tears of Petra von Kant, 1972). When the fashion designer Petra von Kant is left by her girlfriend, her masterfully artificial pose, her precious and distanced language, all break down. In a fit of wanton self-pity, she stamps on a Meissen tea service, smashing it to pieces symbolizing the breakdown of a whole culture: 'What looks like an affront to good taste simply annuls parameters of taste.'[30]

The cultural breakdown takes place not least at the

sartorial level. Where *The Tailor and Cutter* had slightly prematurely feared a reversion to a state of savagery when belts started to replace braces in the 1930s, the early 1970s witnessed sartorial anarchy. Fashion took its inspiration from the 'street', a term that had acquired great significance since demonstrators dug up cobblestones in May 1968 in the hope of finding the beach. Inspiration no longer came from above but from a variety of sources, including specifically workwear and significantly the past. But the reasons for this dissolution of dress codes were not only ideological but also economic: 'As Western countries adjusted to economic crisis following the first oil shock in 1973, expenditures on clothing slowed… This consumer listlessness had been preceded by a crisis in savoir-faire that began in the late 1960s. Social conventions and ritual politeness formerly accepted as part of the social contract had begun to seem like constraints. People stopped dressing up and at the same time dropped traditional forms of courtesy. Handshakes went the way of trouser creases, neckties and formal language.'[31] Fassbinder – mixing divergent elements in his dress with impunity – was certainly representative of this wider trend amongst his age group. Yet he was hardly part of a tribe. His appearance and the somewhat overdone informality of his manners were very much the product of his personal history.

That Fassbinder's protagonist is a woman is no coincidence. Arguably his most successful films are about women and he frequently identified with the female characters in his movies. Margit Carstensen, who played some of his most memorable characters, later recalled: 'I always had the feeling I was there as his representative… He always behaved as if, when I was acting, I was playing his part.'[32] This internal dualism again recalls Quentin Crisp, who – in a reversal of Fassbinder's case – projected his femininity externally while maintaining a pronounced emphasis on rationality that correlates more closely with conventional notions of masculine thought patterns. In *Chinese Roulette* (1976), Fassbinder implicitly comments on his own hermaphrodite psyche when he has the character of Gabriel read from what is supposedly his own writing. It is in fact – though we are never told – a paraphrase of some of the central tenets of Antonin Artaud's *Héliogabale ou l'anarchiste couronnée* (Heliogabalus, or the Crowned Anarchist, 1934) which was published in Germany in 1967 and seems to have made a great impression on Fassbinder. In Artaud's telling, the Roman emperor Heliogabalus, who came to the throne in AD 218 at the age of fourteen and was murdered by the Praetorian Guard four years later, struggled to incorporate not only man and god in his person but also man and woman: 'Heliogabal is man and woman. And the worship of the sun-god is the religion of the man, who without the woman – his double in which he is reflected – can achieve nothing... Within Heliogabal a [dual] struggle is taking place: the WHOLE which splits itself and yet remains WHOLE. The man who becomes woman and yet eternally remains man.'[33]

Fashions of the 1970s were equally trying to blur gender boundaries by celebrating androgyny. The popularity of long hair and denim with both sexes meant that unisex fashions – a concept that had already been pioneered by the much underrated Austro-American designer Rudi Gernreich in the 1960s – became a key concept of the decade. But men's tailoring also became more feminized, with tight, often concave pagoda shoulders, wide lapels and flared, skirt-like trousers. This was a development of the Minet look. While tailoring was under threat both from the street and from the ready-to-wear industry, the 1970s were the last decade in which bespoke tailors dictated the fashionable cut. In Britain it was Tommy Nutter of Savile Row who was at the forefront of this last flowering of the tailor's art, famously making identical suits for Mick and Bianca Jagger. The 70s-style suit was easily adapted for women and became a staple of high fashion, most famously in Yves Saint Laurent's *smoking* (dinner jacket), which became acceptable evening wear for women (a design he had first featured in his 1966 collection). As the 1970s suit undoubtedly represents the Hellenistic age of tailoring, it has often been ridiculed in retrospect for its exaggerated qualities. Yet the 1970s were a period of great sartorial character and vitality, when skilled tailors could still be found anywhere. The 1970s suit has aged far better than the designer fashions of the following decade. What to some seemed excessively 'trendy' in the 1970s in fact echoed not only the 1930s but also Victorian or Edwardian sartorial traditions. Flares had not only long been worn by sailors, but also had antecedents that can be traced back to Victorian fashion plates. The most significant stylistic development in the suit was the predominance of the two-button jacket. In stark contrast to the abandonment of formality in society as a whole, it was frequently worn with a waistcoat, adding formality to an already very tailored look.

Just as drag frequently emphasizes the wearer's masculinity, the 1970s suit possessed a particularly strident masculinity on men of Fassbinder's rather non-androgynous body type. In *Chinesisches Roulette* (Chinese Roulette, 1976) Fassbinder arguably manages the opposite feat: to project himself as a female dandy. The mother, played by Margit Carstensen, is a creature of a precisely tailored artifice – she wears a hairnet in bed with her lover – that contrives to convey the combination of control and grace that distinguish the dandy. (The effective use of men's tailoring had of course been pioneered by another German: Marlene Dietrich.) Carstensen's glamour is as abstract and dissociated from her sex as it is from her sexuality. Characteristically for Fassbinder, she is also the character who dissembles at the end.

Fassbinder was not alone in embracing an ambiguous and anarchic sexuality. It was part of the assumptions of the '68ers' that the repression endemic in bourgeois society had moved into people's souls and bodies. Equally the idea that social and sexual repression were linked was already commonplace in the counter-cultural milieux of the late 1960s. In his liberal depictions of polysexual couplings, Fassbinder appears to Germany's revolutionary moment of 1968 as the equivalent of the Marquis de Sade post-1789. Yet Fassbinder's cinematic explorations of sexuality are rarely celebratory. They lack a hippyish belief in collective transformation through free love, and continue his theme of emotional exploitation.

Ambiguity of gender and sexuality are of course also characteristic of *À la recherche du temps perdu*. Not only are the real-life models of Proust's characters frequently of the opposite gender to those they inspired in the novel, but the protagonists are also liable to change their sexual

preferences within the narrative. A moral ambiguity towards homosexuality is generated by the suggestion that all are guilty: 'He used homosexuality like snobbism and cruelty, as a symbol of universal original sin.'[34] But Fassbinder does not feel the need to mask homosexual relationships as hetero-sexual ones; he simply does not differentiate between them. The issue he is concerned with is the exploitation of emotions in relationships per se. Fassbinder reaches beyond concerns of moral guilt or good and evil. The outsider protagonists of his movies are as capable of inhumanity and nastiness as their oppressors.

In this, Fassbinder clearly diverged from the black-and-white morality of the contemporary left. What would later be called political correctness was to Fassbinder just another form of discrimination. It is with *Die Ehe der Maria Braun* (The Marriage of Maria Braun, 1978) that Fassbinder truly leaves the cod-Marxism of the 68ers behind and embarks on the search for his lost childhood. The character of Willi, an old friend of Maria, has become a Marxist in the 1950s and tells Maria about the need to raise people's consciousness, as 'consciousness always lags behind real events'. We may safely assume that Fassbinder is speaking through Maria when she replies: 'With me it is just the other way around, real events always lag behind my consciousness.' *Maria Braun* is the first part of the BRD Trilogy, Fassbinder's chronicle of the early years of the Federal Republic, which – despite his frequently expressed and also intermittently enacted desire for exile – defined him as much as he defined it. By the late 1970s retro-culture was in full swing, and the 1950s received their own pop culture revival, not only from connoisseurs

of camp but also in mainstream films such as *Grease* (1978) and a number of bands. As a progressive vision of the future became increasingly hard to discern, the 1970s looked backwards rather than forwards.

While the 1950s are generally remembered visually through American culture, Fassbinder had more specific aesthetic ghosts to summon up. The 1950s were Fassbinder's favourite historical period, a time for which he was intensely nostalgic, despite – or maybe because of – the fact that they represented a time of missed opportunity for him, both personally and historically. This was the decade of his blighted childhood, as well as of the missed opportunities of a new beginning for the Federal Republic. What fascinated Fassbinder about the post-war period, and enabled him to find traces of his own anarchist spirit in it, was that it was a time of transition, a time when established values were temporarily suspended and the individual temperament could blossom. Maria Braun and Lola – the protagonist of the second part of the BRD Trilogy – are just such anarchic figures, women who rise rapidly in the world through a merging of female and male qualities: they are pitiless and affectionate, resolute and ultra-feminine. Not only did Fassbinder find it congenial to express his complex individuality through an appropriation of femininity, but he also found female protagonists more suited to representing a particular period in history, as women are more in tune with the zeitgeist, 'its surface as well as its libidinous ground-swells',[35] its fashions as well as its spirit.

A great admirer of the work of Douglas Sirk, the Danish-German film director who had emigrated first to France and then to Hollywood in 1937, Fassbinder preferred the decidedly undandyistic form of melodrama in which Sirk had excelled in, films such as *Imitation of Life* (1959) and *Written on the Wind* (1956). This was a form that allowed Fassbinder to emphasize *sehnsucht*, the undefined yearning so characteristic of the German 1950s as a stylistic element in itself. *Lola* (1981) is entirely lit in the comforting artificiality of 1950s pastel colours, and the film culminates in the eponymous protagonist's abandoned performance of the song 'Die Capri-Fischer', made popular by Rudi Schuricke in 1949. Yet Fassbinder goes far beyond a knowing and kitsch pastiche of more innocent times. What makes for the complexity of these films is the fact that stylistic awareness is wholly reflected in the intelligence of the characters: 'A form of intelligence which allows the characters to stand up to their personal brokenness and inconsistency in a way that enhances their functioning rather than paralysing it.'[36] There is also evidence of what may be viewed as the dandy's particular form of intelligence: intelligent taste. Both Lola and her mother comment on the male protagonist's purchase of a new sports-suit in order to impress Lola. First the mother reluctantly admits that she doesn't like it, and then Lola later adds that it appears incongruous with the wearer's personality and therefore hypocritical.

Stylized melancholy – be it *sehnsucht* or *weltschmerz*, *heimweh* (homesickness) or *fernweh* (wanderlust) – was a recurrent theme, counterbalancing the hysterical jollity of the years of *wirtschaftswunder* (economic miracle), expressed in its upbeat consumer design and endless strings of musical comedies. While the latter helped in the suppression of the recent past, the former represented its unconscious surfacing. In *Veronika Voss* (*Die Sehnsucht der Veronika Voss*, 1982) the Nazi period throws distinctive shadows over the nation's longing for amnesia. Veronika Voss is an UFA film star who is losing her struggle to keep her artificial personality alive. As in *Despair*, it is evidence of excessive self-scrutiny that sets in motion a fatal chain of events. In the first scene, Veronika watches herself on screen. Her self-image as a star is a *paradis artificiel* precariously kept alive by the morphine she receives from a corrupt doctor (with an obvious but unspecified Nazi past), in return for her money and worldly possessions. Ultimately, Veronika is coerced into committing suicide by this sinister mother-figure – a coercion with which she is in tacit agreement. On this occasion there is a poignant exchange between them, which simultaneously celebrates and exposes the sentimentality of 1950s German popular culture:

> Veronika: 'To say goodbye and to arrive are the most
> beautiful things in life. Marianne you have given me
> so much happiness.'
> Marianne: 'I've sold it to you.'

The parallels between *Veronika Voss* and *Sunset Boulevard* (1950) are clear and deliberate. Veronika Voss and Norma Desmond are larger-than-life creations in a world that – like the pictures – was getting smaller. This was even truer in the 1970s than it had been in the 1950s: 'Fassbinder's achievement lies in having wrestled a vibrant, intelligent and also nuanced image from this rather sombre time, without letting the viewer forget that this potential is not to be ascribed to the circumstances of the time, but rather is founded in characters who convey the essence of life especially because they are "bigger than life".[37] It is no coincidence that Fassbinder's look back at the 1950s took place in the 1970s: the *sehnsucht* of the 1950s was projected into the future, and that future had come and proved to be a disappointment. By the late 1970s, all that had been suppressed had returned to haunt the Germans, not least in the form of terrorism – which in retrospect appears not only as a reckoning directed at the continuity of Nazi elements in the Federal Republic, but also as a repetition of aspects of the Nazi terror itself. Fassbinder's aim in depicting the 1950s was to create not a historically accurate depiction, but rather a representation of the 1950s as they presented themselves in the late 1970s. Through films of the time, stories told by the older generation and family photographs, Fassbinder also goes beyond memory: his examination of his own and the nation's past is akin to a psychoanalytical process with the aim of regaining time, rather than mere nostalgia or a 'look back in cynicism'. By then, in less nuanced cultural circles, a climate of increased cynicism had indeed replaced the euphoria of the 1950s and 1960s. Punk, which had emerged in 1976, loudly proclaimed 'No future' as its slogan. Negativity was replacing the dandy's ambiguity and nihilism his wit. While the first oil crisis of 1973 had ended the optimism of the 1960s and set in train the dissolution of modernism (and indeed of modernity, in the Loosian sense of timelessness), the second one of 1979 set the seal on it. By 1983 a new era was afoot and the signifiers of the end of modernity were overwhelming; to name but two: Monty Python dissolved and Hergé, creator of Tintin, that mascot of modernity, died. A year earlier, Rainer Werner

Fassbinder's future had already ended. Having always been obsessed with the idea that time was running out, he had first neglected his body and then actively destroyed it. Ten days after his thirty-seventh birthday, after years of drug abuse and breathless exhaustion, his heart gave up. More than thirty years after the end of modernity and the dissolution of the ideal of the dandy that went hand in hand with it, it seems apt to close with Fassbinder's favourite sentence: 'Life is so precious, even right now.'

d.

Le dandy
est mort.
Vive le
dandy !

Après le Déluge

From then on nothing much happened.

PAUL BOWLES, *WITHOUT STOPPING*

I don't claim to have taste, but of my distaste
I am very sure.

JULES RENARD

Voltaire was categorical: *'Pourquoi ce garçon a-t-il toujours raison? Parce qu'il a du goût* (Why is this boy always right? Because he has taste).' It would seem impossible to make such a claim today. While taste has always been an elusive notion, the twenty-first century has made it the last taboo. The democratization of taste, which Baudelaire feared as the dandy's death knell, happened long ago. While the twentieth century might have democratized taste, the twenty-first has killed off the notion altogether. To qualitatively discriminate in aesthetic matters today is a habit akin to necrophilia only less acceptable, lacking as it does the forced extravagance that pleases an unshockable cultural climate.

The notion of 'good taste' developed hand in hand with the dandy. At the beginning of modernity, neo-classicism codified tastes in art, architecture and design. As we have seen, the concomitant codification of the gentleman in its artificial epitome, the dandy, was inextricably bound up with neo-classicism. Like the dandy, 'good taste' was a bourgeois construct that exemplified the need of the emerging middle class to assert the superiority of its values over those of both the aristocracy and the proletariat. The Modern Movement of the twentieth century then tried to recapture the certainties of the rules of classicism, which the eclecticism of Victorian taste – viewed by modernists as the very definition of 'bad taste' – had thoroughly obfuscated. The dandy's existence was dependent on a notion of taste, and it was Brummell's greatest achievement to have established this notion with such lasting authority. The parallels between 'good taste' and dandyism are so manifold as to make the two well nigh synonymous. Taste as a description of discernment rather than oral sensation is primarily a feature of western cultures, based ultimately on the idea of a shared Graeco-Roman heritage. Taste is an artificial construct, as it gives absolute authority to subjective perception: while Immanuel Kant maintained that aesthetic judgements have universal validity, the varied and paradoxical history of taste has shown that this is hardly so. Yet the narrative of 'good taste' that begins with neo-classicism assumed its own universality with the same disarming implicitness that led the dandy to take it for granted that he was a gentleman. When 'good taste' went through its Victorian decline, the dandy followed suit into decadence with great relish, until both were resuscitated by the Modern Movement. Oscar Wilde had already replaced exemplary elegance with affected eccentricity, so prefiguring

the inauthentic 'public dandyism'[1] of today. Self-promotion
and stylization are characteristics of a celebrity culture
that fundamentally lacks the capacity for reflection that
alone could lend it authenticity. The Italian dandy Gabriele
D'Annunzio had been one of the first to use the medium of
photography for the purpose of self-propaganda. Ironically,
after losing the sight in his right eye as the result of a flying
accident, he subsequently became photophobic. Today any
publicity is good publicity, and an aversion to being constantly photographed in a world that is deluged with images
is considered quaint at best.

While the dandy of the twentieth century might frequently have asserted his individuality by sinning against
'good taste', his individuality still defined itself around the
tension between the observation of rules and their transgression. Confronted with a world without rules, a world in
which everything is permissible as long as it has had its claws
removed, the dandy's twenty-first-century epigone lacks the
tension necessary to define his individuality. Concocting a
persona out of the combined dressing-up boxes of history
and fashion, when both are accessible without paying a
personal price, is neither heroic nor subtle. In his curious
mixture of asceticism and excess, the dandy was heroic primarily through his sacrifice of the chance of conventional
happiness. While in the twenty-first century the concept of
'happiness' seems more elusive than ever, this is the result not
so much of a commitment to sacrificing on the altar of rules –
aesthetic or otherwise – but rather of the disorientating lack
of a dominant narrative to follow or disrupt.

Even the 'secondary dandyism'[2] of the late twentieth

century, which Susan Sontag identified with camp subcultures and their celebration of 'bad taste ', has become an irrelevance. There is hardly a subculture left that has not been taken up and exhausted by the mainstream. Tattoos, for example, no longer signify crime of the real or the aesthetic type; they are the stigmata of a culture in which the transgressive has become the banal convention. As Sebastian Horsley, one of the more convincing twenty-first-century dandies, put it: 'You make a mark on your body when you feel you can't make a mark on your life.'[3] To substantiate his existence, the modernist dandy relied above all on meaning, whether this lay in 'good taste' or the declaration of the absence of meaning in itself (as with twentieth-century dandies with a penchant for existentialist absolutes). To assure himself of meaning, the dandy sought to make meaning identical with himself, to unite form and content, to find himself and consequently to become identical with himself. Kierkegaard thought 'desperately trying to be oneself' the hardest task there is, and it is a truth universally acknowledged that the advice to 'just be yourself' is impossible to follow even for the most superficially reflective person. Yet both the dandy and the notion of taste relied on the existence of self, however elusive. The nineteenth-century rationalist architect Viollet-le-Duc even maintained that taste and the self were identical: *'Le goût consiste en paraître ce que l'on est, et non ce que l'on voudrait être* (Good taste lies in appearing as one is, not as one would wish to be).'[4] The twenty-first century, on the other hand, conveniently dispenses with the elusive task of becoming one with oneself and indulges in endless role play. The impossible dream is being dreamed no more.

Melancholy, man's mourning of his own alienation from his timeless origin, was the mental state of modernity, and above all of its epitome, the dandy. He instilled meaning into this temperament either by giving himself up entirely to sensuality, by celebrating his alienated state, or by aiming for transcendence, by instilling the visible world and by extension himself with mystery. The twenty-first century has made meaning elusive, which is why attempts to regain it today so often combine great urgency with an awareness of their own futility. In the twenty-first century, melancholy has turned to depression and psychosis, barely held at bay by ubiquitous psychotropic drugs.

Ironically, the dandy's creation carried his demise within itself; the weight of his Janus face was always going to break his neck in the end. Two souls living within his breast, the epitome of über-aristocratic distinction on the one hand and the revolutionary harbinger of democracy on the other, he ultimately found that the seeds he had sown had turned into dandy-eating plants that would devour him. The dandy perpetuated the 'injustice' on which all high culture is based: he created parameters which privilege a minority. 'Elegance is by its very nature not available to the majority. She certainly can appear to be modest, but she can never be ordinary without disappearing. In other words she is not democratizable.'[5] After coming into being as a by-product of neo-classicism, 'good taste' spent the rest of the nineteenth century as a criterion for judging the fine arts. Once the Modern Movement had resurrected the notion in the twentieth century, it eventually moved on to design – partly because 'manners', defined by moral principles (form follows function, integrity of materials), were first applied to design, and partly because the increasing abstraction of modernist art made principles of taste harder to apply. After the Second World War, 'the public would take its aesthetic pleasures where it could find them: in the styling of cars, the cinema and in popular culture. Put another way, the century of consumerism has moved the entire man-made world into the province of aestheticism.'[6] Halfway through the twentieth century, the democratization of taste had thus progressed so far that, according to a superficial definition of the term, a great part of the population of the western hemisphere displayed aspects of dandyism.

The shift from fine art to consumer goods reached its first period of decadence in the 1980s, with the absurd commodification of the design object and of designers themselves, which thereby increased the banality of design – a vocation that had hitherto contained potential for originality – in proportion to its glorification by the market. When the market took over, taste itself started to be confused with fashion and 'design'. The Loosian credo of perfectibility, of objects that last for ever, gradually declined in currency in the course of the 1970s, along with modernism and the belief in progress. It was also in the 1980s that the concept of authenticity first dramatically lost its relevance, and a by then moribund modernity gave way to uninspired and equally lifeless regurgitations of the past. Today the whole of history has been made available for unreflecting consumption. If dandyism has followed a trajectory from revolutionary to reactionary to meaninglessness, so too has aesthetic culture as a whole.

The twenty-first century has seen the return of Art, but it has come back as a zombie. Where Nietzsche had declared that the purpose of art was 'for us not to perish in the face of the truth',[7] art today is conspicuously lacking in such metaphysical healing properties; it has lost its mystery. Art is now marketed in a way that makes it entirely indistinguishable from consumer – or more accurately fashion – items. The bulk of art is sold without any reference to its integrity as though it were share certificates with pictures on them, its market and resale value the exclusive measure of its desirability. Art is to the new millennium what pop music was to the 1960s and 1970s, and design and fashion to the 1980s and 1990s. It is hardly surprising that what passes loosely as 'the new dandyism' is incestuously bound up with the art world and reflects its values. Significantly, it is particularly in the art world that taste has become an irrelevance. Discernment, specifically in the form of distaste, is implicitly discouraged as undemocratic or politically incorrect, while democracy has become synonymous with saleability. Capitalism has made the lowest common denominator its cultural focus much more thoroughly than the Cultural Revolution or socialist anti-elitism could ever have managed. While social democracy still allowed for distinction within equality, free-market capitalism ironically does not: Theodor Adorno has noted the puzzling paradox that under capitalism taste is not autonomous, as one would expect of a system that promotes competitive individualism, but tends rather to be collective.[8] Dandyism carried within itself also this aspect of its own destruction: Stephen Bayley has called neo-classicism 'the first consumer cult'.[9]

The market requires that everything must be likeable, as everything must be saleable. While contemporary culture contains a diverting stream of absolute negativity, as in say the writings of Michel Houellebecq, it is so hyperbolic as to be no more than a well-matched counterpoint within the endless muzak of meaningless positivity. While it is perfectly possible to propagate cultural pessimism on Facebook, the automated response for reactions to this view is a 'like' button.

Retro-culture has grown enormously since its 1970s inception, but is now completely subsumed within the fashion system. In the process, it has lost the fine irony of its pioneers, while an excess of virtuosity curiously gets in the way of sublimity. London and Paris are full of creatures in perfectly researched period outfits, but with a few exceptions they give the inescapable impression they will get back into jeans and fleeces once the fancy dress party is over. Bespoke tailoring has experienced a renaissance, and the number of people who are having their clothes made has not been so large since the 1950s. Sartorial advice is everywhere, and even the most subtly stitched furrow has been comprehensively ploughed. But it is precisely this exaggerated self-consciousness that precludes true elegance: leaving a hand-stitched buttonhole undone on one's sleeve is a gesture of true vulgarity precisely because it sets out to draw attention to the generic market value of the suit, while at the same time ignoring its inherent value. Something that ideally has been carefully designed around the wearer's individuality is rendered exchangeable.

What of the twenty-first-century dandy, then? While the market negates the existence of 'good taste', to the OCD sufferer there is still a 'right' way and a 'wrong' way of doing things. In his autobiography *Dandy in the Underworld*, a memoir that veers between the lucidity of Quentin Crisp and the entertaining dementia of Helmut Berger, the late Sebastian Horsley admitted: 'Tidiness has always been my vice and it meant I would never really be chic. Only a fool would make the bed every morning. I couldn't help it. A complete meltdown would follow if the kettle was not facing due east. For me controlling interior space and keeping order in an inherently chaotic existence were intimately connected. As I got older, my craving for classification, seen in the uniformity of my clothes, the obsessive need for perfection in my work, and the symmetry in my art, was a means of staving off the chaos I saw at the centre of my being.'[10] Born in 1962, Horsley found inspiration not only in a mother with 'the loyalty we all feel to unhappiness'[11] but also in the nascent punk movement of his teenage years. Sebastian understood that dandyism, like punk, was about flamboyant failure. Of Johnny Rotten, lead singer of the Sex Pistols, he observed: 'He had all the unmistakable signs – the charismatic aura, the dandy's narcissism, the canny look of the holy tramp.'[12] Horsley soon merged into a convincing hybrid of punk and dandy. In adulthood he dabbled in anything transgressive – from passive sodomy with Scottish murderers to penetrating quadruple-amputee prostitutes, from offering his services as a gigolo to having himself crucified in the Philippines – without ever losing sight of the destination of his journey: himself. As self-scrutiny inevitably provoked exasperation as much as inspiration, oblivion proved to be the only passion that could balance his compulsion. A connoisseur of heroin and its twenty-first-century plastic cousin, crack, Horsley was ever faithful to the vice that would kill him. In his forty-eighth year he died of an overdose, on the night of the West End premiere of a play based on his autobiography.

The Parisian illustrator Floc'h was born in 1953. Old enough to have experienced the end of modernity and be a little wistful. Immaculately dressed in a suit that echoes the 1930s without stooping to fancy dress, he claims to have 'stopped wearing jeans after a bad LSD trip'. He illustrates his own books and others in the irreproachably modernist style of the *ligne claire*, made famous by Hergé. Floc'h is also a great anglophile: his early *bandes dessinées* have titles such as *Le Rendez-vous de Sevenoaks* and *Une trilogie anglaise*. His apartment in the fifth arrondissement is decorated in the style that captures the essence of Britishness as seen from a distance, a beautiful abstraction that is unknown within the sceptred isle itself: what should they know of England, who only England know? Floc'h is a dandy in the grand tradition of classic modernism: he is passionate in his belief in perfectibility. Rather than playing the lottery of fully bespoke tailoring, he is an obsessive alterer, permanently tweaking existing garments to fit his vision. The strikingly well-fitting 1930s-style single-breasted suit he wears started life as a baggy 1980s double-breasted affair. Defining taste as '*le don de discernement*', he is acutely aware that a dandy in the tradition of Brummell is an anachronism in the current climate: 'From the 80s onwards we had to live with *mauvaise foi*' he explains. The existentialist term perfectly describes the state of being at odds with the zeitgeist. Yet while Marxists used the term as 'false consciousness' in order to alert those lagging behind history, the 'right consciousness', that wishes to be at one with the body it inhabits, is now itself history.

What remains of the dandy? Has all the good gone from the word goodbye? Baudelaire begs 'every human who thinks to show me what remains of life',[13] and dandyism appears to be a form of life that is all but dead. For an enlightened resurrection we might turn again to Proust, whose concept of 'regaining time' was described by Camus in terms of an alternative (to) religion: 'It has been said that the world of Proust was a world without a god. If that is true it is not because god is never spoken of, but because the ambition of this world is to be absolute perfection and to give to eternity the aspect of man. *Time Regained*, at least in its aspirations, is eternity without God.'[14] Where the modernist Proust tried to regain the spirit of the Belle Époque of his childhood, today's *bourgeois rêveur* seeks to recapture the consciousness of modernity itself. 'Actively decadent',[15] he uses the disillusioning experience of the last three decades to come to a considered notion of taste. Aware that 'good taste' and fashion are both constructs, he looks to his own past, his own moments of pain and inspiration to arrive at an intelligent notion of taste. Intelligent taste in the Proustian sense is 'analytical intelligence mutated to a poetic sensorium'.[16] In a world that has lost its grip on meaning, the dandy understands that taste is not an arbitrary collection of likes and dislikes, but rather a rare form of intelligence: an intelligence that transcends the ubiquitous knowledge of styles past and present. Gaining this intelligence is a perpetual process, which is part and parcel of the gaining of self-knowledge. But to have gained it, *cela justifie une vie.*

Loch Hourn, 8 June 2013

NOTES

Translations from the German and French by
the author unless otherwise stated.

NOTES TO INTRODUCTION: I. MODERNITY

1   Max Beerbohm, *Dandies and Dandies*, cited in Ellen Moers,
     The Dandy: Brummell to Beerbohm (London, Secker & Warburg,
     1960), p. 21
2   ibid
3   Thomas Carlyle, *Sartor Resartus* (Oxford, Oxford University
     Press, 1987), p. 207
4   Pearl Binder, *The Peacock's Tail* (London, Harrap, 1958), pp. 30–31
5   Lady Hester Stanhope cited in Moers, op. cit., p. 18
6   Anecdotal citations regarding the life of Brummell largely from
     Jesse, *The Life of Georges Brummell, esq., commonly called Beau
     Brummell* (London 1844)
7   Anne Hollander, *Sex and Suits* (New York, Kodansha
     International, 1994), p. 7
8   ibid, p. 86
9   ibid, p. 88
10   ibid, p. 89
11   Walter Benjamin, *Passagenwerk, Gesammelte Schriften*, Band V. 1
     (Frankfurt am Main, Suhrkamp, 1991), p. 131
12   Hollander, op. cit., p. 101
13   ibid, p. 68
14   Egon Fridell, *Kulturgeschichte der Neuzeit* (Munich, C. H. Beck,
     1996), p. 836
15   ibid
16   Charles Baudelaire, Œuvres complètes, *Le Dandy* (Bouquins,
     Robert Laffont, Paris, 1999), p. 817

17   Beerbohm cited in Moers, op. cit., p. 33

18   Cited in Farid Chenoune, *A History of Men's Fashion* (Paris, Flammarion, 1993), p. 14

19   Ian Buruma, *Voltaire's Coconuts, Anglomania in Europe* (London, Phoenix, 2000), p. 9

20   Evelyn Waugh in Nancy Mitford, *Noblesse Oblige* (London, Penguin, 1961), p. 67

21   Shirley Letwin, *The Gentleman in Trollope. Individuality and Moral Conduct* (Cambridge Mass., Harvard University Press, 1982), p. 268

22   William Hazlitt, *The Look of a Gentleman* (London, 1889), p. 184

23   Letwin, op. cit., p. 14

24   Roland Barthes, *Dandyism and Fashion* in *The Language of Fashion* translated by Andy Stafford (Oxford, Berg, 2006)

25   Simon Raven, *The English Gentleman* (London, Anthony Blond, 1961), pp. 15, 59, 63

26   Oscar Wilde, 'Pen, Pencil and Poison' (*Fortnightly Review,* Janauary 1889)

27   Franz Blei, *Die Mörder*, cited in Verena von der Heyden-Rynsch, *Riten der Selbstauflösung* (Munich, Matthes & Seitz, 1982), p. 192

28   Otto Mann, *Der Dandy, Ein Kulturproblem der Moderne* (Heidelberg, Rothe, 1962), p. 91

29   ibid, p. 90

30   Sándor Márai, *Schule der Armen: Ein Leitfaden für Menschen mit geringem Einkommen* (Munich, Piper, 2006), p. 101

31   Mann, op. cit., p. 90

32   Gilles Lipovetsky, *The Empire of Fashion* (Princeton, Princeton University Press, 1994), p. 241

II. DECADENCE

33   Ernst Jünger, *Rivarol* (Frankfurt am Main and Hamburg, Fischer, 1962), p. 26

34   Beerbohm on Disraeli, *Dandies and Dandies* (*Dandies and Dandies,* London, New York, 1896), p. 5

35   Michel Leiris, *L'âge d'homme* (Folio, Gallimard, Paris, 1993), p. 208

36   ibid, p. 26

37   Richard Walker, *Savile Row: An Illustrated History* (London, Rizzoli, 1988), pp. 178, 179

38   Dolf Sternberger, *Über den Tod* (Frankfurt am Main, Suhrkamp, 1977), pp. 12, 13

39   Baudelaire, op. cit., p. 808

40   Mann, op. cit., p. 40

41   Luis Buñuel, Jean-Claude Carrière, *Mon dernier soupir* (Paris, Robert Laffont, 1994)

42   Susan Sontag, *Against Interpretation* (London, Eyre & Spottiswoode, 1967), p. 277

43   Hollander, op. cit., p. 5

44   Barthes in von der Heyden-Rynsch, op. cit., p. 306

45   ibid, p. 307

46   ibid

47   Sándor Márai, *Bekenntnisse eines Bürgers* (Munich, Piper, 2002), p. 420

48   Benjamin, op. cit., I2, p. 578

49   Breton citing Rigaut in von der Heyden-Rynsch, op. cit., p. 228

50   Pierre Drieu la Rochelle, *Le feu follet* (Paris, Gallimard, Folio, 1991), p. 150.

51   Malraux cited by Joachim Sartorius in the preface to Drieu la Rochelle, *Geheimer Bericht* (translation of *Récit secret*, Matthes & Seitz, Munich, 1986), p. 13

52   Sándor Márai, *Schule der Armen* (Munich, Piper, 2006), pp. 113, 114

53   Mann, op. cit., p. 42

54   Mann, op. cit., p. 43

55   Walter Benjamin, *Charles Baudelaire* (Suhrkamp, Frankfurt am Main, 1974), p. 95

56   Oscar Wilde, *De Profundis, Epistola in carcere et vinculis* (Oxford, Oxford University Press, 2005), p. 64

57   ibid, p. 107

58   Gibbon cited by Strachey, *Portraits in Miniature* (London, Chatto & Windus, 1931), pp. 166, 167

59   Joris-Karl Huysmans, *Against Nature* (translated by Robert
      Baldick, London, Penguin, 1959), p. 143

60   Connolly, *Enemies of Promise* (London, Routledge, 1949), pp. 50,
      51

61   Praz cited in Moers, op. cit., p. 303

62   Mann, op. cit., p. 125

63   Yeats cited in Moers, op. cit., p. 288

64   Oscar Wilde, *The Picture of Dorian Gray*, Chapter 11 in the
      Complete Works of Oscar Wilde (Oxford, Oxford University
      Press, 2000–2013)

65   George D. Painter, *Marcel Proust, A Biography*, Vol. II (London,
      Chatto & Windus, 1959/65), p. 10

66   Connolly, *Selected Works* (London, Picador, 2002), p. 215

67   Emil Cioran, *Syllogisme de l'amertume*, Gallimard, Pléiades,
      Paris, 2011, p. 172

68   Cassou cited in Georges Simenon et Frédérick Franck, *Le Paris
      de Simenon* (Charles Dessart éditeur, Brussels), p. 1

NOTES TO ADOLF LOOS

1   Elsie Altmann-Loos, *Adolf Loos, der Mensch* (Vienna, Herold,
     1968), pp. 43, 185

2   Anders V. Munch, 'In welchem Stil sollen wir leben?' in Inge
     Podbrecky and Rainald Franz (eds), *Leben mit Loos*, (Vienna,
     Bohlau, 2008), p. 124

3   Burkhardt Rukschcio, Roland Schachel, *Adolf Loos* (Salzburg and
     Vienna, Residenz Verlag, 1982), p. 31; originally: Robert Scheu,
     'Adolf Loos' in: *Die Fackel*, 283/284, Vienna, 29 June 1909

4   ibid

5   Cited by Anne-Katrin Rossberg, 'Loos' Frauenzimmer' in
     Podbrecky, op. cit., p. 151

6   Hollander, op. cit., p. 107

7   'Die Herrenmode, Ins Leere Gesprochen, Gesammelte Schriften
     1900–1930' (Vienna, Prachner, 1982), p. 55; originally *Neue Freie
     Presse*, 22 May 1898

8   Chenoune, op. cit., p. 114

9   Walker, op. cit., p. 85

10   In Loos's column in *Neues 8-Uhr Blatt*, 4 October 1919

11   'Die Herrenhüte, Ins Leere gesprochen', p. 112; originally: *Neue Freie Presse*, 24 July 1898

12   Carl E. Schorske, 'Österreichs Asthetische Kultur, 1870–1914, Betrachtungen eines Historikers' in Tino Erben (ed.), *Traum und Wirklichkeit, Wien 1870–1930* (Vienna, Eigenverlag der Museen der Stadt Wien, 1985), p. 12

13   ibid

14   ibid, p. 21

15   Michael Hofmann, 'Joseph Roth: Going Over the Edge' (*NYRB*, 22 December 2011)

16   Carl E. Schorske, *Fin-de-siècle Vienna, Politics and Culture* (New York, Alfred A. Knopf, 1981), pp. xvii–xviii

17   Joseph Roth, *Die Kapuzinergruft* (Cologne, Kiepenhauer und Witsch, 1987), pp. 117–18

18   Alfred Pfabigan, *Geistesgegenwart* (Vienna, Deuticke Verlag, 1991), p. 53

19   'Über Josef Hoffmann', Adolf Loos, Manuscript from 1931, cited in Rukschcio, op. cit., p. 63

20   ibid

21   'Die Herrenmode', p. 56

22   Baudelaire, op. cit., p. 807

23   'Die Herrenmode', p. 57

24   Richard von Schaukal, *Leben und Meinungen des Herrn Andreas von Balthesser* (Stuttgart, Ernst Klett, 1986), p. 17

25   'Die Herrenmode', p. 55

26   ibid, p. 57

27   Jünger, op. cit., p. 26

28   Hermann Muthesius, 'Landhauser der Architekten J. W. Bedford und S. D. Kitson in Leeds' (*Dekorative Kunst 6*, 1903), p. 82

29   Manfred Russo, 'Hätte Loos adidas getragen?' in Podbrecky, op. cit., p. 32

30   Hollander, op. cit., p. 92

31   Baudelaire, op. cit., p. 807

32   'Die Herrenmode'

33   'Die Damenmode, Ins Leere Gesprochen', p. 126; originally *Neue Freie Presse*, 21 August 1898

34   ibid

35   ibid

36   Marcel Proust, *À la recherche du temps perdu* t. I, *À l'ombre des jeunes filles en fleurs* II, *À la recherche du temps perdu* t. I, *À l'ombre des jeunes filles en fleurs II* (Paris, Pléïades, Gallimard, 1954), pp. 619–20.

37   Mark Wigley, 'White Out, Fashioning the Modern' in Deborah Fausch et al (eds), *Architecture in Fashion* (New York, Princeton Architectural Press, 1994), p. 217.

38   'Das Prinzip der Bekleidung, Ins Leere gesprochen', pp. 139–45; originally *Neue Freie Presse*, 4 September 1898

39   Rukschcio, op. cit., p. 173

40   Ludwig Hevesi, 'Adolf Loos' in *Konfrontationen*, Adolf Opel (ed.), *Schriften von und über Adolf Loos* (Prachner, Vienna, 1988), p. 16; originally *Fremden Blatt*, 22 November 1907

41   Cited in Rukschcio, op. cit., p. 304

42   Altmann-Loos, op. cit., p. 156

43   'Lob der Gegenwart' in Opel, Adolf (ed.), *Die potemkinsche Stadt, Verschollene Schriften, 1897–1933* (Vienna, Prachner, 1983), p. 117; originally: *März*, Heft 16, Munich, August 1908

44   Altmann-Loos, op. cit., p. 97

45   Loos cited by Willy Haas in Adolf Opel (ed.), *Kontroversen, Adolf Loos im Spiegel der Zeitgenossen* (Prachner, Vienna, 1985), p. 179

NOTES TO THE DUKE OF WINDSOR

1   The Duke of Windsor, *A Family Album* (London, Cassell, 1960), p. 12

2   Philip Ziegler, *King Edward VIII, the Official Biography* (London, Harper and Collins, 1990), p. 9

3   The Duke of Windsor, *A King's Story* (London, Cassell, 1961,) p. 1

4   Walker, op. cit., p. 47

5   Ziegler, op. cit., p. 8

6   James Lees-Milne, *The Enigmatic Edwardian. The Life of Reginald, 2nd Viscount Esher*, London, 1986 cited in Hugo Vickers,

The Private World of the Duke and Duchess of Windsor (London, Harrods Publishing, 1995), p. 36

7   Ziegler, op. cit., p. 6

8   Duke of Windsor, *A Family Album*, p. 13

9   ibid

10   Ziegler, op. cit., p. 19

11   Duke of Windsor, *A Family Album*, p. 105

12   ibid, p. 50

13   *Max Beerbohm Works*, London 1896, p. 74; 3 August 1921, Dudley Ward Papers cited in Ziegler, op. cit., p. 108

14   Martin Green, *Children of the Sun* (New York, Basic Books, 1976), p. 48

15   Duke of Windsor, *A Family Album*, p. 93

16   Ziegler, p. 97

17   Cecil Beaton, *The Glass of Fashion* (London, Weidenfeld and Nicolson, 1954), p. 149

18   Green, op. cit., p. 24

19   Suzy Menkes, *The Windsor Style* (London, Grafton, 1987), p. 34

20   In conversation with a friend of the author

21   Green, op. cit., p. 194

22   Paul Keers, A *Gentleman's Wardrobe* (London, Weidenfeld Paperbacks, 1987), p. 27

23   Ziegler, op. cit., p. 251

24   Walker, op. cit., p. 24

25   BBC Interview, January 1970

26   Chenoune, op. cit., p. 164

27   Duke of Windsor, *A Family Album*, p. 99

28   ibid, p. 42

29   Diana Mosley, *The Duchess of Windsor* (New York, Stein and Day, 1981), p. 84

30   Marie-Jacqueline Lancaster (ed.), *Brian Howard, Portrait of a Failure* (London, Anthony Blond, 1968), p. 8

31   Vickers, op. cit., p. 83

32   Walker, op. cit., p. 97

33   ibid, p. 99

34   The Duke of Windsor, *A Family Album*, p. 108

35 ibid, p. 133

36 ibid, p. 84

37 G. A. Lawnston, 'Le tenues du Prince Charmant', *Adam*, November 1930 cited in Chenoune, op. cit., p. 169

38 The Duke of Windsor, *A Family Album*, p. 112

39 ibid, p. 41

40 ibid, p. 14

41 Menkes, op. cit., p. 16

42 Beaton, op. cit., p. 153

43 Walker, op. cit., p. 17

44 ibid, p. 42

45 ibid, p. 13

46 Ziegler, p. 104

47 Baudelaire, op. cit., p. 804

48 Walker, op. cit., p. 94

49 Jacques Dumaine cited by Christopher Wilson, *Dancing with the Devil: The Windsors and Jimmy Donahue* (London, Harper and Collins, 2000), p. 144

50 Wilson, op. cit., p. 168

51 ibid, p. 8

52 Nicholson cited in Vickers, op. cit., p. 540

53 Menkes, op. cit., p. 92

54 Pope-Hennessy cited in Vickers, op. cit., p. 220

55 Sidney Johnson cited in Menkes, op. cit., p. 99

56 Wilson, op. cit., p. 8

NOTES TO BUNNY ROGER

1 James Knox, *Cartoons and Coronets: The Genius of Osbert Lancaster* (London, Frances Lincoln, 2008), p. 30

2 Cyril Connolly, *The Missing Diplomats* (London, Queen Anne Press, 1952), p. 25

3 ibid, p. 44

4 E. M. Forster, 'What I Believe', *The Nation*, 16 July 1938

5 Graham Greene, Introduction to Kim Philby, *My Silent War* (London, McGibbon & Kee, 1968)

6   Rebecca West cited in Green, op. cit., p. 405

7   Green, op. cit., p. 399

8   Green, op. cit., p. 303

9   Andy Medhurst, 'Can Chaps be Pin-Ups? The British Film-Star of the 1950s' (*Ten 8 Magazine* 17)

10 Green, op. cit., p. 353

11 Beaton, op. cit., p. 8

12 Virginia Cowles, *Edward VII and His Circle* cited in Walker, op. cit., p. 85

13 Beaton, op. cit., p. 16

14 ibid, p. 64

15 Evelyn Waugh to Nancy Mitford, January 1945 in Charlotte Mosley, *The Letters of Evelyn Waugh and Nancy Mitford* (London, Hodder & Stoughton, 1996), p. 15

16 Waugh cited in Green, op. cit., p. 55

17 Evelyn Waugh, *Labels* (London, Duckworth, 1980), p. 40

18 Osbert Lancaster, *Here of All Places* (London, John Murray, 1959), p. 4

19 *New Statesman*, July 1949 cited by Robert Hewison in *In Anger, British Culture in the Cold War, 1945–1960* (Oxford, Oxford University Press, 1981), p. 4

20 Hewison, op. cit., p. 50

21 Nicholas Haslam, *Redeeming Features* (London, Jonathan Cape, 2009), p. 169

22 Moers, op. cit., p. 111

23 Green, op. cit., p. 245

24 Roger cited by Haslam, op. cit., p. 78

25 Beaton, op. cit., p. 46

26 Laver, 'When Styles Change We All Change' (*Tailor and Cutter* approx. June 1953), pp. 59, 60

27 James Fox, *The Langhorne Sisters* (London, Granta Books, 1998), p. 515 cited by Philip Hoare, 'The Dandy Esprit de Corps' (*Journal for Fashion Theory – the Journal of Dress Body & Culture*, vol. 9, no. 3, 2005), pp. 263–82

28 John Le Carré, *The Spy who Came in from the Cold* (London, Penguin, 2011), p. 12

29   The Duke of Windsor, *A Family Album*, p. 52
30   Robert Robinson, *Skip All That* (London, Century, 1996), p. 113
31   Waugh in Mitford, *Noblesse Oblige* (London, Penguin, 1961), p. 69

NOTES TO QUENTIN CRISP

1   Quentin Crisp, *The Naked Civil Servant* (London, Flamingo, 1985), p. 5
2   Andrew Barrow, *Quentin and Philip: A Double Portrait* (London, Macmillan, 2002), p. 193
3   Crisp cited in Simon Hattenstone, 'Miracle on 3rd Street' (*Guardian Weekend*, 12 December 1998), p. 41
4   Crisp, *How to Become a Virgin* (London, Duckworth, 1981), p. 8
5   ibid
6   Crisp, *How to Have a Life-Style* (London, Alyson Books, 1998), p. 15.
7   Crisp, *The Naked Civil Servant*, p. 19
8   ibid
9   ibid, p. 22
10   ibid, p. 25
11   ibid, p. 34
12   ibid, p. 35
13   ibid, p. 39
14   ibid, p. 49
15   ibid, p. 60
16   ibid
17   ibid, p. 54
18   ibid, p. 77
19   ibid, p. 91
20   ibid, p. 92
21   ibid, p. 110
22   ibid, p. 122
23   ibid, p. 131
24   ibid, p. 133
25   ibid
26   ibid

27   ibid, p. 134
28   ibid, p. 177
29   ibid, p. 156
30   ibid, p. 157
31   ibid
32   ibid, p. 161
33   ibid, p. 181
34   In the style of Ronald Firbank: English writer (1886–1926)
35   ibid, p. 187
36   ibid, p. 197
37   ibid
38   ibid, p. 205
39   ibid, p. 194
40   ibid, p. 211
41   ibid, p. 215
42   ibid, p. 222
43   Paul Robinson in Paul Bailey, *The Stately Homo* (London, Bantam Press, 2001), p. 112
44   ibid, p. 117
45   ibid
46   ibid, p. 118
47   Crisp cited in ibid, p. 100
48   *An Englishman in New York*, film directed by Richard Laxton, 2002
49   Marcel Proust, *Le temps retrouvé*, p. 30p
50   Barrow, op. cit., p. 210
51   Crisp, *How to Have a Life-Style*, p. 8
52   Crisp, *Manners from Heaven* (London, Hutchinson, 1984), p. 50
53   Crisp, *How to Have a Life-Style*, p. 10
54   Crisp, *Manners from Heaven*, p. 16
55   ibid, p. 88
56   Crisp, *The Naked Civil Servant*, p. 191
57   Bailey, op. cit., Introduction, p. 26
58   Albert Camus, *L'Étranger* (Paris, Gallimard, 1980), p. 186
59   Crisp, *Manners from Heaven*, p. 44

60   ibid, p. 25

61   Crisp, *How to Have a Life-Style*, p. 100

62   Crisp, *The Naked Civil Servant*, p. 121

63   Marcel Proust, *Le côté de Guermantes*, p. 144.

64   Barrow in Bailey, op. cit., p. 146

65   Crisp, *The Naked Civil Servant*, p. 168

66   Patrick O'Connor in Bailey, op. cit., p. 89

67   Crisp, *The Naked Civil Servant*

68   ibid, p. 153

69   Crisp, *Resident Alien* (London, Flamingo, 1996), p. 16

70   ibid, p. 136

71   Andrew Barrow in Bailey, op. cit., p. 146

72   Barrow, op. cit., p. 213

73   Simon Hattenstone, op. cit., p. 42

74   Crisp, *How to Become a Virgin*, p. 107

75   ibid, p. 148

76   ibid, p. 149

77   ibid, p. 152

78   Crisp, *The Naked Civil Servant*, p. 161

79   Crisp, *How to Become a Virgin*, p. 190

80   Crisp, *How to Have a Life-Style*, p. 146

81   Crisp, *How to Go to the Movies*, (London, Hamilton, 1990), p. 109

82   Cited by Adam Mars-Jones in Bailey, op. cit., p. 188

83   Crisp, *How to Go to the Movies*, p. 114

84   ibid, p. 17

85   Cited in Barrow, op. cit., p. 517

86   Crisp, *Resident Alien*, p. 59

87   Cited in Barrow, op. cit., p. 517

88   Crisp, *How to Have a Life-Style*, p. 150

89   Robinson in Bailey, op. cit., 117

90   Crisp, *Manners from Heaven*, p. 19

NOTES TO JEAN-PIERRE MELVILLE

1   Baudelaire, op. cit., 'La Beauté' *Les fleurs du mal*, pp. 15, 16

2   Jules-Amédée Barbey d'Aurevilly, *Pensées detachées, aphorisme* XCI (Gallimard, Paris, 1966), p. 1249.

3   Jules-Amédée Barbey d'Aurevilly, *Œuvres romanesques complètes*, T. II, *Du dandysme et de Georges Brummell* (Pléïades, Gallimard, Paris, 1966), p. 671.

4   D'Aurevilly, *Du Dandysme et de Georges Brummell*, translated by George Walden in *Who's a Dandy* (London, Gibson Square Books, 2002), p. 148

5   ibid, p. 79

6   ibid, p. 98

7   ibid, p. 101

8   ibid, p. 113

9   Moers, op. cit., p. 265

10   D'Aurevilly, *Du Dandysme et de Georges Brummell*, p. 715

11   ibid, p. 705

12   Benjamin, *Baudelaire*, p. 3p

13   Proust, *À l'ombre des jeunes filles en fleur* II, p. 761

14   Moers, op. cit., p. 273

15   Baudelaire, *Salon de 1846*, ch XVIII, p. 688

16   Baudelaire, *Journaux Intimes, Hygiène*, p. 401

17   Peter W. Jansen and Wolfram Schütte (eds), *Jean-Pierre Melville* (Munich, Hanser, 1982), p. 75

18   Rui Nogueira, *Melville on Melville* (New York, Viking, 1971), p. 14

19   Robert Fischer, *Kino der Nacht* (Berlin, 2002), p. 17

20   *White Shadows in the South Seas*, W. S. Van Dyke, 1928

21   Jansen, op. cit., pp. 79, 84

22   Ginette Vincendeau, *Jean-Pierre Melville: An American in Paris* (London, BFI-Publications, 2003), p. 121

23   Nogueira, op. cit., p. 8

24   Fischer, op. cit., p. 76

25   ibid

26   Pierre Grasset, 'Melville par Pierre Grasset', *Cahiers du Cinéma* p. 502

27   Nogueira, op. cit., p. 117

28   Chenoune, op. cit., p. 198

29   See Vincendeau

30   Rui Nogueira and François Truchaud, 'A Samurai in Paris' (*Sight and Sound*, Vol. 37, no. 3, Summer 1968), p. 119

31   Chenoune, op. cit., p. 196

32   Jansen, op. cit., p. 106

33   ibid, p. 22

34   Nogueira, op. cit., p. 37

35   ibid, p. 123

36   Jean-François Rauger, Alain Delon, 'L'unique et son double' (*Cahiers du Cinema* 501, April 1996), p. 32

37   Sigmund Freud, 'Zur Einführung des Narzißmus' in *Psychologie des Unbewussten* (Frankfurt am Main, Fischer Verlag, 1989), p. 61

38   Judith Butler, *Gender Trouble: Feminism and the Subversion of Identity* (London, Routledge, 1990), p. 28

39   Benjamin, *Arcades Project*, American edition cited, Dia, 9, p. 104

40   Nogueira and Truchaud, op. cit., p. 119

41   Nogueira, op. cit., p. 128

42   Jansen, op. cit., p. 101

43   Charles Baudelaire, *Journaux intime* x: fusées no. 46

44   Bruzzi, op. cit., p. 84

45   ibid

46   Pierre Drieu La Rochelle, *Récit Secret* (Paris, Gallimard, 1989), p. 40

47   Fischer, op. cit., p. 70

48   Jacques Rigaut, 'Je serais sérieux', *Littérature* 17, December 1920

NOTES TO RAINER WERNER FASSBINDER

1   Lars Albaum, 'Cognac für den Mörder', (*Süddeutsche Zeitung*, 7/8 June 2008)

2   Jean-Patrick Manchette, *La princesse du sang* (Paris, Payot & Rivages, 1996), Preface

3   Guy Debord, *Panégyrique* (Paris, editions Gerard Lebovici, 1989), p. 13

4   *Warnung vor einer heiligen Nutte* (Beware of a holy whore, 1971)

5   Marion Schmid and Herbert Gehr (eds), *Rainer Werner Fassbinder: Dichter, Schauspieler, Filmemacher. Werkschau* (Berlin, Rainer Werner Fassbinder Foundation, 1992), p. 178

6   Hilmar Hofmann and Walter Schobert (eds), *Abschied von Gestern: Bundesdeutscher Film der sechziger und siebziger Jahre* (Frankfurt am Main, Deutsches Filmmuseum, 1991), p. 31

7   Oswald Wiener, 'Eine Art Einzige', in von der Heyden-Rynsch, op. cit., pp. 35ff

8   Wolfgang Koeppen, *Das Treibhaus* (Frankfurt am Main, Suhrkamp, 1972), pp. 19, 127

9   Harry Baer, *Schlafen kann ich wenn ich tot bin* (Cologne, Kiepenhauer & Witsch, 1992), p. 27

10   Jean-Jacques Schuhl, *Ingrid Caven* (Paris, Gallimard, 2000), p. 74

11   Fassbinder cited by Ian Birnie of the LA County Museum of Art, Extras to *Fear Eats the Soul*, DVD

12   Albert Camus, *The Rebel*, translation by Anthony Bower (London, Hamish Hamilton, 1953), p. 46

13   ibid, p. 17

14   Ronald Hayman, *Fassbinder Filmmaker* (London, Weidenfeld and Nicolson, 1984), p. 133

15   Camus, *The Rebel*, p. 46

16   Christian Braad Thomssen, *Fassbinder: The Life and Work of a Provocative Genius* (London, Faber and Faber, 1997), p. 9

17   Robert Katz and Peter Berlin, *Love is Colder than Death: The Life and Times of Rainer Werner Fassbinder* (London, Cape, 1987), p. 8

18   Michel Houellebecq interviewed in *Frankfurter Allgemeine Zeitung*

19   See Thomas Elsaesser, *Rainer Werner Fassbinder* (Berlin, arte/Bertz, 2001), p. 8

20   Hayman, op. cit., p. 129

21   ibid

22   Schmid and Gehr, op.cit., p. 192

23   Camus, *The Rebel*, p. 222

24   ibid, p. 48

25   Gottfried Benn, *Briefe an F.W. Oelze. 1932–1945* (Wiesbaden, Limes, 1977), pp. 92, 93

26   Peter W. Jansen and Wolfram Schütte (eds), *Rainer Werner Fassbinder* (Frankfurt am Main, Fischer, 1992), p. 86

27   Elsaesser, op. cit., p. 130

28 Charles Baudelaire, op. cit., 'L'Héautontimorouménos' in *Les fleurs du mal,* p. 57

29 Camus, *The Rebel,* p. 229

30 Wilhelm Roth essay in Jansen and Schütte, op. cit., p. 154

31 Chenoune, op. cit., p. 285

32 Hayman, op. cit., p. 145

33 Antonin Artaud, *Héliogabale ou l'anarchiste couronné* (Paris, Gallimard, 1990), pp. 94, 95

34 Painter, op. cit., Vol. 2, p. 314

35 Elsaesser, op. cit., p. 185

36 ibid, p. 188

37 ibid, p. 202

NOTES TO EPILOGUE: APRÈS LE DÉLUGE

1 See Günter Erbe, 'Der Moderne Dandy' (*Politik und Zeitgeschichte,* B46/2004), pp. 32, 33

2 See Oswald Wiener in von der Heyden-Rynsch, op. cit., p. 59

3 Sebastian Horsley, *Dandy in the Underworld: An Unauthorized Biography* (London, Sceptre, 2008), p. 85

4 Viollet-le-Duc cited in Stephen Bayley, *Taste, the Secret Meaning of Things* (London, Faber and Faber, 1991), p. 11

5 Georg Franck, 'Eleganz, ein Abgesang' (*Merkur* 739, December 2010), p. 1209

6 Bayley, op. cit., p. 20

7 Friederich Nietzsche, *Sämtliche Werke,* vol. 15 (Munich/Berlin, dtv/de Gruyter, 2005), p. 500

8 See Bayley, op. cit., p. 47

9 Bayley, p. 40

10 Horsley, op. cit., p. 56

11 ibid, p. 37

12 ibid, p. 57

13 Cited as a motto in Roberto Callasso, *Der Traum Baudelaire's,* translation by Reimar Klein (München, Hanser, 2012)

14 Camus, *The Rebel,* op. cit., p. 235

15 Herbert Lachmayer, 'Produktive Dekadenz' (*Wiener Zeitung,* 27 January 2006)

16 ibid

LIST OF ILLUSTRATIONS

1. The Broken Bow: portrait of the author by Massimiliano Mocchia di Coggiola, 2016. Photo provided by Philip Mann.

2. Beau Brummell: portrait, 'from the painting in the National Portrait Gallery'. Image taken from Armstrong Bridgeman Jerrold, Clare: *The Beaux and the Dandies: Nash; Brummell, and d'Orsay* (London, Stanley Paul & Co., 1910). © The British Library Board, Papyrus 1531, verso.

3. Beau Brummell in the grip of the blue devils. Photo by Bibliothèque Nationale, Paris, France.

4. Michel Würthle: Your head is too big! November, 2015. Photo provided by Philip Mann.

5. Jacques Rigaut: objectifier of man and life, suicide artist. By Man Ray. Photo © Peter Horree/Alamy Stock Photo.

6. Dandy in a cul-de-sac: Maurice Ronet in Le Feu Follet (Louis Malle, 1963). Photo © AF archive/Alamy Stock Photo.

7. The correct shape? Adolf Loos by Trude Fleischmann, 1930. Photo by Private Collection, Courtesy Neue Galerie New York © 2017. Neue Galerie New York/Art Resource/Scala, Florence.

8. Edward VII, then Prince of Wales: side creased and unbuttoned. Photo © Paul Popper/Popperfoto/Getty Images.

9. Joseph Roth: making full use of his cavalry strides, Place d'Odeon, Paris. Photo © Leo Baeck Institute/Lebrecht Music & Arts.

10. Richard von Schaukal in atypically folkloristic dress, 1922. Photo © Imagno/Getty Images.

11. Adolf Loos, 1909 (oil on canvas), by Kokoschka, Oskar (1886-1980) /Schloss Charlottenburg, Berlin, Germany/Bridgeman Images.

12. A claustrophiliac's wet dream: the Loos Bar in Vienna. Designed

BIBLIOGRAPHY

BOOKS

Altmann-Loos, Elsie, *Adolf Loos, der Mensch* (Vienna, 1968)

Artaud, Antonin, *Héliogabale ou l'anarchiste couronné* (Paris, 1990)

Baer, Harry, *Schlafen kann ich wenn ich tot bin* (Cologne, 1990)

Bailey, Paul, *The Stately Homo* (London, 2001)

Barbey d'Aurevilly, Jules-Amédée, *Œuvres complètes*, 2 vol. (Paris, 1966)

Barrow, Andrew, *Quentin and Philip: A Double Portrait* (London, 2002)

Barthes, Roland, *Œuvres complètes*, 'Le dandysme et la mode', 3 vol. (Paris, 1993)

Baudelaire, Charles, *Œuvres complètes* (Paris, 1999)

Bayley, Stephen, *Taste, the Secret Meaning of Things* (London, 1991)

Beaton, Cecil, *The Glass of Fashion* (London, 1954)

Beerbohm, Max, *Dandies and Dandies* (London, 1962)

Benjamin, Walter, *Arcades Project*, translation by Howard Eiland and Kevin Mclaughlin (Cambridge Massachusetts and London, England, 1999)

Benjamin, Walter, *Charles Baudelaire* (Frankfurt am Main, 1974)

Benjamin, Walter, *Passagenwerk, Gesammelte Schriften*, Band V. 1. (Frankfurt, 1991)

Benn, Gottfried, *Briefe an F.W. Oelze. 1932–1945* (Wiesbaden, 1977)

Binder, Pearl, *The Peacock's Tail* (London, 1958)

Bruzzi, Stella, *Undressing Cinema: Clothing and Identity in the Movies* (London, 1997)

Buñuel, Luis and Carrière, Jean-Claude, *Mon dernier soupir* (Paris, 1982)

Buruma, Ian, *Voltaire's Coconuts, Anglomania in Europe* (London, 1999)

Butler, Judith *Gender Trouble: Feminism and the Subversion of Identity* (London, 1990)

Calasso, Roberto, *Der Traum Baudelaire's*, Translation by Reimar Klein (Munich, 2012)

Camus, Albert, *L'étranger* (Paris, 1980)

Camus, Albert, *The Rebel*, Translation by Anthony Bower (London, 1953)

Carlyle, Thomas, *Sartor Resartus* (Oxford, 1987)

Chenoune, Farid, *A History of Men's Fashion* (Paris, 1993)

Cioran, Emil, *Œuvres complètes* (Paris, 2011)

Connolly, Cyril, *Enemies of Promise* (London, 1949)

Connolly, Cyril, *The Missing Diplomats* (London, 1962)

Connolly, Cyril, *The Selected Works* (London, 2002)

Crisp, Quentin, *How to become a Virgin* (London, 1981)

Crisp, Quentin, *How to Have a Life-Style* (Los Angeles, 1998)

Crisp, Quentin, *Manners from Heaven* (London, 1984)

Crisp, Quentin, *Resident Alien* (London, 1996)

Crisp, Quentin, *The Naked Civil Servant* (London, 1985)

Debord, Guy, *Panégyrique* (Paris, 1989)

Drieu La Rochelle, Pierre, *Le feu follet* (Paris, 1991)

Drieu La Rochelle, Pierre, *Récit secret* (Paris, 1989)

Elsaesser, Thomas, *Rainer Werner Fassbinder* (Berlin, 2001)

Erbe, Gunter, *Dandys-Virtuosen der Lebenskunst* (Koln-Weimar-Wien, 2002)

Erben, Tino (ed.), *Traum und Wirklichkeit, Wien 1870–1930*, exhibition catalogue (Vienna, 1985)

Fausch, Deborah (ed.), *Architecture in Fashion,* (New York, 1994)

Fischer, Robert, *Kino der Nacht* (Berlin, 2002)

Fox James, *The Langhorne Sisters* (London, 1998)

Freud, Sigmund, *Zur Einführung des Narzißmus* in *Psychologie des Unbewussten,* (Frankfurt am Main 1989)

Fridell, Egon, *Kulturgeschichte der Neuzeit* (Munich, 1996)

Green, Martin, *Children of the Sun* (New York, 1976)

Greene, Graham, Introduction to Kim Philby, *My Silent War* (London, 1968

Haslam, Nicholas, *Redeeming Features* (London, 2009)

Hayman, Ronald, *Fassbinder Filmmaker* (London, 1984)

Hazlitt, William, *The Look of a Gentleman* (London, 1889)

Hewison, Robert, *In Anger, British Culture in the Cold War 1945–1960* (Oxford, 1981)

Heyden-Rynsch, Verena (ed.), *Riten der Selbstauflösung* (Munich, 1982)

Hofmann, Hilmar und Schobert, Walter (ed.), *Abschied von Gestern: Bundesdeutscher Film der sechziger und siebziger Jahre* (Frankfurt am Main, 1991)

Hollander, Anne, *Sex and Suits* (New York, 1994)

Horsley, Sebastian, *Dandy in the Underworld: An Unauthorized biography* (London, 2008)

Huysmans, Joris Karl, *Against Nature,* translated by Robert Baldick (London, 1959)

Jansen Peter W. and Schütte, Wolfram (ed.), *Jean-Pierre Melville* (Munich, 1982)

Jansen Peter W. and Schütte, Wolfram (ed.), *Rainer Werner Fassbinder* (Frankfurt am Main, 1992)

Jesse William, *The Life of Georges Brummell, esq., commonly called Beau Brummell* (London, 1844)

Jünger, Ernst, *Rivarol* (Köln, 1989)

Katz, Robert and Berlin, Peter, *Love is Colder than Death: The Life and Times of Rainer Werner Fassbinder* (London, 1987)

Keers, Paul, *A Gentleman's Wardrobe* (London, 1987)

Knox, James, *Cartoons and Coronets: The Genius of Osbert Lancaster* (London, 2008)

Koeppen, Wolfgang, *Das Treibhaus* (Frankfurt am Main, 1972)

Lancaster, Marie-Jacqueline (ed.), *Brian Howard, Portrait of a Failure* (London, 1968)

Lancaster, Osbert, *Here of All Places* (London, 1959)

Le Carré, John, *The Spy who Came in from the Cold* (London, 2011)

Lees-Milne, James, *The Enigmatic Edwardian. The life of Reginald, 2nd Viscount Esher* (London, 1988)

Leiris, Michel, *L'âge d'homme* (Paris, 1993)

Lepenies, Wolf, *Melancholie und Gesellschaft* (Frankfurt am Main, 1972)

Letwin, Shirley, *The Gentleman in Trollope. Individuality and Moral Conduct* (Cambridge Mass., 1982)

Lipovetsky, Gilles, *The Empire of Fashion* (Princeton, 1994)

Loos, Adolf and Opel, Adolf (ed.), *Ins Leere Gesprochen, Gesammelte Schriften 1900–1930* (Wien, 1982)

Loos, Adolf and Opel, Adolf (ed.), *Die potemkinsche Stadt, Verschollene Schriften, 1897–1933* (Wien, 1983)

Loos, Claire, *Adolf Loos Privat* (Wien, 1985)

Manchette, Jean-Patrick, *La princesse du sang* (Paris, 1996)

Mann, Otto, *Der Dandy, Ein Kulturproblem der Moderne* (Heidelberg, 1962)

Márai, Sándor, *Bekenntnisse eines Bürgers* (Munich, 2002)

Márai, Sándor, *Schule der Armen: Ein Leitfaden für Menschen mit geringem Einkommen* (Munich, 2006)

Menkes, Suzy, *The Windsor Style* (London, 1987)

Miller, Toby, *The Avengers* (London, 1997)

Mitford, Nancy, *Noblesse Oblige* (London, 1961)

Moers, Ellen, *The Dandy: Brummell to Beerbohm* (London, 1960)

Mosley, Charlotte, *The Letters of Evelyn Waugh and Nancy Mitford* (London, 1996)

Mosley, Diana, *The Duchess of Windsor* (New York, 1981)

Muthesius, Hermann, *Das englische Haus* (Berlin, 1904/05)

Nietzsche, Friederich, *Sämtliche Werke*, 15 vol. (Munich/Berlin, 2005)

Nogueira, Rui, *Melville on Melville* (New York, 1971)

Opel, Adolf (ed.), *Konfrontationen, Schriften von und über Adolf Loos* (Vienna, 1988)

Opel, Adolf (ed.), *Kontroversen, Adolf Loos im Spiegel der Zeitgenossen* (Vienna, 1985)

Painter, George D., *Marcel Proust, A Biography*, 2 vols. (London, 1969)

Pfabigan, Alfred, *Geistesgegenwart* (Vienna, 1991)

Podbrecky, Inge and Franz, Rainald (eds), *Leben mit Loos* (Vienna, 2008)

Proust, Marcel, *À la recherche du temps perdu*, 3 vol. (Paris, 1954)

Raven, Simon, *The English Gentleman* (London, 1961)

Robinson, Robert, *Skip All That* (London, 1996)

Roth, Joseph, *Die Kapuzinergruft* (Cologne, 1987)

Rukschcio, Burkhardt and Schachel, Roland, *Adolf Loos* (Salzburg and Vienna, 1982)

Schaukal, Richard, *Leben und Meinungen des Herrn Andreas von Balthesser* (Stuttgart, 1986)

Schmid, Marion und Gehr, Herbert (eds), *Rainer Werner Fassbinder: Dichter, Schauspieler, Filmemacher* (Werkschau, Berlin, 1992)

Schorske, Carl Emil, *Fin-de-siècle Vienna, Politics and Culture* (New York, 1981)

Schuhl, Jean-Jacques, *Ingrid Caven* (Paris, 2000)

Simenon, Georges and Franck, Frédérick, *Le Paris de Simenon* (Brussels, 1969)

Sontag, Susan, *Against Interpretation* (New York, 1966)

Sternberger, Dolf, *Über den Tod* (Frankfurt am Main, 1977)

Strachey, Lytton, *Portraits in Miniature* (London, 1981)

Thomsen, Christian Braad, *Fassbinder: The Life and Work of a Provocative Genius* (London, 1997)

Vickers, Hugo, *The private world of the Duke and Duchess of Windsor* (London, 1995)

Vincendeau, Ginette, *Jean-Pierre Melville: An American in Paris* (London, 2003)

Walker, Richard, *Savile Row: An Illustrated History* (London, 1988)

Waugh, Evelyn, *A Little Learning* (London, 1966)

Waugh, Evelyn, *Labels* (London, 1930)

Wilde, Oscar, *De Profundis, Epistola in carcere et vinculis* (Oxford, 2005

Wilde, Oscar, *The Picture of Dorian Gray* (London, 2011)

Wilson, Christopher, *Dancing with the Devil: The Windsors and Jimmy Donahue* (London, 2000)

Windsor, Duke of, *A Family Album* (London, 1960)

Ziegler, Philip, *King Edward VIII, The Official Biography* (London, 1990)

ARTICLES

Albaum, Lars, 'Cognac für den Mörder', *Süddeutsche Zeitung*, 7/8 June 2008

Erbe, Günter, 'Der Moderne Dandy', *Politik und Zeitgeschichte* (B46/2004)

Forster, E. M., 'What I Believe', *The Nation*, 16 July 1938

Franck, Georg. 'Eleganz, ein Abgesang'. *Merkur* 739 (December 2010)

Grasset, Pierre, 'Melville par Pierre Grasset', *Cahiers du Cinéma*, 502

Hattenstone, Simon, 'Miracle on 3rd Street', *Guardian Weekend*, 12 December 1998

Hoare, Philip, 'The Dandy Esprit de Corps', *Journal for Fashion Theory – the Journal of Dress Body & Culture*, vol. 9, no. 3, pp. 263–282, 2005

Hofmann, Michael, 'Going Over the Edge', *New York Review of Books*, 22 December 2011

Lachmayer, Herbert, 'Produktive Dekadenz'. *Wiener Zeitung*, 27 January 2006

Laver, James, 'When Styles Change We All Change', *Tailor and Cutter*, June 1953

Loos, Adolf, Column in *Neues 8-Uhr Blatt*, 4 October 1919

Medhurst, Andy, 'Can Chaps be Pin-Ups? The British Film-Star of the 1950s'. *Ten 8 Magazine* 17

Nogueira, Rui and Truchaud François, 'A Samurai in Paris', *Sight and Sound* Vol. 37, 3, Summer 1968

Rauger, Jean François, 'Alain Delon: L'unique et son double', *Cahiers du Cinéma*, 501, April 1996

Rigaut, Jacques, 'Je serais sérieux', *Littérature* 17, December 1920

Woods, Gregory, 'High Culture and High Camp, the Case of Marcel Proust', *Camp Grounds: Style and Homosexuality*, Boston, 1993

ACKNOWLEDGEMENTS

Thanks for literary and/or moral support:

Richard Millbank, Clémence Jacquinet, Jessie Price, Matt Bray
and Ellen Parnavelas at Head of Zeus, Jason Amesbury, Sir
Hardy Amies, Jean-Luc Bitton, David Brown, Stephen Campbell-
Sutherland, Olivier Copet, Barry Curtis, Jakub Dolejš, Diana
Dunwoody, Guenter Erbe, Brigitte Felderer, Floc'h, Sandra
Friesen, Nicholas Haslam, Lisa Hilton, Jane Hoare, Nicholas
and Sarah Hopkins, Carry Kania, Babette Kulik, Herbert
Lachmayer, Martina Larsson, Edmund Leites, Alexander Lieck,
Kiki Lindskog, Franck Loric, Stoddard Martin, Barbara Mellor,
Massimiliano Mocchia di Coggiola, Martin Mosebach, Anne
Mallégol, Ruth Skilbeck, Michael Sullivan, Harry Walton,
Ian Wright, Michel Würthle, Klaus Zwangsleitner and the
London Library.

INDEX